THE LIFE SWAP

THE LIFE SWAP

BY NANCY WEBER

AN AUTHORS GUILD BACKINPRINT.COM EDITION

For information address:
iUniverse, Inc.
2021 Pine Lake Road, Suite 100
Lincoln, NE 68512
www.iuniverse.com

Originally published by Dial Press

"Alcestis on the Poetry Circuit" and lines from "Seventeen Warnings in Search of
a Feminist Poem" by Erica Jong: From HALF LIVES by Erica Jong. Copyright
© 1971, 1972, 1973, 1991 by Erica Mann Jong. Reprinted by permission of the
author.

"A.M.A. Speaker Declares Manic Phase Helps Gifted": © 1973 by The New
York Times Company. Reprinted by permission.

Nancy's classified ad, on the cover, is reprinted by permission of *The Village
Voice*, © The Village Voice, Inc. 1973.

Design by Lynn Braswell

ISBN-13: 978-0-595-37821-0
ISBN-10: 0-595-37821-8

Printed in the United States of America

Most of us
in this book are
wearing made-up
names.
If this were a novel, it would
be a *roman à clef*.
—TRIGGER MIKE KAGAN

CONTENTS

CHOOSING

I didn't dream up the ad; it dreamed up me. Marched into my mind without warning and took the whole joint over, sparing none.

LET'S SWAP LIVES. Woman
writer, 31, will exchange her joyful,
productive existence with yours for a
month. I offer small Village apartment
with fireplace & courtyard; size 8
wardrobe starring St. Laurent and
Levi-Strauss; 1,000-plus books, fine
paintings, Bach, tennis racquet;
sterling friends & loving lovers, not
all of whom are married. I'll do your
work, adore your family, see your
shrink, whatever, wherever. Why? I want
to know if people can get out of their
skins. References, lawyers,
all safeguards both ways.

The ad laughed away my attempts at exorcism. It would not become a novel or be talked away in bars. The imperative grew plain: I had to live the bastard out or be its prisoner forever.

On a Monday morning shot through with New York winter light, I walked to *The Village Voice* and placed the ad. Came home and spent the two days until it appeared trying to figure out why it had chosen me to write the check that would bring it to life.

I looked at things I'd written and tootled through my memory and lined up glimmerings and dreams and fears, and the realization came: Everything had conspired to make this choosing happen. Sweet, such realizations. I started making notes on blue paper for myself and anyone else who might care.

My mother's mother, a woman we all wildly adored, became completely senile in her seventies. She no longer recognized children or grandchildren, no longer made coherent sentences, had no sense of time or world. But something survived. Some special Rosalie essence went on existing even when she was cut off from everything familiar. It was a spectacular mix of kindness and warmth and dignity: her character. Everyone noticed it, even nurses, strangers. Something survived the death of her consciousness. So the urge was born in me to find the essential character in everyone I loved, in myself, to know what would survive the most severe dislocation, even perhaps the death of the body.

This discovery of the soul when I was twenty-five in no way disturbed my dearest belief that each of us has at hand all the components of personality, to do with what he will. Nothing could have disturbed this belief. If it isn't our right and our gravest obligation to invent ourselves, reinvent ourselves, can we be said to exist at all? To be a single personality, fixed and final, would be to render ourselves unable to love all those we might love, serve everything we consider worthy, honor the magnificent contradictariness of life.

My great friend George Warneke, a psychologist, insisted that I attend an encounter session last year. Several hours after we began, George asked a woman named Rhea to choose someone to play her in a role-switching event. She'd spent a lot of energy attacking me (I was "charming" and therefore "dishonest"), confessing that she was jealous of me (a matter of ten years and twenty pounds), and otherwise creating a hostile air between us. I was the one she chose. I stood in the middle of the group with someone named Arthur and responded as I felt Rhea would have to his gestures of anger, abandonment, need. Afterward she said, and the group concurred, that I had exactly done what she would have done. I'd known little about her, really seen only that resentment of me. But her face, body, walk, clothes, the way she smoked cigarettes, did or didn't sit close to people—these were clues enough to spark a light trance in which I felt a range of feelings as foreign as could be, as real as could be. Her possessiveness. Her fear. Her forgiveness. I realized when the exercise was over that my notion of self-invention had never gone near as deep as it could have, had never concerned itself with the emotions that manifest themselves in personality, in style.

The two seemingly opposing impulses—to find my essential character; to come up with all the different personalities that could live with it—fused in the idea of swapping lives with another woman.

I'm convinced that if I could be Rhea after knowing her not at all intimately for two hours, I will to an infinitely greater extent be able to be another woman when I'm in her contextual place, getting the responses she gets from the people in her life, obeying her metabolism, wearing her clothes and perfume, drinking what she drinks, doing her work. And I believe in so doing I'll find emotions, impulses, tastes that belong to me, too. Maybe something as small as a liking for coffee ice cream, something as big as a talent for monogamy. I'll also find out some things I'm not, never can be; I'll find the walls I've been too blind or cocky to see. Very important, I'll also be discovering things about this woman that she doesn't know and that she'll now be able to work consciously to amplify or destroy. And she, back in my life, will be making the same discoveries for herself, for me.

Wednesday I woke up giddy, was at the newsstand at nine. *The Voice* hadn't come. I walked up Sixth Avenue to Balducci's, the most seductive market in New York. Mo was tenderly arranging the fat first asparagus of the year. "How's the novel selling?" he asked, as he always did. "Not well enough to buy asparagus in February," I said, bought some anyway.

"Now if I do a nonfiction book about swapping lives, she thought . . .," I thought as I walked back to the newsstand. I'd been sneaking around corners to avoid running into that thought. Did I want to do a book? Shouldn't this be pure adventure? But how could I resist sharing all the magic I would find? What gave me the right to resist it?

The Voice was there now, crisply piled. I bought a copy. Superstition forbade buying two copies or reading it on the street. I walked back through my courtyard and up to my apartment, sat down in the corner of the couch that no one is allowed to sit in but me, opened the paper to the public notices. And there it was. No smudges, no typos. My poem, with a box number attached.

I read it a dozen times. Was I really going to go through with this madness? I looked around my apartment, at the New England tea table my brother, Nick, had built, at my no-kitchen kitchen, at the yellow snowdrifts Trigger Mike had sent because *The New*

York Times Magazine had commissioned another cover, at the painting I had to go through a windshield to buy and it was worth it: Gabriele Münter's oil of a white house against the cobalt mountains of Murnau. It all looked too good to leave. It all looked too good not to share.

I put blue paper in the typewriter.

Do we own our lives, or do they own us? The beauty of being cast free from all we've come to think of as us, finding out how talented we are at surviving on the wild seas, seeing how freedom becomes us! I'm the ironic person to want to reach the bare place, try on a new clutter. I'm grounded in details, a fascist about small things. Must always have yellow fresh flowers in my apartment, drink Irish whiskey in a goblet just so, have worn Shalimar perfume for fifteen years. I have my ways; oh, do I have my ways. Love them. And love the thought of taking a vacation from them, thumbing my nose at them, finding out how they get along with somebody else, coming home to them with different eyes.

I have such death fears, such a pervasive longing for immortality. Is this intentional schizophrenia I have in mind simply a trick to extend life sideways, the only direction we control for now?

I know little about women, love few women. Yet I'm prepared utterly to trust whoever enters into this madness with me, suspend all notions of competition. I don't know why I feel that way, but I do. Who do I want it to be? A mother; a courtesan. Anyone but a writer with a sweetly chaotic single life and a lousy second serve.

I'm thirty-one. I've lived in this apartment for ten years to the month. In this life for ten years. I'm on the verge of a leap—I can feel it, and it's time: I'm beginning to repeat myself, in love, in my work, in the dailiness I so cherish, even in my fantasies. (My metaphorical trips to Geneva as a spy are becoming as dull as any commute.) Maybe the leap is into marriage, or at least into some focusing of affection, and motherhood. I think I hope that's what it is. Not to renounce what's been or run from it; to make sense out of it in a way that repetition cannot. But how can I make the leap until I know what I'm leaping from? I never take photographs; my journals are fragmented; no one but Nick grasps and shares everything I'm about—and his grasping, sharing are circumscribed by his being a man and my brother. Probably the most important thing the woman I swap with will do is certify for me, for my children, for the world, that my life for the past ten years has been the life I meant it to be.

Would Trigger Mike want to make the leap with me? Did I want him to? How would the gods vote? I called the Algonquin, his February hotel.

"My girl!" he said in his nice morning voice.

"Sweetheart! Go buy *The Voice* this minute—they centered all the lines, it looks terrific."

"Sure it looks terrific. You're a genius, kid. She just better have your legs."

"She will. She'll have everything. She'll be the most extraordinary woman in the world."

"Yes, honey, good-bye, I'll talk to you later."

Blue paper.

The most important thing is for my swapee to be someone who can keep my people happy. Do I really want that? Yes. Prettier than me would be good; smarter, funnier. It's got to be a great experience for everyone involved, or it isn't fair. (I'm not worried about her people. I know I'm good at making others happy when they let me.) And I don't want anyone suspecting my motives, thinking I did this thing only so everyone'll be relieved when I get back. I want them to be glad, but I really don't want to be missed while I'm away.

If it's someone who doesn't get headaches, will she get mine? Will I have her allergies? If they're caused by the lives we live rather than by some absolute chemistry, why not?

Is there someone out there who'll be better at being me than I am? How indispensable are we to our own lives?

Things to think about: financial arrangements (the month should cost us both the same), legal stuff. Start making lists for her, things she should know about me, about my people, all the details.

If she does big drugs, will I do big drugs? Will this finally be the time to take acid? I suppose we should draw the line at doing things that might have drastic aftereffects, but maybe becoming someone else for a month alters chromosomes, too.

There were two letters and a postcard on Friday. The people at *The Voice* looked excited. I ran all the way home, threw myself into my corner of the couch, tore open the envelope with the Staten Island postmark.

To whom it may concern,

I am a 19 year old artist with a very unusual life style. I live with my lover, have 2 cats, a a 6 room apt. My lover is a photographer-musician, easy to get along with. My cats are male/female and they too are easy to get along with.

I would like very much to meet you and discuss swapping lives for a month. Even if we don't, I think it will be an enjoyable experience meeting you.

Berry Weybright
224 Lincoln Av, New Brighton Staten Island

Oh God, no phone number on the letter or in Information. I sent a telegram asking her to call *tout de suite*. Staten Island—her next-door neighbor was probably a cop, how terrific. Her taste in stationery was less than terrific; becoming a printer's daughter for a month would be good for her. Miss Weybright of New Brighton. Oh, yes. Would I have any trouble being nineteen? My knees had started to go, but Trigger Mike was always telling me that I looked eighteen, and my brother insisted that I had the mentality of fourteen; sure, I could pull it off. I was more worried about the cats, but if Berry didn't mind the smell, I wouldn't mind the smell when I was Berry. LET'S SWAP NOSES. What time would she get the telegram? Should I have sent a Dollygram?

I looked at the rest of my mail.

Dear Miss,

I wish I was married. Ha!

Rainbow

Dear Woman writer 31 —

You're nuts! Your physical presence in someone else's life will be no more productive than your imagining yourself there. Unless your imagination is not very good. In which case, you're in the wrong profession. Think about it! Life is only as interesting as your imagination;

Woman writer 36
(been there)

I sent answers in my head.

Rainbow, I love you; you're crazier than me.

Woman writer, 36, you're infuriating.
Why didn't you give me your address so I
could tell you that I tried imagining
this thing, tried writing a novel, and came away
feeling like the world's biggest cheater?
Life is only as interesting as life, you ˙
dummy; the greatest thing about imagination
is that it gives us glimpses of what we can
do with the real stuff. If you don't
understand that, you're using your profession
to cheat life and yourself.

Woman writer, 31
(been there)

Trigger Mike called to tell me to meet him at Gallagher's at seven. I said okay. George Warneke called to say it was high time we did a book on tantric yoga. I agreed. Magda Jepson, whom I think of as my blood sister, called to giggle. I giggled back. All I could think about was Berry.

And then. At six thirty-two. As I was standing in front of the mirror hating my hair.

"Hello, is Nancy there?"

"This is Nancy."

"This is Berry."

"Hi! I loved your letter."

"I loved your ad—you must be a far-out lady."

"I don't know, not so far out. What kind of artist are you?"

"I'm kind of into an erotic trip these days. A lot of pen-and-ink stuff."

"I'd love to see something."

"They have some drawings over at the Pleasure Chest near Sheridan Square. I think they'll be up another couple of days."

"Great. I'll stop over on my way uptown right now. I'd love that, being a painter. My mother's a terrific painter. I have lots of her things here; her self-portrait's looking at me very peculiarly at the moment. Do you think you could do some of my writing? Magazine articles, maybe some fiction?"

"I could try."

"Well, listen, let's meet. You sound really nice. Do you come into the Village much?"

"I'm coming in tomorrow."

"Perfect. How about around six at the Lion's Head? Hey, have you discussed it with your lover? What does he think about it?"

"Not he. She."

                                                                      "Oh."

                                                    "I have to
                    admit I hadn't thought of that. I'm pretty

                                                    heterosexual."
        "I hadn't thought of *that*."
        "How would you feel about   being   lovers   with
my men?"

"Okay."

"Well, gosh, I don't know, it would be interesting as hell, I suppose I'm bisexual, maybe just sexual, we all are; I don't know. Let me have your phone number. I have to think it over a little."

"That's cool."

Oh, Berry, I wasn't cool at all. I went to see your drawings; they were beautiful and full of Persephone desires, and they scared the hell out of me. "Not he. She" was an easy laugh I played all over town. I never called you back. I told myself it was because I hadn't conceived of the swap as a primarily sexual adventure and didn't want it to become one. True enough, but I still should have called you back.

There were three letters on Saturday, all from men.

```
Dear Joyful productive thirty-one-year-old woman
    in search of something, Hi.
Have heart.
You are not alone anyway.
Are you really in search of karmic exchange . . .
    i.e., do you really want to get out of your
    head . . . or is it just your skin you want to
    give up along with your St. Laurent—Levis.
I guess it depends on how into your fantasy you
    are
but
If it's truly change in the fullest sense that
    you seek, why do it
ALONE
or is that part of the trip the trip the trip
meaning why take care of a husband and friends who
    could never really get into what you are
    looking for (could they?) when in fact you
    could take care of me. And I could dig you . . .
    and you could dig me digging you and have that
    whole other look at yourself . . . and I
    promise that I would let you see me from the
    first moment.
(if you have stopped understanding . . . stop
    reading . . . this ain't for you)
Anyhow (I know you're still reading because if
    you were together enough to put this letter down
    at that point you would understand it and if
    you weren't you'd still be here out of
    curiosity) I'd be interested to know if you
    were slightly defensive at this point since I
    still haven't said a thing other than
Hi
```

I mean, isn't that what it's all about?
(so you put an ad in the VV . . . what do you
  expect . . . coherence?)
What I'm suggesting is that rather than take my
  wife's place and live with me why not just
  come directly . . . my wife split two years
  ago . . . and she probably would have spilled
  things on your clothes anyway.
But don't bring all your bullshit . . . take $100
  and come over and we'll go buy the clothes you
  need (my life-style is casual) and join me on
  my scene . . . but I can't tell you what my
  scene is because a guy's scene is the same as
  a chick's looks and it's heads we're talking
  about and my head is right out here for you to
  dig . . . the same way that yours is in your ad
but I'm not unattractive
so if you're into it let's do it
I mean no bullshit with coffee, tea, and
  introductions
gutty like
call me
move in
and when the time comes
leave
Mel Green
119 Wooster Street
NYC
966—XXXX

Michael Littauer
110 W 17th St. N.Y.C. 10011
777-XXXX

Hello
I think that you have a thoroughly
delightful idea as well as a very valuable
experiment in human potentiality in mind.
I think I'd love to exchange with you —
my only immediate reservation is that we might
be a wee bit too much mirror-images of each
other. I'm a 31 year old writer with a (largely)
joyful productive existence, wood burning
fireplace (no court yard) with superb friends
and lovers of every background and
enthusiasm. I fear that both St. Laurent &
Ibis would be a trifle snug but I am
resourceful & adaptable enough to at least try
tennis instead of bicycling. No shrink — but
a dynamite men's consciousness raising on
Tuesday nights (for consciousnesses already
raised). Let's try.
Warmly,
Michael

Dear Box A 3240,

I was totally delighted to read your ad in the Voice. I'd like to swap. Why? Well life gets dull here: Allday long I swing up & down. Occasionally they bring in someone from St Louis or St Antonio to screw, but it's a stranger & I get nothing out of it. But don't get me wrong. I too have a joyful life in many ways. Lots of admirers. People give me food all the time. Weekends are a popcorn orgy.

I offer a small studio situated in the heart of Central Park. My pad is cleaned twice a day & I have no fireplace, but I bet my courtyard is bigger than yours. I'm afraid I have no wardrobe— I don't believe in clothes. Books, of course, I have no need of, as I'm all basic. You might say I'm at that primitive level everyone's trying to reach these days. I love tennis racquets.

I know you'd enjoy a month here. You can swing as much as you like. I hope I'll hear from you right away. If you'd like to interview me, just come to cage 5 and throw in 2 hot tamales so I'll know it's you.

With all my love,

X

King Kong IV
Central Park Zoo
New York, N.Y. 1000000

I liked Mel Green's letter, chicks and scenes and digs and all, but I'd decided that I wasn't going to answer any come-ons from men. Could Michael Littauer be for real? I called T.M. and read him the letter. "Now don't get totally crazy," he said. "You're not trading with a man, I don't care how good his legs are." I kept calling the 777 number anyway; I had to find out if he meant it. The number never did answer.

The King Kong letter was from Lou, of course. Lou was a lawyer, an old college friend of T.M.'s; we'd had some good times until we decided to save each other. The swap idea had first come up while we were seeing each other, and it had shocked him, wounded him a bit, set him to muttering about my needing to be institutionalized. The letter was a jolly gesture, but it didn't hold off a wash of the blues. I wanted real letters from real women. I wanted to get on with the swap.

I walked up Sixth Avenue to Jerri's Cleaners. One of the triumphs of my joyful, productive existence is knowing a wonderful manic in a profession packed solid with depressives.

"And here comes Nancy," Jerri sang out.

"The great Jerri!"

"What's new, babe?"

"Sublime madness. Of which you and Florence will be a part." I handed him a tear sheet from *The Voice* with my ad circled in purple.

"Hey, that's wild. So you mean when she walks in here with your chamois number, I don't ask her whose closet she's been ripping off, I just say, 'Hi, Nancy; good-bye, Nancy,' or do I use her name?"

"Hadn't thought about that. I guess we exchange names, sure."

"Tree-mendous. Gonna be a book?"

"Maybe, I guess, though it's not why I thought it up; I really want to just do it. Can I have these for Monday?"

I got them on Monday. That was all I got. No letters. I didn't understand it. How could any woman not answer the ad? I made faces all afternoon and told T.M. I was unfit for human consumption and wouldn't have dinner with him. I ate a summery melon and wished I were in France.

My film maker friend Andy Baron called later that evening. He said he had a story to tell me. He'd been having a drink with a writer named Al Wexler, and Al had pulled my ad out of his pocket and said, "Wouldn't it make a terrific film?" "I know the girl who ran the ad," Andy said. "We've talked about it as a film." "Who is she?" asked Al. "My wife and I thought it was the most terrific thing, even fooled around with the notion of answering it." Andy told him my name. "Oh, my God," said Al. "She was my wife's best friend all during grade school. They were inseparable."

"Jane Blackman!" I said.

"Right. And when Al went home and told her that a friend of hers had written that ad, she said, 'I bet it was Nancy.' "

Incredible. We hadn't seen each other in fifteen years, and there it all still was. I got her number from Andy and called her. We were shy and emotional and giggly and self-recriminating about having let the friendship go and full of questions about each other's parents and brothers and just very glad to be in touch again. I invited her and Al to come to dinner the next week, then called Andy and invited him, too. It didn't matter anymore that no mail had come that day. This reunion was magic enough for the moment.

I called my parents. I knew they would love the story, and they did, though they were not at all excited about my excitement over the project *en général*. It was such a terrific idea, they kept saying, would make such a great novel if only I'd keep trying; why did I always have to walk off the edge of the world with everything?

"She may make it a better mixed-doubles game," I said.

They weren't moved. They told me again that they couldn't possibly take part in it, Jane Blackman or no.

I was upset. I was trying to prove something about liberty, and they were behaving like parents. Even my brother was down on the whole thing, though he said he'd go along. I knew it was mostly that they were afraid for me; my mother kept saying that a sane woman could have put that ad in *The Voice* but only a crazy one would answer it. That still didn't square it. I wanted to take a train to Hartford and say brilliant things and look impervious to all madwomen and make them feel about the ad the way I did. I wanted to make sure that my swapee would know what it was like to love them, be loved by them. I wanted them pulling for me.

I didn't go to Hartford. I poured some Tullamore Dew into a goblet and started to write a story of sorts.

Anne and Nat and their parents had once been playing tennis on the kind of midsummer Connecticut day when the heat becomes a frosted-glass window around the court, dims the colors and sounds beyond the clay, distorts all motion out there, finally leaves the players with the sense that the lines of the court define the entire breathing world. Anne looked at her father next to her, crouched (gallantly back a bit farther than he had to be) to receive her mother's first serve of the point; at her mother, across from him, two balls in her hand and her racquet ready, centering her strength; at Nat, frozen low at the net, in tournament concentration, but—too hot to see for sure—maybe making a face to set his darling sister agiggle; and the darling sister herself, the least-good player of the four, nearer the baseline than she should have been, trying to look ferociously ready for whatever might come, but in fact undone by the beauty of the moment.

The four of them there like that, held in perfect tension, as connected with one another as though the lines of a Mondrian bound them, all the elements of their family life present in such rich measure—the love, the sharing of pleasure, the humor, the friendly-fierce competitiveness, even (in the pairing of the teams) safe sexuality: The moment gave Anne so deep a sense of completeness that she wanted it to last a few hundred years, knew all future moments, however fine, would be marred by a longing for this one. Instantly she realized the curse she'd put on herself, wanted to shout, be obscene, rip off her clothes, defile the picture that by its beauty promised to mock all beauty to come. "Let me go!" she screamed in her head. Her mother served into the net and scattered the ghosts.

Trigger Mike called from the Lion's Head. I said I'd be over in a minute.

I knew I'd never finish the story, but it wasn't really a story anyway. Old analysand Lou would have liked it, my dumping my psyche on paper like that. He'd said from the start that my real motivation for the swap was a wish to break with the family I loved too much. My parents were great fans of the unconscious? My brother and I looked and sounded so much like our father and mother that we were advertisements for the power of genes? The environment of my childhood home still claimed me and soothed me as no other place did? Obvious, then. It was simple postadolescent rebelliousness that motivated me to prove that unconscious, genes, environment were tiny factors in determining personality, that self-invention was, at least could be, the real determinant.

But Lou: My parents and brother are among the most consistent celebrants of freedom I know, so how do you reconcile that?

T.M. looked terrific. His hair, where there is hair, was a little longer than usual and looked more than ever like oatmeal. I kissed both ends of his ridiculous moustache.

The Head was crowded, noisy. I still had a certain shyness in bars, but I knew a lot of the people who hung out there and was getting to like it very much. Paul poured Paddy into a wine glass without even asking; that felt good. T.M. was talking it up about the mayoralty race. I listened a little bit, but we'd figured out a while back that we got along better at bars when we didn't stand around pretending to be amused by stories we'd heard a hundred times. I went over to the jukebox, dropped in a quarter, turned, put my hands behind me, pressed buttons here and there. The Stones started singing, which is what randomness will get you. Jack Barleycorn waved his beer glass at me.

Jack and I had met at a party months before. He'd been wearing a blue and white striped shirt with the sleeves rolled up two notches, and I'd wanted to marry him. He must have known; he never called. Now here he was, being friendly as could be.

We spent ten minutes discussing his latest New England epic novel and something like three hours raging about the swap, questions and answers jamming up against each other. I can still feel the heat of it, but most of the words fell out of my head as they happened, maybe because T.M. kept bobbing up with another glass of Irish. I've never seen Trig so delighted with me in a bar. I do remember one exchange Jack and I had toward the end.

JACK: I just don't see how you can ask a lover of yours to accept some other woman in your place. What if she doesn't turn him on?

NANCY: She won't be another woman; she'll be me.

JACK: Come off it, goddammit.

NANCY: She will be, goddammit. She'll talk like me, smell like me, and if my lovers just treat her as if she is me, then she'll——

JACK: No more of that ya-de-ya; I'm going out of my mind. Does Mike get a look at her first?

NANCY: Oh, no. We all take the plunge. If she and I like each other enough to trust each other with our whole lives, then the people we care about have to like us, don't they?

JACK: You're insane.

NANCY: I'm a nice Jewish girl from New England.

JACK: I suppose the way to find out about it all is to get to be better friends with you.

NANCY: Do you still have your blue and white striped shirt?

Later on that night Trigger Mike asked politely if the ardor I had visited on him had anything to do with Jack Barleycorn.

"He's sweet, isn't he?" I said.

"He has mean eyes. He's trouble, kid."

T.M. got his usual attack of four a.m. restless legs and went back to the Algonquin. I put blue paper in my typewriter.

In a crazy way T.M. will be the easiest man to turn over to my swapee because I love him the most, know how much he loves me, know there's no way I'd ever just be fungible goods for him. It'll also be easiest for him to accept my swapee as me, for her to be me when she's with him. Our existence together is so defined, we're both so grounded in it, that life will proceed like a well-written play, call it a comedy, with a last-minute switch in the cast. Does that make sense? I had much much such-a-much to drink tonight. Jack Barleycorn is going to break my heart. I guess I *am* insane: I love T.M. for being so cool about having my swapee as his dearest lover for a month, and I love Jack Barleycorn for being horrified (though somewhat turned on) by that idea. Go to sleep, Annunciata Mandolin. PLEASE BE MAIL TOMORROW.

I woke up very early Tuesday with a head that wanted to die. I took it to the counter at Bigelow Pharmacy and soothed it with two chocolate Cokes, best thing I ever learned from my mother. Went next door to my florist. Playing with flowers can cure me of almost anything.

"Calendulas," shouted Phil. "Freesia. Yellow daisies. Buttons. Abbeys." My blood did a jig. For a yellow-and-orange-flower junkie, February is one long high.

T.M.'s snowdrifts were demoted to the bathroom. The new flowers went all around the room—next to the Münter (the centers of the yellow daisies exactly the yellow of the tree between the house and the mountains), in front of my records, on the floor next to the fireplace, on Nick's tea table, on the yellow bookcase next to the couch. My head felt more kindly disposed toward the day. I called my answering service, made Louise promise never to let me drink again, asked her to take any calls, turned off the bell on the phone, and knocked out a short piece for *Cosmopolitan* attacking people who interpret everything sexually. It was a rather witty piece, even intelligent here and there, which meant they would probably reject it. (They did.) Wrote a letter to Mike Murphy at Esalen.

I'd reviewed his spectacular book *Golf in the Kingdom* for *The New York Times,* and we'd become mail friends; and I wanted him to show the ad to any potential swapees, let me have his thoughts on it.

There was no point in calling *The Voice* yet. The second mail wouldn't be sorted until eleven thirty. I answered the phone calls that had come in while I was working. Made a pass or two around the apartment.

> *Oh, Ben, Ben, do you have any idea what it feels like to remember all this, the innocence of it, the simplicity, a Coke here, a letter there, do you know what it's like to write all this without a hint of what was to be, the crossing over, the terror, the pain this thing caused others, the stillness with you, I dream about the pain to the others but I think about the stillness, your body so fluid on the bed with the crucified moon outside, I think about your eyes open so wide when we touched, your mouth looking so moved and astonished, and no one else's touch feels quite right, and I think of how she's poisoned you against me, not just for now and later but also to kill what was, is this how I pay for the pain to the others, that we don't even have what was*

There were letters that day, exactly the letters I wanted. I realized it made sense, all of them coming on Tuesday like that; the people who were serious about the ad had waited for the weekend, and leisure, to answer it. I pictured four serene women doing the Sunday *New York Times* crossword puzzle with their husbands, then sitting down at their portable typewriters to draft letters to me, reading them out loud, being kissed on the top of the head, dropping envelopes in the mailbox on the way to the movies. Did any of them get the attacks of elevator stomach that I get when a letter I care about has slid past the point of no retrieve into the belly of the mailbox? One of them, maybe; and would she be the one I swapped with, or would I have to learn a whole new way of mailing letters? It dizzied me, the thought of all the learning.

dear box a3240 i am very interested in your
life-swapping offer and hope you will contact me
at 553—XXXX ask for susie during the day

i am thirty and size eight so that's one thing
in our favor
i have an Irish beautiful setter and a little
brown puppy and a husband in the field of magazine
publishing
i have a background in fine arts, media, and
education, an MA in art ed and am seeking
alternative lifestyles and growth as a human
being

my interests include feminism, yoga, skiing, scuba
diving, tennis, video tape, still photography,
sex, and royal air force exercises

i also climb lots of stairs and have an "open
marriage" with lots of problems not lots relative
to many

i am also willing to gamble

Dear "Let's Swap Lives,"

I've read your ad in the Voice, dated February 8, 1973, and I find it both intriguing and exciting.

I:
  am thirty-three
  happily married
  have a successful, good-looking husband
  have two fine children
  live in a large modern home
  am an avid tennis player
  an equally avid reader
  enjoy music from rock to Bach
  am very athletic and active
  just started a yoga class
  am a size seven or eight
  am very good looking and sexy
  own my own car
  don't need a shrink
  enjoy dancing, films, and plays
  enjoy lunching with friends frequently
  share some of my husband's hobbies—photography
    —I enjoy modeling
  don't share his interests in camping and fishing
  enjoy sex
  have very few hang-ups
  would enjoy hearing from you. . . . .

        B. Miller
        P.O. Box 22
        Somerville, N.J.

Dear Box A 3240, VV:

I am thirty-two and a housewife with a husband of
same age and a daughter of soon six. We live on
Manhattan's East 84th Street. We are all Swedish
and have lived in the U.S. for three years. My
husband is an importer-exporter.

I have been working on and off during my
seven-year-marriage, lately as a tour escort and
guide. Right now I'm only caring for the
household. Our daughter is in school five days a
week from nine to three.

Your idea to find out if people "can get out of
their skins" interests both myself and my husband.
We believe people can, it just takes an open mind.
A change in lifestyle, we believe, is good and
healthy.

I find myself being bored by doing the same thing
for a certain amount of time and this includes
work, home, child, sex, etc. A change for me for
a month could very well prove if it is my
surroundings that bore me or myself. Therefore
your offering of a single life, apartment,
friends, etc., in exchange for mine for a short
period of time interests me.

My wardrobe is eight-nine (Cacharel types). You
will get a four-bedroom apartment, a family life
with not too many friends.

If you think my offering is to your liking and
purpose please call me at 371-XXXX so we can get
together and further discuss the venture.

Elke

% Danny Richards
115 W. 85th St.
New York, N.Y. 10024

I am ready to swap lives with you.

Have house in Bucks County, apartment in
Manhattan, husband in Buffalo, loving lovers here
and there.

No shrink to see. In fact, I am one. But don't
worry, the work is no sweat.

I am already out of my skin, and am willing to
try yours.

You can reach me at the above address, or call
me at (212) 663-XXXX.

Micki

I called Susie. Someone at her office said she was "in the field." I pictured Persephone gathering wild flowers. Sent B. Miller a telegram. Called Elke and set up a meeting for six thirty at the Lion's Head. A man answered at Micki's number and said she wouldn't be home until later. I told him why I was phoning, and he said, "Oh, yes," in a knowing voice. I wondered if he were a lover here or there and what he was wondering about me.

I manicked around the apartment. They all sounded so good. Could I swap with the four of them? A little wild for my friends, but maybe not out of the question. I tried to imagine myself in each of their lives. I saw myself with Elke's daughter on my knee, our heads close together, mine by osmosis blonder than it is, both of us smiling at some secret—a Clairol ad. As B. Miller I was in a car, an American four-door, maybe a station wagon. Her/my husband was wearing an Abercrombie's hooded parka, and the kids —both boys, I was sure—were being squirmy and adorable as we drove to our favorite ice-skating pond. I was somewhat older, more formidable as Micki, wearing a Peck & Peck suit, sitting behind an enormous modern desk as I delivered healing words to one of her/my patients. Then I was Susie, racing her/my husband up the stairs to our dog-filled apartment.

Five hours until I met Elke. My sanity was in luck; I had a hundred things to do.

Went to talk to the editor of *New Ingenue* about some articles I wanted to aim at young writers. We decided I should begin with a science fiction write-in. I'd ask eight or nine great sf writers to supply one ingredient apiece for a short story; we'd print the ingredients and invite *Ingenue*'s readers to send us stories built around four or more of them; then we'd buy and publish the best. I wondered where the swap and this project would intersect. Would my swapee get to write the letters to Isaac Asimov, Harlan Ellison, and the other sf writers I most like, or would she have the fun of getting their answers, or would it be up to her to judge the stories the girls wrote? Did she like science fiction? Care about discovering new writers? What would she think if Asimov made his usual teasing reference to the see-through shirt I'd been wearing when I was an editor at *Scanlan's* and he came in to deliver the piece I'd asked him to do for us? Would she think I was crazy to do something so time consuming for a few hundred dollars, or would she agree that this was more important than ten thousand weighty words for *Harper's?*

Into a phone booth to call Nick in Hartford. He was starting to get enmeshed in my dither, love all the questions that kept popping up. We decided to spend the weekend together in the city, see the two Saul Steinberg shows and lots of movies, play cribbage and Scrabble, be as decadent as possible. I hoped Trigger Mike was going to Chicago or had a basketball game or something. Nick didn't particularly like T.M., which meant T.M. was out of the picture when Nick was in town. My oatmeal-haired lover took this situation with fairly good grace (he was fond of his own sister, who wasn't fond of me), but still. Would the woman I swapped with understand how loyal Nick and I were to each other? Loving T.M. as much as I did would make it easy for me to put him into my swapee's care for a month; loving Nick would make it unbearable. Maybe the difference was that the other woman would have a husband or lover she was wild about, someone I could be wild about that way, but wouldn't so likely have a Nick on whom I could hang all my sisterly adoration. Our jokes, our games! I would teach them all to her and every once in a while during the swap punch a hole in her/my persona and watch them playing together and have the ecstatic experience of being in two places at once.

Took a cab to Chinatown. Had a spectacular meditation, full of highs and lows, dark cool spaces and flashes of light. I would have to give my mantra to my swapee, a violation of all the rules, if the Transcendental Meditation people were right. Even if they were, I'd be okay. During that month she would be me, not somebody else.

Ecstatic shopping. Bought snow peas, young Chinese cabbage, fresh coriander, dried mushrooms, cellophane noodles, and all the other things I needed for fondue à la Chinoise. Magda was coming over with her upstairs neighbor John (her husband, Will, was in Canada pushing his new book), and my new friend Abbe, an Israeli violinist who hung around the Lion's Head, would be there too. I felt very happy. Thought, as I often had before, that I should probably live in a market. The colors, the smells. Walked down Mott Street, bought a gigantic almond-paste cookie shaped like a fish—pure Paul Klee. Something about the cookie made me think of Jack Barleycorn. He tickled my witchiness, called just as I walked in the door, invited me to dinner. I invited him to come join all of us; he said, no, he didn't trust me to cook. I liked that. It was a day for liking everything. I skipped to the Lion's Head, singing all the way.

Elke was stunning. Her looks filled me with longing because if my imperfections were perfections, I'd look more like her than like most people. She had orange-blossom-honey hair (mine is more like buckwheat honey and bends in peculiar ways where hers curves sublimely); she had silky fair skin that, unlike mine, looked safely beyond adolescence; she had a lot of nose, but there was nothing hilarious about it; she was wearing the kind of European womanly elegant secretly sexy sporty clothes that I loved, but she looked soignée in a way I never did, clearly never dropped her drink or tripped up a flight of stairs.

She smoked menthol cigarettes and drank tea and asked me lots more questions than I asked her. What did Trigger Mike look like? Where did I hang out? She had very few friends—would I feel lonely? How did I feel about taking care of her daughter?

Extraordinary, how shy I felt answering her, how intrusive I felt asking her if she felt capable of doing my work and being unmonogamous, if she had any hesitancy at all about my being lovers with her husband. She told me she and her husband had separate bedrooms, and I felt shier still. I listened to her and watched her and wondered what it would be like to be so cool, to be all the things she was. I imagined myself sitting on the other side of the table, wearing white wool pants and a pale blue shirt, flicking the ashes off a Salem, and suddenly it didn't seem as if it would be hard at all; I just needed to do a little studying, have a few props. There was an Elke inside me and a Nancy inside her, I was sure of it. I suggested that we keep detailed journals for a week to give each other an idea of the drift of our days, then meet again. We shook hands outside the Lion's Head. She looked very tall.

I went home and put on *Tristan und Isolde* and made the sauces for the fondue. Would Elke buy too much food, the way I always did for guests? Would she cook as much for the eye as for the palate? Would I have to make Swedish meatballs for her husband who had his own bedroom (or was it she who had her own)? Took a shower and put on the embroidered black Bedouin dress I'd once worn to the Wailing Wall out of some mad ecumenical impulse and nearly had torn from my back. I'd have to remember to tell Abbe-from-Haifa that story. I pinked my cheeks, put on the

Dior lipstick that T.M. says looks like chopped liver. (He thinks Shalimar smells like a vanilla egg cream. What does it all mean, Lou?) I wondered exactly how much of a gift Elke's physical beauty would be for the men in my life. T.M. had this crazy affection for my crazy face, and other people who loved me loved looking at me; how would the man who lived with Elke's perfection feel about me? I put fresh towels in the bathroom. My apartment looked serene, alive. I knew it would be a fine evening. I madly longed to call George Warneke's wife, Kylie, and say, "Come on over and be me tonight. I've done all the cooking that doesn't get done at the table, and I'll do the dishes," turn my Bedouin dress over to her, put on my blue-jeans, go to the Riviera, order a hamburger and a beer on the rocks, and spend the evening reading Troyat's biography of Tolstoy and thinking of the great party I was throwing for Abbe and Magda and John.

The phone. Micki. Sounding crisp and hurried and seriously interested in the swap and very friendly. She told me that she was thirty-one, that she taught sociology and headed the women's studies program and did counseling—her shrinking—at Hawthorne College in Brooklyn, and that she was too out-of-her-mind busy to see me until next Tuesday. We agreed to meet at the Lion's Head at six thirty. A heavyweight academician! I realized I'd forgotten to call back Susie of the many stairs and open marriage. Tristan died and Isolde shrieked. The doorbell rang.

Magda and John and Abbe and I drank a spectacular amount of sake. They all said they would treat my swapee just the way they treated me; what could be simpler than that. The Chinese fondue was superb, and I was glad I was there and sorry Jack Barleycorn wasn't. Everyone left around two. I sat down with blue paper.

Not only taking someone else's name; carrying her identification papers. All my spy fantasies come true.

If I tell my swapee a lie about myself—say that I like someone I actually dislike—will her acting as if this were true build up a dynamic that will eventually make it true?

Everyone tonight was talking about the sexual aspects of the swap. Inevitable, I guess, but I don't think that's the most dramatic part. Why am I convinced that it will be easier to make love the way she does than cook the way she does? Maybe because each of us is many lovers but only one or two cooks. I would never make eggs Benedict of my own volition, or use margarine, or buy frozen fish or un-Heinz ketchup, but there's nothing sexual I can't imagine feeling, doing, being under certain conditions. And I'm counting on her husband/lover/lovers to approach me not as a new body but as their dear and familiar one. They can, after all, always have the experience of making love to a new woman; they'd be mad not to pursue this unique chance to make love to a new/old woman. (Shouldn't I also be able to count on her pots and pans and refrigerator speaking to me? Yes. But.)

The week jumbled by. Susie came in from the field and agreed to meet me for breakfast Sunday at the Lion's Head. I got a phone call from B(arbara) Miller, the tennis-playing mother from New Jersey, who giggled constantly and said she was scared and sounded delightful and agreed to meet me Monday for breakfast at the Brasserie.

My best friend from childhood Jane and her husband Al came for dinner with Andy Baron (Chinese fondue again), and there was much hugging and warmth and laughing and fun. I had my biggest fight in years with T.M. (he was being nastily jealous—a lovely trait in a polygamous lover), and I did something wicked. I called up Mel Green, whose invitation to dig him digging me I'd found sweet, and said my name was Darryn Dangerfield and I'd just come in from Switzerland and my friend Nancy who'd placed the ad in *The Voice* had showed me his letter, suggested I call him. He didn't sound the least bit like a strangler, and I went to his loft wearing pearls but no shirt or sweater with my plaid New England coat and skirt. He was incredibly gentle and had a funny bone sense of humor and let me know that he didn't believe I was Darryn or Swiss but it didn't matter, he would just call me M.W. for Mystery Woman and let me tell as many truths or lies about myself as I pleased. We spent a day being entirely kind to each other, and then I went home—I knew there would be flowers from T.M., and I didn't want them to die. There were flowers, and I put them in water and called T.M. up, and we went to Jimmy's for dinner and were worldly and happy indeed. I worked on the journals for my potential swapees: "Up this morning at eight thirty, nine, nine thirty, nine forty-five for real. Went through a pot of Irish tea (milk goes in the cup first). T.M. called three times. . . ." Sent two bottles of Swiss white wine to Mel Green. Got a jolly note from Mike Murphy at Esalen:

The ad in the Village Voice lifts my spirits. Congratulations! It is in the grand tradition of the mystical quest. Though it might have horrified him at first, the Buddha would be proud. Only in America, I think, could the ego be amputated so decisively.

There was a great letter from a might be swapee named Nancy in Savannah with a picture of her baby. I also worked in a few non-swap events. If I didn't live something like my normal life, what would I have to trade when the time for trading came? Did a lot of reading about tantric yoga and got George and me an assignment to write about it for *Viva*. I had a wonderfully serene evening with Bill and Katharine Andrews, oldest and dearest friends. Met with Yuric Lermentov, the Polish film maker, whom I was helping to adapt a screenplay for American production. Broke out maniacally and went to see darling Dr. Verde, my dermatologist, for a little "acupuncture." For no reason that I particularly understood, received from Viking a copy of *The Psychology of Consciousness* by Robert Ornstein and opened it at random to see if it contained a secret message, and it did:

[An] exercise attributed to Gurdjieff consists simply in maintaining continuous awareness of a part of one's body—an elbow, hand, leg. Another exercise of this tradition is to perform ordinary habitual actions slightly differently, such as putting shoes on in the opposite order, shaving the other side of the face first, eating with the left hand (if one is right-handed). These exercises can be seen as attempts to return habitual, "automatic" actions to full awareness.

Had dinner with T.M. and the Jepsons and a certain senator at Elaine's and didn't like the senator, or was it just that he paid more attention to Magda than to me? Wished Jack Barleycorn would call, wished it about once an hour. Went for a walk with Abbe and told him I wouldn't go to bed with him just yet; I was going to leave it up to my swapee to decide if he and I were meant to be lovers. Did he think I was serious? Was I? Then at last Saturday and Nick and looking at paintings and being eight years old again.

Blond blue-jeaned Susie met me at the Lion's Head on Sunday and eyed me up and down and seemed to wonder whether or not to trust me. She told me she led a busy, ordered life—lessons for this, groups for that; she hinted at rather many lovers. Her job, in the field and out, was with the Board of Education, running a special program in the arts. She said she'd stopped painting years before and had taken up still photography and video taping. I heard a wistfulness in that and decided if we swapped I'd become a painter again for her. I was shy, though not quite so shy as with Elke, and made the suggestion about trading journals at the end of a week or so. She said she was a lousy writer but agreed to try. She was on her way to see her parents, which I liked. We decided that if we swapped in early April, we could go to each other's parents' seders. What every Jewish mother wants.

I liked her a lot, and the meeting exhilarated me, but I came away from it as wiped out as if I'd played four sets of tennis. Even meetings with several out-of-the-question swapees had done that. Nick wanted to see lots of movies—perfect for me. We went to *Cesar and Rosalie, Save the Tiger,* and *Night of the Living Dead,* ate junk food in between, had word-derivation contests while standing in line, fell asleep the minute we got into bed. Jack Barleycorn called at two in the morning and asked me to go for a walk with him, and I jumped out of bed all awake and went. He was wearing the blue and white striped shirt, though alas not at all on purpose, and we talked about growing up in New England and behaved as if we hadn't. I brought warm croissants home for Nick, but they were cold by the time he woke up.

February played out, and March took over, most of it going at that tempo. Snow did and didn't happen. Trigger Mike moved to the Plaza for a month. My dear young writer friend Fran Berman fell in love by a pinball machine and decided to get married. T.M. and I had some fine times; Jack Barleycorn made me suffer, which was good for my figure. An editor interested in a book on the swap asked if I had any respectable backing for my ideas, and George Warneke gave me a letter on his Ph.D. stationery, like a note from home to teacher:

The most difficult thing in psychotherapy is to convince a role-bound person that there actually are other possibilities for him, other ways to feel, think, structure a life. In psychodrama a person begins to act out the figures in his or her dreams, to try on new roles as though they were pieces of clothing and see how they fit. Nancy Weber's life swap fascinates me because it may confirm that we can put aside our "givens," explore other givens, then integrate the fruits of our exploration into our lives—as Nancy and her companion in this adventure hope to do when they return home. I think what these women plan to do will give other people the courage to expand their notions of themselves and their destinies, to live more fully than they may have dared dream was possible.

Mostly I thought about the women who had answered my ad. It was down to Susie and Micki and Barbara, though there'd been a mess of canceled appointments, and I hadn't yet met Micki and Barbara, just logged a lot of hours with them on the phone. Elke was out. She'd said her husband wanted to meet me; I'd agreed, though I believed he'd have a harder time treating me as Elke if he got a fix on me as Nancy; we'd set a date; then she called and broke it without giving an excuse, never called again. I didn't pursue her. I'd begun to be put off by her coldness and by the feeling that she wanted to use the experience simply to decide whether or not to remain with her husband. Nancy from Savannah was out, too. We'd both decided that two-year-old Timothy was not quite up to coping with a new mommy. None of the other women who answered panned out.

I started making notes on pink paper:

SUSIE: I like her more all the time, like her sense of herself as a woman. Her feminism is mostly an impulse to be independent, is little tainted by ideology, though now and then the word "chauvinism" creeps into her talk—agggh. She doesn't have a feminist's contrived indifference toward her appearance, is brash and shy—endearing. I think she's surprised when people are really good to her. I'd like to surprise her. We have very similar moral constructs: Morality for both of us has everything to do with kindness, nothing to do with sex. I think she could really understand me, really get inside a lot of the connections in my life.

MICKI: Are we ever going to meet? She keeps having emergencies up at school, trouble with her wisdom teeth. What I know of her life is intriguing as hell. During the week she lives on the upper West Side with her twenty-one-year-old lover, Peter, a former student; and a male homosexual friend and academic colleague, Danny (not Peter's lover). She spends weekends in Bucks County with her husband, Ben, who teaches Latin and linguistics at a private school near Buffalo. She's a big feminist theorist, a fairly militant bisexual; she wanted to know if I was scared. I said no, I rather longed to resolve all that—Micki, I want to meet you!

SUSIE: Her husband is insisting on spending some time with me. I agreed; we're going to have dinner in a couple of nights.

BARBARA: Absolutely marvelous meeting, finally. Of all the women I've met and talked with, she seems the happiest—giddily in love with her husband (which Susie certainly isn't and Micki doesn't seem to be) and generally content to be what she is. Content—but not content about being content, which is why she answered the ad. I love the sound of her kids—I was right, two boys—of the uncompulsive orderliness of her life. She says the kids and Bob are all for the adventure; she's the only one who isn't sure. Half an hour after meeting her, I told her I was sure about her, the first absolute commitment I've made. One thing I like about the idea of doing the swap with her is that I think it would be terrific for her, more so even than for me or Susie or Micki. Not that I remotely want to make her restless with her life. But she admits that within that life she's too reluctant to try new things, too sure she won't like them or be good at them—like going camping with her husband. I asked her to keep journals. She said she can't write. I told her I liked the letter she wrote me; turns out her husband wrote it!

SUSIE: No journals. Says she hates writing. Told me she mentioned the swap to her supervisor at the Board of Education and got a flat no, but the woman agreed to meet me. Seeing her husband tomorrow night.

MICKI: And at last. The great Micki. A formidable creature—cerebral and manic and very self-assured. Should do something about her hair. I was faintly terrified as I crossed the slushy Hawthorne campus and walked into the gothic horror that houses her office—I was back at Chaffee, about to face Mrs. Parker and tell her why I was incapable of learning history. Micki's looks relaxed me. Pixie face, pants, striped jersey. Nothing like the Peck & Peck grown-up I'd expected. We talked for a while, mostly about the theoretical basis for the swap and my antifeminism and tantric yoga. It knocked me out that so much psychological theory, about which I know nothing, supports what I want to do, and I was very excited by all the thinking Micki could bring to bear on it. Students came in and out, and one of her colleagues called to ask her to lecture on sex to a class the next day. I loved the way Micki instantly agreed and said, "Oh no, I can't take money for that from you." Very jazzy, all of it. She kept telling me the work would be no problem, especially with her secretary, Carla, to help me. She was just as sure that she could do my work, even do something frothy for

Cosmopolitan. She promised to start keeping journals that night, no matter what her wisdom teeth did. After a while we drove back into Manhattan and had a couple of drinks at the Cedar Tavern. I'd been picking up the checks at all the meetings I'd been having about the swap (though both Susie and Barbara had protested), and I thought it was funny and sweet that Micki bought us a round while I was off phoning T.M. Though I wondered if that, like getting me to meet her at her office, wasn't a way of making sure I wasn't running the show. She told me she was a little worried about T.M. She'd seen his cartoons, of course, and was afraid they'd clash on politics. I reminded her that she'd have my politics during the swap, and she smiled and said she guessed it would be okay. I told her I definitely wanted to do the swap with her, that if Barbara or Susie or both of them worked out, I'd do it with each of them for two weeks. She said two weeks was probably better for her anyway. I said that her life sounded very open and ordered and that I thought I'd learn something important from her. She told me it would be good for her to learn about chaos from me.

SUSIE: Dinner with Susie's Ken. Met him at his office—he publishes several trade publications—and we talked about magazines. It was nice that we had something like that in common, it took away the strangeness, but in a way I hated talking about what was such a big part of my Nancy life. Japanese restaurant; conversation about food and travel. Afterward we had a brandy in the bar, and he started putting the hard questions to me, mostly about what kind of cut Susie would get if a book came out of all this, how they could be sheltered if they wanted to be anonymous. I liked his protectiveness of her, but I wondered a bit about his own motivation for going along with the swap. There was no particular spark between us; I don't think we would have gotten much going across a crowded room. Funny, maybe, almost scary, but that really didn't matter to me. If things worked out with Susie's job, then I would take on everyone in her life without hesitation. I knew that if I were living with Ken as his wife, I would find a spark, make a spark. The challenge excited me. When I saw T.M. later, I asked him how he'd feel about having three new Nancys on his hands that spring.

BARBARA: Long gossipy talks on the phone. I love her throaty voice.

SUSIE: She and T.M. had dinner together. They seem to have liked each other a lot. He's worried, though, that he knows her too well as Susie.

MICKI: Dinner. Chinese. She told me she'd started her journals. Talked about a symposium she'd taken part in that weekend, another coming up. She asked if she could read my novel and such. Sent a copy of *Star Fever* and a batch of magazine pieces down to her place in Riverset, Pennsylvania, where she's gone for spring vacation. I have a feeling she'll find it all frivolous. A lot of it *is* frivolous, but I secretly think it's all secretly serious, a lot of it, anyway; hope she thinks so, too.

SUSIE: Lunch in Chinatown, then a meeting with her supervisor. I got no further than she had; there was no way I could take over her job; the computers would all blow up; the *New York Post* would make it a page-one scandal. We were both sad, but in a way I felt relieved. A closeness had sprung up between us that would make it more like swapping with an old friend, and that's not what I want. I realized that one of the best things about running the swap ad is that I've met such fine women, have spent so much time talking intimately with women. Susie lives three blocks away from me, and I know we're going to see a lot of each other, have other kinds of adventures. She'll be an important part of the swap because she'll be an important part of my life.

BARBARA: It was the life swap in miniature: Barbara off to a worldly night at Sardi's and Jimmy's with T.M., me off with blue-jeaned, moustached Bob to a discotheque on the upper East Side. I liked the way Bob talked about Barbara. I get a feeling from both of them of a true camaraderie. He told me not to believe her when she said she couldn't write, that even her shopping lists were like poems. I wasn't quite sure I believed his casual shrug when I asked him how he'd feel about Barbara going to bed with my lovers. (Amazing how much easier it was talking about the sexual side of the swap with a man than with the women involved.) This time the spark was there, though he told me I should wear eye makeup, and I knew he would want Barbara to go through with the swap in part for his own sake. Not that he was more eager than she would have wanted, than I would have wanted for her; he was just the right amount eager. T.M. told me later that he'd liked her very much and that the boys at Sardi's had thought she was great looking and delightful, but he was sure she'd never do it; it was just too much of a leap from her quiet, monogamous life.

MICKI: Called to share my excitement over having a firm offer for a book on the swap. She's as eager as I am to get our findings out into the world, and she was pleased that a fine publisher was interested, but she thought the money sounded low. We talked about having to work out our own contract, but that will have to wait until I know if I'm swapping with Barbara, too. She said she'd kept pretty good journals for the past three weeks but didn't want to give them to me yet; they were a mess, and she was going to have her secretary type them over. I sent her thirty-two single-spaced pages of mine, a mad stew full of T.M., Jack Barleycorn, spelling mistakes, ravings about art shows, hypochondria, science fiction, food and clothes, mystical experiences with crazy, terrific Fran Berman, flowers and showers and megalomania at large.

BARBARA: She sounded scared when I told her a publisher definitely wanted the swap book and I definitely wanted to write it, whatever it might be. I think she's slipping, wish I could give her an injection of the self-confidence she needs to say yes.

MICKI: Said my journals made her laugh; she loved all my different names for T.M. Was solicitous about my hypochondria.

BARBARA: A sweet sad lunch. She said that although Bob and the boys were disappointed in her, she just couldn't go through with the swap. She liked me; she liked T.M.; she knew she'd kick herself afterward for saying no—but no was what it had to be. I was torn. I told her I understood her decision completely, accepted it, but I wondered if she didn't still want me to make her want to do it, if I didn't owe her that. But what if she started the swap, then panicked in the middle? Most horrible thought. Better to let her go. We embraced in the street and vowed to stay friends. When I was a block down Fifth Avenue, she came running after me and handed me the letter she'd written in response to the ad and never mailed. I read it when I got home and realized that if I'd gotten it instead of Bob's, I would never have thought she'd do the swap. I was glad I'd gotten the other letter, had talked as much and as closely with her as I had.

B Miller
PO Box 22
Somerville NJ 02276

Dear "Let's Swap Lives."

Having read your ad in the Village Voice, decided to write and tell you that your idea was simply super. Whether I would be capable of going through with it is probably beyond me.

To the average suburban housewife the swap sounds great. Having thought about the freedom of single life many times. To fantasize is one thing — but to actually do it — well!

I'm 33 years old — married to a successful, bright, and attractive man who makes me quite happy most of the time. Two boys ages 11 & 7 round out my family, which my life settles around.

Having a very uncluttered and comfortable life style — I am active, slim and attractive. My personal pleasures consist of tennis, yoga, dancing and reading (mainly current fiction and periodicals. Simply love films any and all (foreign, good, bad) — never guided by the critics.

I'm 5'3" — 112 lbs. — with a very fine self-image.

My husband is a broad minded, liberal person. In fact, he spotted your ad and was quite impressed with the idea.

Two possibilities could develop after this exchange of life style — my family could learn to adore you and as a result not be too pleased to have me return — or — the other alternative — they might be so glad to have you leave that they will be overjoyed at my return (interesting thought).

This whole thing is really too much. Awaiting your reply —

With anticipation,

B. Miller

MICKI: Half a bottle of Gewürztraminer and some pâté *chez moi.*
Micki said she really likes my liking for fine wines and such, which made
me feel good: I knew that although she sometimes teased me about my
extravagance and said I'd find her life "funky," she'd enjoy that part of
my life and would entertain my friends in full style. Went out to dinner
(Japanese). Micki was still feeling the aftereffects of having two wisdom
teeth out, and had her period and was in pain from that, but her spirits
were high. I told her that one of the advantages of being me would be
sublime cramplessness. She told me more about some of the problems
of being a teacher—like being relaxed enough with her students to be
a successful counselor, but still wanting their papers in on time. We
talked a little bit about Barbara, and Micki told me that someone else
had written her letter, too—a psychologist friend, Sig Lewis, at Princeton. (She'd read it, signed it before it went off.) She gave me her
curriculum vitae—four pages of incredibly impressive scholar's credentials—and a batch of papers she'd written as part of her research work
for the women's movement. She's going to give me her journals next
week; I can't wait, though I feel I'm getting to know her very well as
it is. As I was walking her to her car, she said, "My other wisdom teeth
are killing me, too. I don't know whether to have them out now or wait
until the swap and let you have them out." I wish Barbara were doing
it also, but Micki understands it all and is very terrific—I can't imagine
anyone better to share in this mad adventure.

NEARING

MICKI'S JOURNAL

Nancy—Some random thoughts before I turn this mess over to Carla to type. I use Madame Rochas and Femme perfume, pinetar soap in Riverset, Ivory in NYC, Revlon Moon Drops moisture balm and cleansing cream. I don't shave my legs or under my arms, and I don't wear a deodorant. I sometimes wear jewelry. I have pierced ears. I take the following vitamins every day: C, A&D, E, B complex, dolomite (calcium and magnesium), calcium pantothenate, sometimes inositol and choline. I use Tampax when I menstruate and take Excedrin for cramps. I smoke at least one joint a day. I wash my face with a face brush. I usually bathe every other day, although in warm weather I sometimes take two or three showers a day. I love bubble bath and bath oil and buy my supply at the Soap Opera in NYC. I buy coffee and tea at McNulty's and take it to Riverset. I shop at Pathmark when in Riverset and at the store next door to my apartment in New York; owner of store is very friendly to me. My favorite restaurants in New York City are Tien Tsin on 125th Street (near Broadway) and Mother Courage on West Eleventh. I usually pay my own way whenever I go out. I often take Peter to dinner and pay for him, too. I cook a lot in Riverset, very little in NYC. Danny does much of the cooking in NYC, and I am chief assistant and sometimes do the dishes. I do very little housecleaning in NYC, and Danny usually does my laundry with his. In Riverset, a woman does general housecleaning about every three weeks, and I use the cleaners and the laundry in the Riverset shopping center. I often eat breakfast in the Riverset drugstore (two eggs over easy, no toast, ham and coffee—I take two sugars and cream in my coffee or tea and read the *New York Times* there). I like mocha java blend (French roast) coffee and Mu, jasmine, chamomile tea. In Riverset, I make coffee with a Chemex using a blend of Martinson's and Medaglia d'Oro. In NYC, we use Medaglia d'Oro, in an espresso maker. I don't eat much meat, lately very little beef. I love vegetables except peas, lima beans, and turnips. I love messages and massages. I douche at least twice a week with Massengill powder. I am quite fastidious about my body. I like to be clean and sweet smelling. My feet are never dirty. I hate dirty feet. I look at people's eyes and mouths and hands when I talk to them. I look at men's crotches and women's breasts. I prefer blue or green eyes to brown. A lot of my friends are left-handed, and I have a soft place in my heart for left-handed people. I notice people's handedness. I do not wear a bra except when not wearing one is going to make someone uptight (sometimes me). My nipples are often erect. I like being kissed on the undersides of the arms, the sides of my breasts and my neck, the insides of my thighs, and the backs of my knees. My favorite position (?) is cunnilingus. I like fellatio, but my small mouth and sharp teeth create difficulties in this area. I am right-handed. I do from fifteen to thirty minutes of yoga a day (hatha). I often meditate (Transcendental Meditation) and sometimes do autogenic exercises (your right leg is getting heavy, warm etc.; your left leg etc., your arm . . .your head). I also do some programmed exercises designed by Maggie Lettvin *(The Beautiful Machine)* for my legs, thighs, and ass, about three times a week. I am weight conscious. I presently weigh between 118 and 120 and would like to weigh 112. I try not to eat carbohydrates of any kind except I don't seem to be able to cut out the sugar in my coffee or tea. I am an atheist and a mystic at the same time, and in most things schizoid. I always feel like a participant-observer. I love word games and double entendres and secretly am amused by almost all conversations having to do with any subject because I always see a sexual meaning in words. Sex is a big part of my life. I like engaging in it, thinking about it, reading about it, talking about it. I am a rather silly person and like to frolic and detour. I'm fairly strong and quite tolerant of individual differences. I swear a lot.

"Fuckadoodle," "shit," "fucked-up," and "piggydoon" are some favorite words. I speak English and French, some Portuguese, some Spanish, some Italian. French, Chinese, and Mexican food are my favorites, more random notes later. What an ego!?

(In notes to follow have indicated making love with Peter as #1 and making love with Ben as #2 to save Carla's sensibilities, though God knows she's typed up more revealing!)

WEDNESDAY, MARCH 7

Nine a.m.: Get up; have coffee with Peter, drive to school for class in environmental sociology (reading *The Pursuit of Loneliness* by Philip Slater).

Twelve thirty: Lunch in student center with Jim and Donna Holub from environmental class. Have fish and chips, which are awful. Cannot finish lunch. Back to the office at one thirty to talk to Donna H and answer mail.

Three thirty: Nancy Weber arrives in brown leather skirt. Feel awkward but speedy-happy. Part of usual manic state that I seem to float into now and then. Serena calls to ask me to teach part of her human development class the next day. Wants me to answer questions on masturbation, frequency of sexual intercourse, premarital sex, bisexuality, and lesbianism. Agree to do it and be serious about it.

Four thirty: Drive to Cedar Tavern with Nancy (University Place) and have two beers (NW has two Irish whiskeys) and talk about Trigger Mike Kagan and his politics. Talk about Jim Cook, whose new book Nancy is carrying. Nancy tries reaching T.M. a few times. Agree to do the thing with Nancy. Have apprehensions about relationship with Mike, but decide if N.W. likes him, he's probably okay.

Six forty-five: Shower and wash hair.

Seven o'clock: Stephen Seldes (Hawthorne advisee, bisexual, one of the beautiful people, elegant con, marvelous body, has turned me on to great bath products, was one of six roommates who shared apartment with Ben and me on upper West Side last year) calls and says he'll come by at 7:20.

Seven twenty: Stephen arrives; we pick up bottle of Rhine wine on way to car and drive to Mother Courage. I have veal Marsala, and he has chicken Kiev. Run into Susan Brady, who gives me Arlene White's telephone number so I can contact her about a therapist. We talk about Stephen's work at school and going to Jamaica. Stephen can get cheap tickets, he says.

Nine thirty: Drive Stephen to his newest sweetie's house on the upper east side, then drive to Jean Stern's apartment on the upper west side.

Ten–one a.m.: Talk to Jean Stern and Betty Kling (both Jean and Betty are feminist therapists that I met three years ago in a discussion group), about what's happened to us since we last saw each other two years ago. Jean confesses that she has become jaded as a therapist. That she has no more empathy for her patients. She gave one woman, who couldn't breathe through her nostrils, psychological nostrils for the last six years, and now she feels like saying, "Why don't you just blow your nose and you could breathe better." Another patient is a midget, who is married to a dwarf with cerebral palsy, whose main problem is that she has a normal-size daughter who beats up on her. Some problem! I can understand why Jean is jaded. She's planning to take a trip to Nassau to a yoga camp for a week and then she's going for another retreat to a Buddhist camp. She's doing a very heavy mystic trip this month to try to become "revitalized," or so she says. She thinks she doesn't want to be a therapist anymore and thinks she might like to become a writer. We discussed what it would be like to change lives with you (Nancy Weber). We also discussed tantric yoga and whether I should become a therapist and we smoked a lot of very heavy grass. Jean is wearing a blue Indian-print dress and looks quite provocative. Betty discussed her current love life and her therapy with an ex-priest lover who was having trouble relating to his penis and so she used the following Gestalt therapy technique with him: She told him to place (imagine) his penis in a chair and talk to it. In this manner he learned to relate to his penis. I finally go home. It's raining, so I offered Betty a ride home. On the way we discussed Gurdjieff and the fact that she had been in a Gurdjieffian group for five years. Drive home, park car, go to bed, and cuddle up with Peter.

THURSDAY, MARCH 8

Nine o'clock: Wake up, have coffee, drive to Hawthorne, ask Carla to call Danny and tell him that it's Peter's twenty-first birthday and that he should contact whatever mutual friends he can get hold of for a surprise party for Peter.

Ten o'clock: Meet with Serena Tisch (colleague in Hawthorne soc. sci. department, developmental psychologist), discuss questions on sexuality that class wants to know something about: extramarital sex, premarital sex, masturbation, lesbianism, homosexuality, clitoral versus vaginal orgasms. Whether one is naturally hetero or homosexual. Will women's liberation make men impotent?

Ten thirty: Discuss questions with class. Class enthusiastic. They clap. Big ego trip for me. A number of women in the class ask me if I'm planning to teach a course at Hawthorne next semester.

Twelve thirty: Lunch with Serena in faculty dining room. Tell her it's Peter's birthday and invite her and Liz Hibbert (her friend) to come to a spontaneous party for Peter.

One thirty: Return to office, call Danny and ask him to invite some friends to Peter's party. Called Maisie Leonard, Pat Barry, Steffie Kahn, and Jean Stern and invited them to party. Answered mail.

Four o'clock: Drove to Papyrus (bookstore) on Broadway and 115th Street with Serena and picked up copy of *Nomadic Furniture* for birthday present for Peter. Picked up bottle of Cold Duck, a gallon of Gallo Hearty Burgundy and a gallon of Almadén Chablis.

Five o'clock: Liz Hibbert, Serena, Peter, and I drink Cold Duck and get stoned.

Six o'clock: I take Peter to dinner at a Szechuan restaurant on Broadway.

Seven thirty: Come home, took twenty-minute nap, #1.

Nine o'clock: Shopped next door for cheese, pretzels, paper cups, napkins.

Nine thirty: Called Ted Holzman (N.Y.U. student doing paper on women's studies program at Hawthorne) to invite him to party. Took shower and washed my hair.

Ten thirty: Party. Everyone smashed and stoned. Steffie (person most like me in the world, clinical psych student, NYU) tells amazing stories about: getting picked up on subway, her flu, her cat and kittens puking all over her apartment, and other amazing anecdotes. Everyone loves her. Peter gets totally smashed and sits in a chair without moving from twelve o'clock on. Everyone leaves at two except Steffie who makes vanilla pudding (two kinds: instant and regular) with Danny and then goes to bed with Danny, throws up, and ends up sleeping on mattress in middle of living room.

FRIDAY, MARCH 9

Ten o'clock: Wake up, have omelet with Steffie and Danny.

Twelve thirty: Drive to office, answer mail, get lots of phone calls.

Four o'clock: Drive to Riverset, Pa. Meet Ben there.

Seven thirty: #2.

Eight o'clock: Call Stephen about tickets for Jamaica. He says he's going to Dallas, will be back Monday and will get them then.

Eight thirty: Call Sig and Alice Lewis in Princeton and arrange to have pizza ready to take to their house for dinner.

Nine thirty–twelve: Spend evening with Lewises. Tell Sig that you've called (NW). Sig was planning to trick me by having friend call and pretend she placed ad in *Voice*. I ask Sig's son Jonah (twelve years old) how he's enjoying puberty. He says, "What is it?" I said it's when your voice changes and you grow hair under your arms and on your genitals and you get pimples. He says he's not there yet. Very cool kid. Ben does not know at this point that the real swap person called until Sig tells him while I'm in the bathroom. Ben voices his misgivings about the whole thing. Sig and Alice are enthusiastic. Sig wants to video tape each of us in our respective new lives. Went home exhausted.

SATURDAY, MARCH 10

Beginning of Ben's spring vacation.

Twelve o'clock: Wake up, #2, did almost nothing all day, played go with Ben, did my exercises, watched TV, went to bed early.

SUNDAY, MARCH 11

Twelve o'clock: Had breakfast in Riverset drugstore, read Sunday *NY Times*, went shopping at Pathmark, did my exercises, had codfish for dinner, ate 30 prunes compulsively in front of TV. Went to bed early.

MONDAY, MARCH 12

Nine–twelve o'clock: Was sick to my stomach from prunes and totally stiff from exercises. Stay in bed.

Twelve thirty: David Gross in Princeton calls and wants to come visit. We say okay.

One o'clock: Have yogurt for lunch.

Two thirty–five thirty: David Gross arrives. Ben and David and I make anise cookies.

Six o'clock: Have yogurt for dinner.

Seven thirty: Played go with Ben.

Nine–one A.M.: Watched TV. Went to bed.

TUESDAY, MARCH 13

Nine o'clock: Had breakfast in Riverset.

Ten–eleven o'clock: Worked in garden. Called Carla at Hawthorne.

Eleven fifteen–twelve fifteen: Went shopping at Pathmark.

One o'clock: Did exercises.

Two thirty: Played go with Ben and tried to contact Stephen Seldes (no answer). Called Jamaica car-rental places for information.

Five o'clock: Had yogurt and cheese for dinner.

Six–twelve o'clock: Watched TV and tried calling Stephen—no answer.

WEDNESDAY, MARCH 14

Nine o'clock: Cloudy day, drugstore for breakfast. Stephen calls. It seems he's no longer "friends" with ticket person and so no Jamaica. Ben very disappointed.

Eleven o'clock: Transplanted plants indoors. Potted some for Peter to take to his studio in the attic, some for Sukie (cleaning woman), and some for Ben's friends in Buffalo.

Eleven thirty: Talked to Nancy Weber about her sending materials to me.

Twelve o'clock: Played go with Ben.

One o'clock: Made tuna fish for lunch.

Six o'clock: Had leg of lamb for dinner and Chinese vegetables. Called Serena at feminist research meeting in NYC to encourage her and invite her to Riverset this weekend.

Eight o'clock: Played Scrabble with Ben.

Eleven–one o'clock: Watch TV and go to sleep.

THURSDAY, MARCH 15

Nine o'clock: Cloudy again. I love rainy days in Riverset. Go to the drugstore for breakfast.

Eleven o'clock: Wrote letters to friends about jobs for next year.

Twelve o'clock: Had trout meunière for lunch.

Two o'clock: Nancy Weber's materials arrive in mail.

Three–four thirty: #2.

Five o'clock: Peter arrives by train in Trenton, pick him up and pick up pizza for dinner (mushroom and pepperoni).

Seven thirty: Ben goes to Princeton to play go.

Eight o'clock: #1.

Ten–twelve o'clock: Watch TV with Peter.

Twelve fifteen: Ben comes home and we go to bed.

FRIDAY, MARCH 16

Nine o'clock: Drugstore in Riverset for breakfast and paper.

Ten o'clock: Did exercises.

Twelve o'clock: Seeds from Parkers arrive. Look at them and make map of garden.

One o'clock: Had yogurt for lunch.

Two o'clock: Wrote Sally. my sister, in Portland, Oregon.

Three–five o'clock: Worked in garden.

Six o'clock: Had leftover lamb for dinner.

Seven o'clock: Called Marjorie Newman in Chicago to tell her I wasn't coming to women's studies symposium this weekend. I just didn't feel up to it. I couldn't sit in meetings for eight hours a day because of my bad back. I feel slightly guilty about not going but then relieved that I have a real excuse not to spend eighteen hours driving to Chicago and then spend three days in meetings.

Eight o'clock: Called Steffie in NYC—no answer. Called Jean Stern and talked to her.

Eight thirty: Drive to Princeton to see *Save the Tiger* with Lewises. Very depressing movie. Then go to visit Williamses (Anne and Dick)—new friends of Lewises, very peculiar couple. Anne is person Sig wanted to have call me and pretend she was you. A friend, Kathy, is visiting them, and when we arrive Kathy is freaking out from drugs or? I get into a very strange "thing" with her. We're there until five in the morning—very bizarre evening! The drive back to Riverset with sun coming up very beautiful.

SATURDAY, MARCH 17

Nine o'clock: Ben goes to drugstore, #1.

Ten o'clock: Ben returns with paper, #2.

Eleven o'clock: Do exercises.

Twelve o'clock: Have yogurt for lunch.

Two–four thirty: Garden.

Five–six o'clock: Shop at Pathmark with Ben.

Seven thirty: Dinner with Ben, Peter, Sig, and Alice.

Nine thirty–eleven o'clock: Watch TV and go to bed.

SUNDAY, MARCH 18

Nine o'clock: Breakfast drugstore in Riverset and read *Times*.

Eleven o'clock: Gardened.

Twelve o'clock: Called Sheila Kling about having dinner with her next week. Called Sue Ann in Pittsburgh to find out when she's coming to NY.

One o'clock: Had yogurt for lunch.

Two–three o'clock: #2, helped Ben to pack.

Three thirty: Ben drives back to Buffalo.

Three thirty–five o'clock: #1, did exercises.

Five thirty: Drive back to New York City.

Seven–twelve o'clock: Party in apartment with Peter and some of his friends.

Twelve o'clock: Go to bed.

MONDAY, MARCH 19

Nine thirty: Breakfast with Danny—omelet.

Ten thirty–twelve o'clock: Read your novel *Star Fever*.

One o'clock: Had wisdom teeth on right out.

Two thirty–four o'clock: Slept.

Four thirty–five o'clock: Called Steffie, called Pat Barry and Gina Bellardo.

Nine thirty–one o'clock: Pat and Gina came over and we got smashed on Cold Duck and grass. I've also had a few pain-killers and am feeling numb all over.

One o'clock: Sleep.

TUESDAY, MARCH 20

Nine–seven o'clock: Office. Made appointment to have haircut at Cinandre, ordered *Altered States of Consciousness* by Tart, taught group dynamics, wrote to several students about late term papers, called Arlene White to tell her about a therapist; made call about job in California, ordered feminist art journal, answered fifteen letters in answer/do file, went back to apartment.

Nine thirty–one o'clock: Spoke to Danny and Bernie Whitehead about Jim Owles campaign for councilman. Bernie says he's never met a sadist he didn't like. He told the story of the masochist he slept (?) with who wanted his nipples threaded and subway tokens hung upon the thread. This seemed like an absurd practice to me, but as some Mexican sage once said, *"Cada loco con su tema."*

I read them again and again. I thought they were wonderful journals—funny and concrete and nicely lean, though as peopled as *War and Peace*. So many women! I hadn't been friendly with that many women in my whole life. I carried the journals with me everywhere I went, and they smelled of my Shalimar and had Gauloise crumbs all over them, like everything in my bag. (I'd started smoking again partly because of Jack Barleycorn and partly—is this awful?—because I thought it would be interesting for the book if I had to quit smoking when I became Micki.) I had a thousand reactions to the journals. Some things scared me or put me off—and ended up exhilarating me exactly because they were Micki's identification marks and not mine, would make becoming her that much more of a challenge.

Some of those things, small and big:

not shaving my legs or armpits for two weeks

bathing only every other day and no deodorant

paying my own way with men rather than reciprocating in the atavistic manner by making dinner for them and having twelve-year-old Scotch and very good Cognac and such around the house

a joint a day

Danny's homosexuality (despite my nice liberal attitude toward everyone's sexuality, I had no really close male friend who was an upfront homosexual)

sugar and cream in coffee and tea

having to be fastidious about my feet

bed life dominated by cunnilingus	feminism
swearing a lot	Cold Duck, Gallo, Almadén
twenty-one-year-old Peter	driving so much
sex: talking about it	watching TV
veal Marsala	yogurt, yogurt, yogurt
spending a lot of time with thera- pists	potted plants
	pizza with mushrooms on it

Some things were exciting because I had always meant to do them:

ingesting the panoply of vitamins	teaching
living with someone	being married
exercises	playing go
not eating carbohydrates	gardening

Some things were reassuring because they were part of my life, too:

drugstore breakfasts	feeling like a participant-observer
dark-light blended coffee made in a Chemex	sex: engaging in it
	Chinese and Mexican food
liking to be clean and sweet smell-ing (though how could I do it without two showers a day, deodorant?)	giving parties
	Sunday *New York Times*
	Scrabble
	loving rainy days in the country
not wearing a bra except when not wearing one is going to make someone uptight	pizza with pepperoni on it

I was preoccupied with the swap during April and May, obsessed with Micki. I thought of her when I bought new clothes (which I did inordinately), made a firm ritual of Sunday breakfast at the Lion's Head, had a fight with T.M. (I was terrified that after six years together this would be the time we'd break, and I'd have to scramble around to make a new life to give Micki); took a magazine assignment (would Micki find it diverting or ridiculous to do a long funny list of what was and wasn't elegant for *Gentlemen's Quarterly?*).

She and I phoned each other constantly, had dinner together a few times, spent many hours sitting around my apartment and talking. We asked and answered questions, scrutinized each other's public behavior, made comments on our very different vocabularies and seemingly similar emotional leanings. We discovered that we both kept the slips from fortune cookies, which cheered us on. I felt I was beginning to grasp her; I looked at her sitting in the sacred corner of my couch and was certain she grasped me.

The swap was touching my life in other ways. When Jack Barleycorn let it be known that he had a predilection for cavorting with two ladies at once, it was Susie I recruited. Though when Susie wanted to get something going just between her and me, I shied away. I loved her and could imagine translating that love into something physical, but I wasn't scheduled to become a practicing bisexual until Micki's Sue Ann from Pittsburgh and Pat Barry.

I played a reporter (dressed, and in pearls) in a porn epic that Mel Green was shooting. I took Trigger Mike out to the big Long Island house where Jane Blackman Wexler lived with her husband and three kids. T.M. and Al got on terrifically, and we vowed to play together often. Barbara Miller and I talked on the phone a couple of times a week, and her husband Bob took me out to Washington Square one Sunday and shot dozens of pictures.

A publisher and I committed ourselves to each other, and Micki and I started the backing and forthing on our own contract. It got very ugly. I considered telling my parents that I would take the trip to France after all. Micki thought I was trying to cheat her, and I thought she was trying to hold me up. There were hysterical phone calls between her and me, her lawyer and my agent, me and my agent. I hate thinking about money, and I began to hate Micki for making me think about it. I even began to hate her face, saw it as cold and pinched instead of sculpted and pixieish. Politics kept coming up—her feminism and neo-Marxism versus my antifeminism and Jeffersonian capitalism. Micki panicked, decided she wanted out; I cajoled her back in. Then I wanted her out and called Susie in the middle of the night and told her she was the only woman I trusted to be loving enough in my life and that I wanted to do the swap with her in the summer, when she'd be on vacation. She couldn't change the travel plans she'd made, and I decided to work things through with Micki. We realized eventually that a lot of the hysteria came from misunderstanding. She wanted 50 per cent of whatever money I would make if I wrote about the swap and sold what I wrote because she thought she'd be writing 50 per cent of the book, and I wanted to give her 10, then 12, then 15 per cent, based on the percentage of time and work I thought she'd be putting into the project. She was wrong to think I'd expect someone to do half my work and not get half my money, but I was wrong too: I didn't know that the time we would spend as each other would be time on a scale all its own. It ended up that she would have 20 per cent of all literary rights, a third of all other rights—films, musicals, sweat shirts. We went to the Algonquin and drank Bull Shots on that, and when the check came, I said, "You've got all my worldly goods now; let me pay for this, too." But I thought it was an equitable deal, and she seemed to think so, too. She had her hair cut short and curly, and I liked her face again.

There were other matters to be negotiated. The most delicate was editorial control. Micki wanted me to promise to respect the spirit of whatever writing she did for the book, and she asked for a guarantee that I would not say anything about her friends or lovers that could be construed as malicious. I thought it was ridiculous to want all this in writing. The swap was going to be a love bath. But I agreed to put what she asked in our contract.

I still felt a lack of trust on her part that was greatly unsettling. There are as many terrible things about me as there are about anyone, but I don't steal and I don't betray, and I wanted her to know this. (How could she be me unless she did?) It bothered me especially that she and her lawyer seemed to keep expecting financial and other meanness from me because I wasn't, by their definition, a radical. (Later she got a literary agent who was properly protective of her but fair to my agent and me.)

At one point when the tension was running high, I broke my own rule. I asked her to come have a drink at Jimmy's with T.M. She did, and I was very glad. She called me the next day and told me she'd liked him a lot and felt much better about everything, was totally committed now. I decided if she had enough sense to like T.M., I was totally committed to her.

We signed our contract. We sent out invitations to everyone who'd be involved in the great adventure:

NANCY AND MICKI
REQUEST THE PLEASURE OF YOUR COMPANY
IN THEIR LIFE SWAP
JUNE ELEVEN TO TWENTY-FOUR
ONE THOUSAND NINE HUNDRED AND SEVENTY-
THREE
GREENWICH VILLAGE, THE UPPER WEST SIDE,
BUCKS COUNTY, WESTERN CONNECTICUT,
AND FINER BARS EVERYWHERE,

**NANCY PUT THIS AD IN THE VILLAGE VOICE
LAST FEBRUARY:**

LET'S SWAP LIVES. Woman
writer, 31, will exchange her joyful,
productive existence with yours for a
month. I offer small Village apartment
with fireplace & courtyard; size 8
wardrobe starring St. Laurent and
Levi-Strauss; 1,000-plus books, fine
paintings, Bach, tennis racquet;
sterling friends & loving lovers, not
all of whom are married. I'll do your
work, adore your family, see your
shrink, whatever, wherever, Why? I want
to know if people can get out of their
skins. References, lawyers, all safeguards both ways. Box A 3240, VV,
80 University Place, NYC 10003

MICKI ANSWERED IT:

*I am ready to swap lives
with you.*
   *Have house in Bucks County,
apartment in Manhattan, husband
in Buffalo, loving lovers here
and there.*
   *No shrink to see. In fact, I
am one. But don't worry, the
work is no sweat.*
   *I am already out of my skin,
and am willing to try yours.*

WE'RE REALLY GOING TO DO IT. YOU'RE INVITED TO COME
ALONG. THE RULES ARE SIMPLE. CALL US BY EACH OTHER'S
NAME, TREAT US AS IF WE WERE THE PERSON YOU'VE AL-
WAYS CALLED BY THAT NAME, AND BELIEVE THAT WE'RE
GOING TO DO EVERYTHING WE CAN TO BE WHAT THE OLD
NANCY, THE OLD MICKI ARE TO YOU. WE WANT NOTHING
LESS THAN TO BEGIN TO BECOME EACH OTHER AL-
TOGETHER, TO PROVE THAT PEOPLE ARE FREE TO BE WHO
THEY WANT TO BE IF THEY JUST RECOGNIZE THIS FREEDOM.
HIGH TIMES FOR US ALL. HOPE YOU'LL COME.

The swap was no longer just two people's project. I rode high
on a wave of everyone's expectations. My brother Nick was as
elated as I was now, though we were both unsettled by how much
we'd miss each other. We don't go two weeks without talking,
even if one of us is in Europe. My parents were being droll and
supportive, if a little choky now and then, and promised to call
Micki/Nancy on the phone. T.M. was the best he'd ever been, and
I knew Micki would get the whole treatment. Abbe—still not my
lover—solemnly invited me for dinner on June thirteenth, and I
wrote it down on the calendar I'd be turning over to Micki. Jack
Barleycorn decided he'd take off for Rome on the fourteenth,
which was probably just as well. Micki thought, not unreasonably,
that he sounded awful. George Warneke promised to work with
the new Nancy on our tantric yoga book, and Yuric Lermentov
said he'd consult her about his next film, the way he'd consult me.
Magazine editors were great about giving me assignments that
they knew she'd be tackling.

It wasn't until we were this close to swapping that I began to get
scared, began to realize it wasn't a totally simple thing we were
doing. I smoked ferociously. Things getting bumpy with Jack Barleycorn made it harder, or maybe it was my tension (and enormous
need for tender acceptance) that made things get bumpy with
Jack. Bill and Katharine Andrews, whose friendship was my oasis
in New York, were leaving for Florida and medical school the
week before the swap, and saying good-bye to them (which would
have been horrible anytime) was devastating. I wanted the world
to stay exactly as it was while I leapt off it.

Micki and I were in ever more fervent touch. One day she came
over and tried on my clothes. She's two inches shorter than I am

and has a smaller waist, bigger hips and ass, and darker coloring, and we were both amazed at how good my favorite pants and dress looked on her. I tried on her pants and jersey, and they fit me fine too, though her pants were short on me. We admired each other's tip-tilted tits and giggled a lot.

I had my hair somewhat blonded and eyelashes darkened (two new events in my life) and, at Susie's suggestion, had my bikini hairline waxed by a spectacular woman, an instant real friend named Rita, who told me that after two weeks of not shaving my legs I'd be able to have them waxed *entièrement*—salvation. I went to my gynecologist, who said everything looked beautiful except for some faintly unfriendly flora and fauna, absolutely non-communicable (she knew about the swap) and deletable in a few days with a cream she prescribed. I decided Micki and I should have our send-off lunch at the Women's Exchange, for both the perfect literary conceit of the name and the freshmanic joy of launching our naughtiness surrounded by women in white gloves, eating tomato surprise. I bought some new undies and a new douche, the only possessions Micki and I were planning to bring into each other's lives. (We weren't going to trade toothbrushes— we hated men who would kiss you all night, then pale if you used their toothbrush in the morning—but I ended up buying new ones for us both.)

My great friend Riff, who loves mystery and intrigue as much as I do (I don't even know his real name), showed up with two dozen roses as a going-away present, though I'd been telling everyone I wasn't going away, just changing bodies, and wouldn't say any good-byes. Nick came in for the last of a series of last weekends we'd been staging all spring, though we'd denied that they were such. We did our usual silly, wonderful things. On Sunday morning he and T.M. and I had breakfast at the Lion's Head, and the two of them got along fine, an event all its own. Jack Barleycorn joined us, uninvited, for a while. He looked pretty bad in that company, but I knew I wasn't yet immune.

Nick went back to Hartford Sunday afternoon. T.M. went off to a party at his sister's (not my friend) a little later. I called my parents, who said they would see Micki if she went to visit Nick —oh, loveliest of parents. Any other calls would have been anti-climactic; I turned off the phone. I gave the apartment a last going-over. (I'd been throwing things out and straightening drawers and arranging records and waxing wood for weeks, insisting it was all for my own sake.) I meditated. I made a few entries in the calendar I'd bought for Micki, wondered if I should arrange more things for her, decided definitely not. One of the important differences between us was that she planned her life ahead, and I liked to keep my life open, never mind the chaos. I worked until well into Monday morning finishing the papers I'd been putting together for her since March:

THE LIST

Alcohol. Heineken on the rocks in a goblet or wine glass. Tullamore Dew, Paddy, Jameson, Power's (in that order), or Bushmills if I must, neat in a brandy glass or wine glass. Clean, thin white wines (Gewürztraminer, Verdicchio); bloody pomegranate reds. Don't usually drink at lunch; it kills the day—but maybe a beer if it's very hot. Cognac usually only at home late at night because bars don't have good-enough brandy. I never drink while I work; rarely drink alone, though I might start on an Irish or wine while waiting for someone here or of course in a bar. I love sitting at bars, as you may know. If you have lunch at Delmonico's with T.M., have a Bull Shot—the best in the world. Sometimes in a good French restaurant, a Kir before lunch or dinner. Lambrusco and retsina for when people just drop in, particularly Magda. Stock Johnnie Walker Black for T.M., who runs through a fifth in nothing flat. If Jack Barleycorn reappears, there should always be at least six bottles of beer on ice.

Allergies: None.

Answering Service: They know what's going on, but only Louise (daytime earthy voice, some weekends, usually on seven to three) totally understands. She's my NY Jewish mother, even though she's Irish. If anything gets fouled up, she'll help, or call Edna Black (who knows) in the main office: 686–XXXX. Number to call for messages is OR 7–XXXX.

Art: Going counterclockwise, from the one over my desk: *House with Brown Roof,* by Gabriele Münter. (She was Kandinsky's mistress and I'm convinced she influenced him, not the reverse; this was done while they were living together.) Lithograph by Josef Albers. Watercolors by my mother (top is view from porch of "our" house in Ireland; bottom, West Hartford) and Irving Katzenstein, great Connecticut painter and close family friend. Top to bottom: Maman, William Horton

(American Impressionist on whom Nick did his master's thesis and with whose son he's in the chart business); Witold K (scrabble scorecard he kept while I was playing *chez lui* with Magda and Adam Max). Two prints by Anni Albers, done in our family printing plant. Katzenstein self-portrait. Louisa Matthiasdottir—great Icelandic painter. Nick, of course. Mama's self-portrait.

I like to wander through the Frick or Modern every few weeks, rarely go to galleries unless Nick tells me there's something I shouldn't miss; I don't know why. My favorite at the Frick is Piero della Francesca's *Saint Simon:* so unpious. At the Modern, the Mondrians. They never fail to electrify me. I hate the Met. Too big. Mostly I like looking at the paintings in my apartment. Sometimes I turn off all the lights and look at the Münter: It becomes a movie after a while, is peopled, usually with a nice lady making chocolate chip cookies for her kids. Nick has fabulous art, too.

My beloved art books are by the phone—Klee, Riopelle, Münter.

Body: Walk a lot. Should exercise more. Always trying to be unfat. Couple of showers or baths a day. Almay body lotion after. Shave my legs and armpits. Have tops of my thighs (the bikini line) waxed by Rita at Saks—she awaits you, if you so desire. Pumice on my feet. Manicures whenever I have the patience; typing kills my nails. Clear polish. I always mean to remember to use Dior Crème Abricot, which works, on my cuticles, but I keep forgetting.

Books: Some that helped invent me: *Shadows Move Among Them, Women at Point Sur, The Elements of Style, Out from Eden, Remembrance Rock, The Revelations of Dr. Modesto, Pride & Prejudice, The Unquiet Grave, Steppenwolf* (in 1962, before they killed it), a lot of sf (especially Heinlein), a lot of spy stories and mysteries (especially Stout and Spillane). Currently reading a new Amanda Cross mystery, if I can get to it; *My Name Is Asher Lev* (at T.M.'s insistence); *The Dead of the House;* Jeff Bailey's new short story (in brown folder in yellow shelf).

Breakfast: I usually go through a pot of Irish tea (with milk, no sugar) before anything else. Then maybe oj and vitamin E—no more if I'm going right to work. When hunger comes, yogurt (Colombo peach melba or lemon custard, with fresh berries) or berries and milk (I'm a berry freak, blink not at Balducci's raspberry prices), or Italian whole wheat bread straight or toasted if I'm patient with sweet butter and buckwheat honey or tangerine marmalade—ah to be a sylph and live on that. Also love drugstore corned beef and poached eggs, especially if I've been up working since 7, which isn't as often as it should be. Melon and sausages and soggy toast on trains. Also croissant moods. Of course lox and toasted bagels and cream cheese and lemon & lots of pepper faithfully at the Lion's Head on Sunday. Try to eat either breakfast or lunch, not both; don't always succeed.

Clothes: You know from journals, I think.

Dinner: Szechuan; great Italian (chicken scarpariella or zuppa di pesce & rugola salad and linguini or fettucini with butter & cheese if I'm not too fat); other seafood as it came from God; meat rarely (and rare) —lambie chops at Frankie & Johnnie's is about all. Home: see separate section of recipes. Wait, though, more out: At Jimmy's, often just prosciutto & melon, or a Caesar salad, or maybe scallops; at the Derby, broiled chicken or shrimp; this time of year soft-shell crabs wherever available.

Dreams: In color, and too violent lately. I'm a baby about nightmares, sleep with the bathroom light on and maybe the Münter light.

Drugs: Marijuana makes me supersexual, but it ruins me for writing the next day (though I was only able to start the review of *Golf in the Kingdom* and the Donleavy piece after a couple of tokes); also I worry, natch, about what it does to my skin. T.M. hates it because it doesn't do anything for him. I smoke with Jeff Bailey—that's really about all these days. Oh, and Susie. And Henry Blanck. Legal stuff: Fiorinal for when I get headaches, which can be bad, but there haven't been many lately. (I know it's cheating, but I'm taking some Fiorinal into my Micki life.) There's Valium and Librium in the john, but I never take them. The hateful pill, which I don't normally take, until the swap is over. (Cheating doubly, since you don't take it, but too many funny people have asked me who the mother would be if one of us got pregnant . . .)

Face: Morning: clean it with Mario Badescu cleaner, with cotton puffs; rinse. At night: use his makeup remover (this is all in middle pail), then cleanser, then rinse. If cleanser is too drying, there's some cucumber cleanser. Use his medicated moisturizer, foundation, blusher, Dior's Sepia lipstick. Mascara sometimes—though I had my eyelashes dyed and plan to again. (The great Rita can do that.) Use drying lotion (in the pail) on bumps. And go to Dr. Verde when necessary for acupuncture: OR 9-XXXX. I love getting facials. I do like the feeling of being made up even when I'm home working.

Family: My father is Saul: I call him Daddy, or Daddums, or Papa (French accented), or Papaloo. My mother is Carol: Moo, Mummy, or Lorac, or BF (short for Best Friend, which she is). Nick is Nick-O, or Herb (to my Arthur), or Sam (to my Princess), or Cher Frère, or Fratèl-lino, or Woolly Lamb, or Palamino, or Sweetness and Light, or Nork-man, or Norkchild, etc. He usually calls me Tard—short for Retarded and Demented Animal. Some other people do, too. Also a member of our family for fifteen years: Clara McIntee, who works for us, often answers AD 3 number. She is one of the few people in the world who can, with impunity, call me Nance. I think you know how I feel about all of them.

Fears: Sirens in the night make me think it's World War III. I'm a hypochondriac, as you know—though when I'm really sick I'm cheery as hell.

Flowers: Orange and yellow, in the containers filled now. The red roses are from Riff—and here's an incredible sign: They came with a little label on them:

FOREVER YOURS

HANCOCK ROSES—RIVERSET, PA.

Florist is Costos, on Sixth just this side of Ninth. They all know what's going on. I hate gladiolas and carnations. Add water to blue vase first thing every morning.

Games: Cribbage, Scrabble, checkers, gin, categories (see sample attached—great for groups).

Hair: I just switched to a new hairdresser, Steve, at Saks. Terrific guy. Wash it every day, use cream rinse, comb into place with beer or use electric brush or both.

Housekeeping: I like to keep the front room neat—but I'm not, as you know, totally compulsive. I like the floors kept waxed, things in their place. When it gets out of hand, I do the whole thing myself (often in the middle of the night) or call Aga Ullmann, 371–XXXX, who'll come down early in the morning or late at night with her baby daughter and big dog. Rug shampooer is rentable from Village Home Shop. Reggie the exterminator comes second Tuesday or Wednesday every month —will you give him the ribbon-tied package (fir-balsam incense) next to the record player? He doesn't know about the swap. Pilot light is persnickety on the stove. Record player stinks. Lights are controlled by two dimmer switches: one in back-south corner of yellow bookshelf, one on a hidden shelf behind my desk, just to the right, and under, the blue vase. Under the grass bench is my linen chest. Tools in old-fashioned suitcase in alcove. Nick can answer any questions about the house.

Incense: Fir balsam only, burned usually in tiny candle holders (see in bar).

Jewelry: You'll have all the stuff I usually wear; pins I sometimes wear as barrettes are in red leather box in top bureau drawer; I adore Nick's coral earrings, wear them when my ears are showing and it's special; other stuff just like to look at. Pearls and pendant come off only for showers and making love with T.M. Rings come off for typing.

Jokes: I invariably screw up the punch line. I hate dirty jokes.

Language: The shy pornographer—I still think there are words better not said in mixed company. Can I even write down which ones? "Shit," mostly. "Fuck," except in its proper meaning. Etc. Sex language: I like "go down on," not the other ones. I can't say "clitoris" or "penis" or "vagina," except to a doctor, without feeling utterly dumb. "Pussy" is friendly. Also "cock." I want to kick something every time I hear "in terms of," "viable," "vis-à-vis," "the fact that." Strunk & White all the way.

Laundry: Sheets, shirts, other pressables go to Liberty, next to Costos. I will do my best to explain to them (they are Chinese) that someone else will be picking up the Web things—no ticket, just Web. If it doesn't work, I'll take a ticket. Laundromat for towels and tights is on the left-hand side of 6th going uptown between 11th & 12th. It's the one ticket I take—I don't know them, or rather they don't know me. Other stuff gets washed by hand in Woolite or with me in the shower.

Letters: Stationery in bottom desk area. Address envelopes to women: "Mme." or "Mlle." "Dear Miss Smith," if I don't know her, or "Dear Alice Smith." Same with men.

Lunch: Going out to a serious lunch kills the working day, and I try to avoid it, but sometimes T.M. lures me. Other lunch friends might be Susie (esp. if you're shopping in Chinatown) or Barbara Miller. At home I have yogurt with/without berries (though not too much yogurt altogether), tuna fish (celery, dill, capers, lots of mayo). I do like lunch out sometimes with the *NY Post:* lox et al. at Bigelow, or chicken salad on whole wheat toast, or (if carnivorous) a rare hamburger outside at the Riviera.

Money: Spend joyfully.

Movies: All-time favorites: *Children of Paradise, Third Man, Yankee Doodle Dandy, Notorious, Nobody Waved Goodbye, The Fountainhead, Razor's Edge, Adam's Rib, Key Largo, Jules & Jim, Un Chien Andalou, Rules of the Game.* Always looking for the perfect trenchcoat mystery.

Music.   Play little of it now because record player's so awful: but jazz in the morning, or Brahms First, or *Water Music. Tristan & Isolde* for cooking or cleaning stints. Violin concerti (esp. Tchaikovsky) late at night alone.

Newspapers: *Times* at night and *News* if T.M. insists, but I find that newsprint is totally countererotic, and I always bitch about that. *The Voice.* The *Post* a few times a week (I'm hooked on Mary Worth).

Politics: I like to think of myself as a Jeffersonian democrat, which means radicals think I'm conservative, conservatives think I'm radical, and liberals think I'm unpolitical. William O. Douglas is my big political hero.

Sex: *Vide* various people.

Shopping Guide: Coffee (espresso, ground for vacuum, although I make it in a Chemex) from Balducci's, between Ninth and Tenth on Sixth; Mo (dark hair, stocky, only visible non-Italian) awaits you eagerly. He will invite you into the refrigerator but he'd really rather talk about his wife and kids.

All produce, butter, milk, cheese, much bread, jams from Balducci's, too. Blackest Irish tea from McNulty's. Eggs (incredibly sweet and fresh) from Murray's on Cornelia Street. Seafood from Sea Cliff on University Place (we are not known by name). Same for Brevoort Meat Market, where I've just started. Fresh-made pasta from the place on Houston between MacDougal and Sullivan. Someday I will write a book about the sensual joys of marketing, the smell of basil, the yellow light in the pasta store, the heft of packages—I like it all disgracefully much.

Sleep: I need at least 7 , alas; like 8 or even a little more.

Superstitions: I have this thing about pennies and Nick. I am always picking them up, or not spending them, or giving them to him—just because. Also I compulsively say, "Hello, puddy tat," every time I see a cat in my garden. Do you want to call this whole thing off?

Taxis: I am a taxi junkie. I tip 20–25%. If the driver wants it off the meter I always say yes, sometimes even suggest it: my only form of dishonesty. (Except for lying.)

Webnesses, as T.M. would put it: I love creating mysteries. It is not beyond me to imply that I am a Swiss spy, or to turn a weekend in Hartford into a weekend in Geneva—even to just happening to have Swiss bank notes on me when I return. Having people mail postcards from other places. Not for aggrandizement; to entertain. *Vide* Riff.

Zap: I like to brush my teeth before I kiss anyone in the morning.

WORK

All material referred to herein and pertaining to can be found in top orange file cube under Current Work.

Erotic Tantra: Book in collaboration with George Warneke (office: 472–XXXX; home: BU 8–XXXX. He'll be abrupt if you call & he's with a patient). Tantra file (within current work file) has outline for book, copy of tantra piece for *Viva,* etc. Books on tantra travel between here and George's; those here are in yellow shelf next to bed; big tantric art book is on floor next to phone. The way George & I plan to do the book is to work separately on different chapters, then turn them over to each other for rewrite, discussion. Pick a chapter you like; my agent may send you the contract for your/my signature.

Review of Eric Forrer's Notes From the Nets of a Salmon Fisherman: For the *NY Times.* Richard Lingeman, who knows about it, assigned this on a free-lance basis. When it's done, it should be sent to John Leonard (Dear John Leonard, I guess) with a note so saying. (Free-lance means no kill fee if it's turned down.) Seven hundred words. I may not get a chance to replace the book, which I left in Hartford; call Doubleday PR and ask for a copy or, much quicker, pick one up at Sheridan Square Bookstore. I liked the book, with some reservations about the style. Wouldn't rave the way I did for Mike Murphy's book, but might write it in a similar style.

Cosmopolitan Article: Call my friend from the Lion's Head, Catherine Houck (265–XXXX), who'll probably tell you to call Bobbie Ashley, who's prepared; or call Bobbie directly. You might have some story ideas when you call them.

GQ: Two pieces on elegance. One is a list thing: elegance is . . . isn't. (Is paper plates, isn't plastic forks.) The piece is supposed to cover the waterfront—people, places, things, thoughts, etc.—from the more-or-less serious to the fluffy. I asked Nick to collaborate on this with me—so. Also for their Big Elegance Issue: a composite of the world's most elegant man—something like Isaac Stern's wrist, Cary Grant's eyebrows, etc. They need to know where to get photos, so you might look through back issues in the library or buy a batch of magazines when you have some notion of who you want. Editor is George Mazzei (Ma-zay), PL 9–XXXX. $350 for each piece.

Viva: Call Arno Karlen's secretary Donna (593–XXXX) later this week and ask her to send a set of galleys on the Donleavy piece (October issue). I've lost my copy (natch!), so if you could ask my agent for hers —and then check the two against each other to see if they've screwed around with it. I made a few changes since sending it out, come to think of it. You might let T.M. have a look at it, too. And hold on to it for me. Though—?

Swap Novel: I'm also leaving, in a yellow clamp folder, the first thirty-nine pages (there were about fifty) of the novel I started to write last fall until I decided I had to do the swap for real. You might find it amusing to carry on with, from Marjorie's point of view (change her name if you want) or Anne's (that's me)—if it works out, it could be a droll addition to the book.

Ingenue. You may get calls about the sf write-in, but I doubt it. You might check with them (688–XXXX) about galleys toward the end of next week, but I'm not sure they'll be ready. If you feel like it, you might look at the red-checked item on page 2 of the writer's workshop proposal; they want me to do that. Haven't yet thought about what writers I'd like to include. It wouldn't necessarily be prizewinners; just greats.

I turn manuscripts in double-spaced on yellow or white paper, name card in upper left-hand corner (cards in top desk drawer). Wide margins —you'll see in my published/unpublished file in orange cube. Xeroxes rather than carbons usually: copy center on sixth between eleventh & twelfth. Paper, large envelopes, letterheads, etc., all in bottom desk drawer. I usually send a short covering note with a manuscript.

For correspondence see correspondence folder in work file.

How wonderful to think of not having to do all this!

I am also helping Yuric Lermentov, the Polish film maker, to translate and adapt his new screenplay for possible American production. It's about a Polish woman who comes to America with her American professor husband, blunders innocently and somewhat madly through American life, and ends up in depression and suicide. What one does is advise Yuric about details of American life, validity of character and plot development, language.

LAST-MINUTE ADDENDA

I use one-half peroxide, one-half water as a mouthwash—yum yum. Not absolutely sure Chinese laundry understood, but if you keep repeating Web, you should be able to get out a sheet or two. My meditation: I do it usually once a day now, often in taxis en route somewhere—well, obviously en route somewhere, if you're in a taxi, Tard. My mantram is: *om mani padme hum!*

Some things I might do in the course of the next two weeks:

buy a baby present for Stephanie Warneke—probably an antique

clean my refrigerator seven or eight times & buy a deodorizer for it

fall in love with someone brand new

lose my pepper mill

lose four purple felt-tip pens

do something incredibly dumb about Jack

put off taking my small desk clock to Jensen's and asking them to fix it

buy something to wear, maybe a sundress

polish my *Star Fever* ashtray

add to my bathroom door/walls

break one to three glasses

I always carry my passport and N.Y.P.D. detective badge 844. My cash is usually loose, coins everywhere.
Stuff wasn't ready at cleaner's; will be after three.

> Other things to do:
> Replace T.M.'s keys, which he lost. (What does that mean, Doc?)
> Somehow get ten dollars plus any bank charges to Everything
> For the Apartment to cover NG check a couple of months ago;
> it is to my eternal shame that I kept putting this off.
> Drink the champagne in the refrigerator for breakfast.

ADDENDA TO ADDENDA

I believe in God.
Things on hook wall should go to cleaners. Ask Jerri to do something to protect white buttons on pink linen skirt or else to spot-clean and press.
I love leaving notes for people.
Make lists on envelopes.
There's no way to end this.

I drew a sample categories game and typed up my recipes for the best scrambled eggs in the world and Irish Whiskey Pâté. I also left Micki my curriculum vitae, three unpublished semiautobiographical novellas, and everything on blue paper about how the swap idea had come about and what I wanted it to be. It seemed like an inundation. With that material, and the thirty pages of journal notes, and the magazine articles (several of them very personal) and other writing I'd shipped down to Riverset earlier, and all the hours we'd logged together, she would know more about me that anyone but a swapee had any business knowing, would ever want to know.

That took care of me. My darling T.M. she knew all about from my journals and conversation. I put a poem he'd written and a few Uppmanns smuggled in from Bermuda in a file folder marked "T.M.'s Cuban Cigars" and left the folder with the others in my orange file cube. She knew all about my family; it seemed to me that from my journals and talk she knew about everyone I loved and liked, would be perfectly equipped to feel the affection I felt, dance to all my music.

But I wanted to put all this information in some readily accessible form and leave her some more coherent list of phone numbers than my chaotic address book. The list would help her do the elegance composite for GQ and any other magazine work she might take on. I also wanted it to be clear which men were my lovers and which weren't. Several who weren't (either because they never would be, or had been and no longer were) had teased me about coming on to Micki, and although I'd told them that this was against all the rules, I wanted her to be prepared for everything. So Monday morning, a bit in haste, I put together an alphabetical list with ninety-nine entries. I should not have done the list in haste. I should not have done it at all.

Monday noon I washed my hair and put on makeup for one last delicious time. I got into a pair of pants that would be too long for Micki unless we bought her stilts, a shirt that had a near twin I could leave behind for her, the Charles Jourdan sandals that make me feel so nicely leggy, and the talisman jewelry I would soon surrender. I put the few things I'd be taking with me to Mickiland in an old Swissair bag and put all my normal purse things in a green linen carryall. I had a couple of funny phone calls with people who were disappointed that the new Nancy wasn't yet installed, and I felt giddy at this proof that people were really going to participate, that it was all going to happen. I called Nick and said, "Talk to you later." Called T.M. and said, "See you tonight." (New Nancy's first evening was going to be the usual Sardi's-Jimmy's round.) I said good-bye to my paintings, though saying good-bye was cheating. I looked through all the words I was leaving for Micki and decided to take the list and the alphabetized notes on people uptown with me so she could start prepping in the taxi home. I stacked the other papers next to my typewriter, left a note on top:

11 June 1973

Micki/Nancy!

I've rehearsed writing this note about a zillion times but I didn't know what it was going to feel like. I still don't know. But I love you & am exceedingly excited and isn't it terrific traveling so light?

Listen, kid. Have a blast: that's the bottom line. And not to worry about your people, because I love them too. In a peculiar way I feel rather bridal, but the love is focused on so many people—or is that "but" always there and therefore not a but.

See you around.

Nancy/Micki

SWAPPING

Monday, June 11

And now I'm here in Micki's bed, in my bed, Peter asleep at my side, the smell of the rose he gave me thickening the air, the size and shape of the room ready to help form my dreams, the ceiling looking as willing as ceilings always do to take down everything I'm thinking, hold it until I'm ready to put it on paper.

I've had a lot of white wine and rather a lot of marijuana, and my thoughts are all mixed up. There are thoughts I meant to have, and thoughts I didn't want to have, and thoughts I didn't expect to have and don't know how to classify, and thoughts that are simply thoughts. I'm Nancy and I'm Micki and I'm the participant-observer and I'm someone I don't know how to name. What seems most important at the moment is that I'm really here in this bed. Micki didn't back out and I didn't back out and World War III didn't up and intervene. I'm here in this bed, in this life, and it feels as right as anything's ever felt. It feels so right that I wish for the moment that there were no reporting to be done, no staring and shredding. I want to be Micki-normal; I want to go to sleep and dream her dreams. Cruel to have to dip back across the line.

Got to the Women's Exchange at two fifteen. Felt the crazy mix that assails me whenever I board a plane: whooshing joy at the thought that I'm about to take the leap and a longing to run back home, hide under the bed. Micki wasn't there yet. I chose a table that would give us privacy and asked the waitress to put champagne on ice. I'm not crazy about the stuff, but I knew Micki was, and the day seemed to demand it.

Ordered a bottle of Löwenbräu—there was no Heineken—and a goblet full of rocks and sipped with a kind of desperate slowness, as if to quench the thirsts of the two hot weeks to come. Bubbles cavorted on top of my tongue and ice tickled the tip—oh, lucky Micki, to be about to inherit that splendid minor joy.

The waitress told me the kitchen was closing, and I asked her to set aside some shrimp and crab meat. I looked through the papers I'd brought for Micki, tried to read a mystery, wondered which salad I'd eat, if either, should Micki not show.

Two forty and there she was, flustered and hot but seeming very up. The waitress thrust food in front of us. Micki opted for the shrimp. A wondrously old gentleman poured champagne. "Here's looking at you," Micki said before I could be clever.

Micki ate little, talked much; I'd never heard such a rat-a-tat from her. I was embarrassingly hungry. We had a second split of champagne.

We started pulling things out of our purses. Micki gave me a calendar with an impressive lot of notations on it and the car papers in an envelope marked "Do Not Lose!"—which rankled. I gave her the papers I'd brought for her and told her where to find the rest at home. She said she hadn't had a chance to make up a list of names and phone numbers and short takes on her friends; she'd do it that day and send it to me along with her address book. That made me a little nervous. It would be hard to be Micki and not constantly make phone calls. She gave me the numbers I'd need right away, and I decided I'd be okay.

I asked the waitress for the bill. Micki took off her watch and gave it to me. "No, on the right wrist," she said. "That's to remind me to be ambidextrous." I gave her the gold ring that has the power to keep planes in the air and the garnet one from Trigger Mike. I helped her put on the pearls my parents had given me when I was confirmed and the antique garnet pendant with which they'd consoled me for turning thirty. We traded purses. We didn't quite laugh. "Well, Nancy," I said to her. "Well, Micki," she said.

New Nancy had to have a pair of high frivolous sandals like the pink and white ones I was wearing, so we oozed through the heat to Charles Jourdan. We were both rather merry now. New N. asked the salesman for my sandals in plain white and size six and pranced around in them. They looked much better on her delicate feet than on my graceless ones, though I hoped for the sake of the legacious T.M. that she'd wear pants more often than skirts. She called the salesman "sweetie" and sportingly handed over the fifty-five bucks he asked for, saved a fervent "Jesus Christ!" until he went to wrap her package. "Now you know how I get rid of it," I said.

Micki suggested Casa Moneo on Fourteenth Street to equip my feet for their new life. It felt funny going back downtown. Micki negotiated in Spanish for my espadrilles—ugly as hell, incredibly comfortable. She picked out some low platform sandals for knocking around as me. I paid for both to ease the sting of *le cher* Charles, though we planned to balance all our spending in the end.

Farther downtown to Instant Pants to buy me Landlubber jeans in Micki colors (lavender, bright green) and my length leg. The saleswoman seemed puzzled by our connection. I had a feeling she was thinking of *The Story of O*. "We're going to be each other for a couple of weeks," I explained casually. "I don't want to hear another word," she said.

We walked to the clutch of phone booths at the triangle that Sixth Avenue, Greenwich Avenue, and Eighth Street make. I looked over Nathan's at the soft green trees in the courtyard that shields my building from the street and felt a wash of homesickness. Micki suggested that we go up to the apartment, make our calls from there. I said I might never leave.

I gave her the number of my answering service, stood by expectantly while she dialed. I'd explained the whole event to them, but would they hesitate over the strange voice? Would there be too few messages, too many, the wrong ones? "This is Nancy Weber," she said into the phone. "Is there anything for me?" (I may have smiled, but I was nowhere near a giggle. She *was* Nancy Weber at that moment.) "Trigger Mike called," she said to me, "will call back between seven and seven thirty. Magda. Riff. George Warneke." A perfect normal run of five o'clock Monday messages. I felt elated, grateful to everyone who'd called and everyone who hadn't.

Micki told me that Peter was going to be out until late that evening (he drove a cab four days a week). I was supposed to see Ted Holzman, the NYU student Micki had met when he was researching a paper on the Hawthorne women's studies program and who'd become her lover just about the time she answered my ad. I dialed the number I'd written down on my calendar at lunch.

"Ted? It's Micki."

"Hi. How's it going?" (Nice voice. Properly casual.)

"Okay. I'm down in the Village with my friend Nancy, we had to do some shopping."

"Want to have dinner?"

"Great. Where?"

"I was hoping you'd turn me on to a new place."

That stopped me. Was I supposed to turn him on to a new place because Micki did that or because I was a new person in his life? I decided to assume he was playing by the rules and the first possibility applied; then I blanked. I suggested we meet at his place at seven thirty.

Old Micki said New Micki had sounded just right. We went around the corner to buy me a pair of Dr. Scholl's exercise sandals to alternate with my lovely espadrilles. It was shopping I could easily have done on my own the next day, but there seemed to be a shared reluctance to part.

Finally we ran out of delays. New Nancy and I walked back to the corner of Eighth Street and Sixth Avenue. She started up to Jerri's Cleaners to get the clothes that hadn't been ready earlier; I hailed a cab. We blew kisses at each other.

It's much much too early to say that any of my hopes for the swap have been confirmed, but the cab trip to 85th Street was a paean to the power of conscious decision. In my mind, in my gut, in my toes, in my sexual places, in every part I could isolate and identify, I felt that I was heading home. Hoping that Peter, whom I had loved for two years with unbroken passion, would surprise me and be there. Wondering if Danny would be around and what kind of day he'd had. Feeling no more sense of transition than anyone feels between afternoon and evening. (Though I was enough the participant-observer to split off from my experiencing self and want to say to the cab driver, "If you knew what you were a part of," enough Nancy to exult that I was already sticking it to my old bête noir, the unconscious.)

Home. I didn't much look over the block, the building. I wasn't

trying to avoid being the notetaker; it simply didn't occur to me.
I let myself into the apartment with my key. Nobody there. I can't
say the place felt familiar, but I knew I belonged.

Opened the first door off the narrow hallway; saw a room just
big enough to hold a double bed and a couple of tall old wooden
cabinets for clothing and two sets of bookshelves. Peter's and my
room. The sheets on the bed were grayish. Perfect. Why should
they have been changed if no one new was going to use them? I
figured out where my things belonged and quickly stuffed my
Nancy possessions into a corner of my armoire.

I went into the long, old-fashioned bathroom. The testing
ground: Micki had told me everyone converged in the bathroom
as casually as in the kitchen, never mind who was doing what. I
was nervous about that, but I liked the idea of my squeamishness
quotient being lowered. Right now there was no one in there but
me and fifty million bugs. I remembered once talking with T.M.
about how much less gruesome cockroaches are in one's own
apartment than in someone else's. These were my bugs, right?
Right. Hi, Otto. Move over there, Gerald.

Into the shower. Away with the last of my Shalimar, Arrid, and
the day's drippings. (No question that this was a day when Micki
would take three showers.) Over to the sink and to work with
Micki's face brush. Off with my evil foundation.

I opened Micki's plastic flowered makeup kit. Smiled and
smiled. Blue eyeshadow like I'd worn when I was sixteen and was
sophisticated and smoked blue cigarettes. Mascara. Campho-
Phenique for bumps. Two pale lipsticks. Cheek gel. A tiny con-
tainer of, yes, liquid base. The child did okay by her face for
someone who twitted me about a little chopped-liver lipstick.

But fair was fair. I'd never seen Micki seriously made up, so it
wasn't for every day. I passed up the liquid makeup and settled
for some Campho-Phenique on my chin. Micki was always telling
me that my skin was fine, that she never would go to a dermatologist for the few bumps I got now and then; but the tension of the
last few days had got to my skin, no question. I put on a little
blushing gel—Micki always wore healthy-looking cheeks. The lipstick made me look embalmed and most un-Micki-ish; I rubbed it
off. The ninety-six-degree day had contorted my hair, and I
thought I looked altogether awful. I decided not to worry about
it, though now that I'd seen Micki's little bag of tricks, I wondered

if she was really as unobsessive about her looks as she said, or if she simply felt that she looked more attractive without foundation, without color on her mouth.

I splashed a lot of her Jean Naté all over me, rubbed some under my armpits. There was already a little feminist stubble—hurray. I was sure I would destroy the city, going out on such a night without deodorant, but that was her way (and it was her clothes I'd be wearing).

The phone rang. I followed the sound into the kitchen. It was the New Nancy. "Where's your colorless nail polish?" she asked rather frantically. "In the bathroom," I said, "in one of the green pails, but don't worry about it, I don't always wear it, it's not important." I looked down at the nails I'd depolished that morning and wondered how quickly they'd grow to Micki length. We wished each other a splendid evening and hung up: I was somewhat knocked out by how right it felt that I was up here and she was down there.

Into my green pants, a bright yellow Mexican top and sash, and Dr. Scholl's sandals for my newly fastidious feet. I looked around the only part of the apartment I hadn't seen, the dark and bookish living room and alcove that was Danny's area. There was a feeling of deliberate indifference about the whole place, and I fell right in with it, was pretty sure that Micki made much the same connection. I was relieved. Misfired aesthetics might have made problems for me; this laissez-faire ugliness was fine.

I left Peter a note on our bed. "Lover. Gone to have dinner with Ted. See you around one. XXXXXXXX, M." Checked to see that I had my keys in my tan canvas shoulder bag, remembered just in time that I hadn't put my watch back on after I showered, fastened it around my right wrist, noticed that in proper Micki fashion I was already ten minutes late. Walked outside and tried to cast a reporter's eye on the neighborhood. I rememberd coming up to a party on this block the year before and being pretty scared. Why on earth had I been? It was quiet here, familyish, much less assaulting than the part of the Village I lived in so nonchalantly. I remembered back further to the time in Israel when I'd asked the inhabitant of a kibbutz hard by the Syrian border if he planned ever to visit New York. "I'd like to, but the streets are too dangerous," he said. The danger you live with every day is like the cockroaches in your own bathtub.

Ted. Very tall—6 feet 2 inches, I'd say. Blond hair to his shoulders. Medium-size moustache. Thin, thin body clad only in cutoff jeans. Greeted me sweetly, but didn't kiss me. Because he didn't kiss Micki in his hallway, or because I was a stranger? I didn't feel like a stranger. I didn't feel utterly intimate with him, but then we'd only been lovers for a couple of months.

We sat around his big West Side apartment with his two roommates, one who had met "me" and one who hadn't. It was exciting talking with the one who hadn't, realizing that I was doing the spadework for his future friendship with Micki. Would she always seem just a little bit off, like Pepsi when you're used to Coke? It was also frustrating as hell. He was a painter, and I was aching to talk to him about the great Klee print on the wall, tell him about the nudge of recognition I'd felt when I saw the big Mondrian book lying on the table. I wasn't sure how Micki felt about Klee and Mondrian, so I let it pass. We started to talk about other things, and I felt the frustration bank around a curve and emerge as relief. It was kind of wonderful not to have to hear my own stories about the magical day with the Klee collection in Bern, about the flashing understanding of Mondrian's politics that I'd had when I first saw his paintings.

Ted offered me a beer; I took it. Miller's straight from the can. Good enough. Micki had told me to get a little stoned before dinner, and I asked if anyone had a joint. Ted rolled one, and we all smoked and talked about small things. Ted kept throwing me clues: "Remember the day at Hawthorne when . . .?" "Remember the Charles Lloyd concert we all went to last week?" It was very forced at first, but after the third reference to the concert, I began to feel as though I'd been there, could actually picture us sitting next to each other at the Bitter End. (I was wearing my face, Micki's clothes.) I thought Ted was terrific to take the project so seriously, to be so eager to fill in all the chinks and craters. I felt that he was devoted to Micki and was transferring the devotion to me, exactly the way I'd hoped it would go.

We ended up eating at the Ideal, a Cuban restaurant a few blocks away. I ordered some special chicken with vegetables, hoping that there would be no peas, lima beans, or turnips to distress my Micki tastebuds. Ted said he'd been neglecting his body's need for protein and ordered steak. Old Nancy perched in a corner of the ceiling and watched with disbelief as New Micki drank glass after glass of sangría. "You look like you're actually enjoying the poisonous stuff," said Nancy. "You've come a long way, kid."

The check arrived. New Micki took out her wallet. Old Nancy half expected Ted to say, "Don't be silly." He said, "Just give me five dollars."

We walked slowly back toward Ted's apartment, stopped to sit for a while in a tiny littered park with a waterless fountain. I wanted my mind to shut up, but it kept wondering if he always ambled and lingered this way with Micki, or if he was nervous for himself or me or the two of us about what would happen when we got home. I thought about how much easier it all was for me than for him: I had no other Ted to match him up against. Then again, he knew the words to the songs I was supposed to sing.

His roommates were asleep when we got back. We went into his room, and he lit candles. I smiled at the poster of the Indian prayer: "Great Spirit, Grant that I may not criticize my neighbor until I have walked a mile in his moccasins." Micki was walking to the moon in my Charles Jourdan sandals; I, in her Dr. Scholl's. Ted asked what kind of music I wanted to hear. "Hot sticky late-summer-night big-city blues," I said, and he put on one perfect record after, another. Now and then we quietly touched.

I felt a hundred different things. The setting made me feel seventeen and shy. I felt Micki's attraction for Ted's strong young body. I felt the sexual indifference Nancy always felt for men with mortal minds, but there was a real Nancy liking for his sporting kindness. I felt a variation of the uncertainty I'd felt when we were walking home. Was Ted taking things slowly because he didn't want to jar my sensibilities, or because he wasn't all that attracted to Nancy, or because Micki was the sexual aggressor between them, or because this was the tempo of all his evenings?

One thing was sure. I (Micki? Nancy?) didn't want him to feel that he had to make love to me. I said that maybe I should be getting home. Even though it was normal for me to get back to the apartment at one, I did want to meet Peter and Danny before they were comatose. That was silly, he said. Peter would probably be working for another hour, and Danny sometimes didn't come home at all. He reached over, and we kissed rather seriously. It wasn't the electrical first kiss of strangers; it was the calmer, sweeter kiss of people who've been lovers and friends for a while, will be lovers and friends awhile more. Nancy knew and liked that kiss, was glad to run into it there.

Ted told me he didn't want me to leave. I'd wanted to hear that, of course, but I hesitated. One of my unfavorite Nancy voices was reciting all the things I'd have to do if I made love with him: shower again, douche, go home to Peter with the edge off. No, that was too horrible a travesty of Micki thinking. I reached for Ted's belt buckle.

It was a confusing but rather splendid circus. Old Nancy was in that bed, and Old Micki, and New Micki, and Ted-with-Nancy, and Ted-with-Old-Micki, and Ted-with-New-Micki. Sometimes everyone was having at it at once, and sometimes we were divided into actors and silent commentators ("Is that off the latest mimeographed handout from your local feminist collective?" "More, Ted, more!"). Sometimes we were just two bodies. I wasn't counting at the coming, but I think it caught us all.

We took a shower together. He washed me all over and told me afterward that I looked better in a towel than in my bright top and pants, that he bet I usually wore soft colors. I was supposed to say, "Oh, no, Ted, you know I always dress like this." "Lots of pink," I said, and mentally dressed for our first post-swap meeting.

Bare-chested, barefoot, he walked me over to Broadway to get a cab. We watched one go by, and he said, "Oh, were you expecting me to hail it for you?" I tried a Micki self-parody: "I'm sorry if I was guilty of sex-role stereotyping." "That's okay," he said. It wasn't parody??? He lit a cigarette. I realized that I'd watched him smoke seven or eight Camels and hadn't once wanted one.

I'd had a fine time with Ted, truly liked him; but as I rode the twenty blocks down Broadway, I felt enormous anticipation: I was going home to Peter. The One. I put my key in the door, fumbled a bit; then it was opened from the inside, and someone was looking at me very nicely, but—help! Was it Peter or Danny? He kissed me, said, "Hello, lover," and I knew this was Peter's beard, Peter's long hair. "Hi, lover," I said.

We kissed and kissed. It felt so good, being home with him again. We went into our room. He rather shyly gave me the rose that now owns the air, and I put it in a glass of water. We partly undressed. He asked me to give him a back rub, and I did. I scratched him lightly all over the way I knew he liked, massaged his feet. We talked about what we'd done that day and drank some cold white wine. I asked him if he felt strange about my being there, and he said he didn't, and I said I didn't either. I let him know that I loved Micki, and I knew how much she loved him, and I thought the swap was going to be wonderful for everyone, and I hoped we never had to break out of the rhythm of it and discuss it again until it ended. He said he felt the same.

We started to make love. I was very turned on to him, but the flora-and-fauna thing was making me tender, and I asked him to take it easy, told him why. He was wondrously gentle, and my Micki passion for him totally overcame the sensitivity of Nancy's body and Nancy's allergy to the Hemingway litany ("Was it good?" "How was it?" "Was it good?").

"It's extraordinary," I said afterward.

"What's extraordinary?" he asked.

"That after two years it still feels so new."

He laughed and laughed, said he knew he was going to like me. I felt a little guilty; that was entirely a Nancy number. But relaxing Peter, taking care of his psyche, was a Micki number, and the laugh had done that, too.

I felt sleepy and nice and sexually pampered and very close to Peter. I knew I could pull back and look at him with Nancy eyes, but I didn't want to. I hoped he felt as easy and good as I did. I rather thought he did.

We heard the front door open. Danny walked into our bedroom. We all said, "Hi," very casual. It didn't seem remotely strange that I was naked in front of Danny, and after a second or two it didn't seem strange that Peter was, too. Danny told us a little bit about the gay activists' meeting he'd been at, then went into the kitchen for some yogurt. He looked like a friendly rabbit, and I liked him and hoped he liked me.

Ablutions. Nobody followed me into the bathroom. I got back into bed next to Peter. We kissed good night, and he turned his back and immediately fell asleep. I had a flashing picture of Trig and New Nancy in bed. I loved them both a lot, was glad they were. together, but they seemed very far away. I stared at the ceiling and started rehashing the day.

Tuesday, June 12

Micki had told me I'd wake up wanting Peter. I did. She told me he'd need arousing in the morning. He didn't. I tried hard not to feel smug and succeeded too well. Figured he was maybe just being polite, just missing Micki.

I'd slept way down under, though we'd both woken up in the middle of the night when a print of "The Garden of Delights" came flying off the wall. I told Peter that 95 per cent of all poltergeist activities occurred when repressed adolescent sexuality was suddenly unrepressed. "Don't look at me, young lady," he said.

I showered (alone) and put on lots of Jean Naté. When I got back to the bedroom, Peter was on a roach-killing rampage. My darling bugs! I got into my new lavender pants and a wonderfully cool Mexican cotton blouse. Danny was still in bed; no omelet. I ate half a black cherry yogurt. Kissed Peter, who was going back to sleep.

Micki had left her car at Hawthorne so I wouldn't have to worry about finding a parking space my busy first night. It was hot and muggy enough to overcome my New England insouciance about weather, and I longed to hail a cab; but dammit, no, Micki just wouldn't. I walked to the subway station at 86th and Broadway. Virtue paid. We didn't get stuck in the tunnel under the East River, and I got to knock off another chapter of a book Micki had told me would explain a lot about her, Philip Slater's *Pursuit of Loneliness*. Slater's compassion and logic added a dimension to my good feelings about Micki, though his politics seemed naïve and made me miss Trigger Mike. I wondered if Micki'd got around to reading *Shadows Move Among Them*, which I'd given her in May, and what she'd thought.

I felt much more self-assured walking across the Hawthorne campus to Micki's office than I had that day in March when I came to interview her. (Felt that way because Micki has more self-assurance than Nancy? Because Nancy's self-assurance had swelled with the starting of the swap? Because it was a different day?)

"Dr. Wrangler!" beamed my secretary as I walked in. She immediately made me feel looked after, spoiled, loved. She led me into my wood-paneled office and pointed out the different folders Micki had left for me, told me to let her know if I needed her help with anything. One thing I knew I'd need help with was asking her for help. Carla was twenty years older than I and had real work to do, and I felt guilty already about being her boss.

Micki had left Micki a splendid variety of tasks. There were letters to answer, references to write, a questionnaire to fill out, a review of *Women and Madness* to work on with a sister feminist, and M.D., Sukie Sandler, (I almost said "fellow feminist," which shows how far I've come), some scholarly papers in need of rewrite. Although most Hawthorne students had gone home for the summer, some were still around, and there were dealings scheduled with them. It all seemed very serious and challenging and terrific fun, like the London Sunday *Times* puzzle.

The questionnaire came from a feminist who was writing a book about "the woman-identified woman." Most of the seventy-four questions dealt with differences between woman-man relationships and woman-woman relationships. Many required very detailed answers. I decided that having to answer the questions as Micki would get my feminist-academic life off to the right start. I took out a legal pad (there was no typewriter in the office), and a ball-point pen, and wrote "Micki Wrangler!" at the top of a piece of paper.

Six or seven years ago I wrote a short novel that was dictated by angels; I just did the typing. After fifteen minutes with the questionnaire I had the same feeling. Some Micki voice that had always sung in my choir, only I'd never heard it before, was dictating to me.

QUESTION: What would you do if you were independently wealthy?

ANSWER: I would drink more champagne, eat more strawberries, keep all my people in fine dope, take people on trips (real and metaphorical)—and essentially keep on doing exactly what I'm doing. I like my life.

QUESTION: Have you come out as a bisexual or lesbian? Why? Have you declared yourself openly to: (a) your female friends, (b) your male friends, (c) your parents, (d) your employers, (e) your husband? What were their reactions? How did they make you feel?

ANSWER: Yes. Why not? I am who I am, and the people I care about have to deal with that—and other people don't matter. My male friends accept it, just as they accept my being polyandrous. Most women either find it natural or maybe somewhat enviable.

I gave my responses to Carla to type (guilt, guilt) and looked at the letters I had to answer. One was from a convict who'd read

about Micki in a newspaper article about women's studies programs and wanted to be pen pals with her. "Heavy," I thought to
my Micki self when I finished reading it. "No wonder I've left it
sitting around since March." I did better with a letter from a
University of Massachusetts graduate student who wanted to
know what I considered an "alternate life-style." I asked Carla for
copies of some other letters I'd written, checked out my style, and
wrote:

I'd define an alternate life-style as one that is based on other than the
written and unwritten laws of a particular society at a particular point in
time. I don't agree with you that "nontraditional" is exactly the point: an
alternate life-style exists in counterpoint to the mores of the present, even
if these mores constitute a rejection of tradition—a generally approved
rejection, of course. Many people who practice alternate life-styles correctly feel, in fact, that they are upholding a great tradition, and that the
practicioners of "conservative" life-styles are actually the destroyers of
tradition. A good example in our culture might be those people who use
drugs for spiritual reasons and consider themselves to be exercising traditional American religious freedom even though what they have is, in
terms of modern American society, an alternate life-style.

"In terms of." Ah, the joy of it. Nick, T.M., and E. B. White will
understand. That violation of my own rules of style made me feel
naughty out of all proportion. I gave the letter to Carla for typing,
told her there was no rush on either that or the questionnaire, and
went to lunch.

In her journals, Micki had mentioned eating in the faculty dining room, but that was out. Only her close friends knew about the
swap, and I didn't want to do anything that might bring me to the
notice of the administration. (Micki was quitting at the end of the
year, but she still wanted me to be cool about my presence.) It
would have been mean to ask Carla where else I had lunch. She
was being so great about calling me Micki or Dr. Wrangler and
thanking me for things I'd done the week before and telling me
that there was plenty of my favorite Seven-Up in the refrigerator,
that I didn't want to mar her efforts by asking any more questions
than I had to. I ended up going across the campus to a drugstore
with a counter and ordering my usual Riverset drugstore ham and
eggs. I wasn't sure the iced coffee was legitimate, so I threw in
extra milk and sugar to compensate and drank it to the beat of

Philip Slater. I bought some ice cream for Carla (it seemed like something Micki—or any remotely compassionate person—would do for an unair-conditioned co-worker on such a day) and an iced coffee to go for me and went back to the office.

Gene Howard, a student, was coming to see me about some letters of recommendation he needed for graduate school. He'd done the drafts; Micki had okayed them; Carla had typed them; and now I had to sign them. I read them carefully and forged my name. A master criminal at last! My calendar said to call Karen Smith about lunch on Friday, and I asked Carla to reach her for me (felt guilty, guilty, guilty about asking Carla to do that, but Micki rarely dialed her own calls). I realized from things Karen said that she was a Hawthorne colleague. We made a lunch appointment for Friday. Peter called, and we made plans to have dinner together. He told me he was with Wendy, someone he's been seeing for a while, and my stomach contracted. Because Old Micki's would have? Because New Micki was afraid she was letting Old Micki down? Because the notoriously unpossessive Old Nancy now and then got jealous? Whatever, my immediate reaction was: I miss Ben; I want to talk to Ben. (Later in the day I realized how extraordinary that was. At the first bump of real insecurity that I'd experienced in the swap, I didn't want to call Nick or T.M. or my parents or Magda; I wanted to call my husband, whom I'd never met.) Just then Ted phoned to tell me how much he'd enjoyed our evening together. His exquisite timing and shy, young voice brought me up again. I decided to wait and call Ben on Wednesday, as scheduled.

Gene Howard walked in when I was five pages into a paper he'd written on black studies programs as a model for women's studies programs. He smiled deferentially and called me "Doctor" in a way that made me feel as though I had eighty-seven Ph.D.'s. I offered him a Seven-Up and gave him the letters I'd signed and some advice on how to deal with his wife's recent immersion in the women's movement. I felt about as qualified to give that advice as I did to perform brain surgery, but he'd asked, and he seemed to think I was helping. Maybe my New England common sense had made the leap to Brooklyn. He thanked me a number of times, and I began to feel as though I really had the right to be sitting behind that desk. I asked him to have lunch with me next week and hoped he'd bring some more problems for me to therapize.

I dashed off a silly, exuberant letter to my friend the writer in Greenwich Village:

Dear Nancy:

I'm sorry to have to tell you that your term paper is not acceptable and you will not be permitted to be graduated from Hawthorne.

Could you dig up a pack of Ovulen from my bureau drawer and send it to me? I took one that's only got enough pills for one more week. If it's not there, it's somewhere, or ask Alan Weissman at Ansonia for a refill. It's cheating horribly, but so is taking the pill as you to begin with.

Please, but I'm sure you thought of it anyway, hold on to all relevant written matter & keep copies of letters, too, as of course I will: even notes, if possible.

If Nick wants to be shnorgled, it means his hair gets ruffled intensely and he is sort of sweetly pummeled all over.

The people in your life love you very much & your work is disgracefully easy & I hope my everything is as good for you.

In sisterhood!

Micki

I stuck it in an envelope and put it on Carla's desk. She handed me a thick typescript of my answers to the questionnaire. I thanked her profusely for having done it so quickly (my guilt was coming out of my toes at this point) and asked her if she thought I'd done a good job of answering it. "You mean Micki didn't leave those answers for you?" she asked. Maybe she just said that to make me feel terrific; whatever, I wanted to hug her. I told her I'd see her in the morning and went out to the faculty parking lot.

It was when I got into Micki's Renault that I knew the swap was really birthing magic because my armpits were not evil, not even a little. Was it possible? I repeated my investigation, left and right: not a trace of dampness. Extraordinary. It had been well over ninety degrees all day. I had ridden in a subway to Brooklyn, sat in an unair-conditioned office all day, eaten ham and eggs in that rather warm drugstore—and the armpits that had been known to outsmart a mix of Dove, Arrid, and Johnson's Baby Powder were not even faintly redolent. Micki hadn't been kidding when she said her work was no sweat.

All the way home (and I mean all the way—I must have crossed

Brooklyn five times before I connected with Micki's route) I pondered this transference of physical characteristics. Those innocent armpits seemed more magical to me than having Micki's orgasms with Ted and Peter or feeling like a full-blown sociologist-counselor with Gene Howard.It was something I'd hoped would happen, something Micki and I had talked about a lot, but the excitement of imagining it hadn't been anything close to the excitement of having evidence. I wanted to send my armpits to Duke University. This was psyche power.

Driving felt marvelous. I'd been an uneasy passenger and driver ever since the accident that bought my Münter, and I'd had apprehensions about all the driving I'd do as Micki; now it seemed a very welcome time-out in a life that I realized made no other provisions for being completely alone. I had one bad moment on a curving downgrade, but I had a strong feeling that it was Micki's bad moment, not Nancy's. Had she had a near accident there? No, that wasn't it. This was crazy, but I was sure of it: Something in that turn and drop gave Micki a suicidal thrill. I made a note to ask her about it sometime, then shrugged the awful thought away.

A gaggle of stickball players on 84th Street helped me into a tight parking space on the right alternate side of the street. I remembered that Peter and I had drunk the last of the Almadén Chablis. I went into the liquor store to replace it (nicely resisting the longing for Gewürztraminer), then went into Micki's grocery store. Danny bought the staples for the household, and she and Peter paid their shares, but I knew she also often bought other things, especially fruit, on her own. As I was counting out a pound of cherries, a nice bald clerk in a green apron said, "Put in a couple of more; I'm not here to make money for the boss." I wondered if he knew I was Micki, but I was pretty sure she hadn't let the people she did business with in on our secret. I couldn't wait to get her notes and know for sure.

No one was home. I put what I'd bought in the refrigerator. Maisie Leonard, whom Micki had described as a gay woman who was a very dear friend but not her lover, called about our plans for Wednesday night. She asked me where I wanted to meet, and I suggested Mother Courage, a Micki favorite place. Maisie sounded nice and was wonderfully matter-of-fact. I blew the mood by telling her that I'd been having bouts of amnesia, had forgotten what she looked like. She told me she had very short hair and looked like a boy.

I remembered that I hadn't taken my vitamins for the day or done my exercises. I swallowed all the pills on the list and got out my exercise cards. There wasn't space enough in our bedroom, so I stretched and bumped and thumped up and down the hallway. A lot more painful and not as much fun as tennis.

Took a cool shower, washed my hair, tucked it behind my ears to dry, did the maximum allowable with my face. Peter came in, kissed me, said he was hungry. I quickly got into my green pants and another Mexican top and beads. "You look nice," he said. With my wet head and naked skin and too-bright clothes? But I think I looked happy.

We hiked up to Tien Tsin. He ordered a Heineken and asked if I wanted one. Micki said no before Nancy could say yes. Oh, unbearable longing! Nancy got back at Micki by suggesting a whole steamed fish and Chinese vegetables. Micki liked the fish as much as Nancy did, and poor Peter still looked hungry at the end.

The conversation centered on my feelings about Peter and Wendy. Old Micki had given me some clues back in May. I knew she'd been jealous, was upset with herself for being jealous, thought she'd overcome her jealousy, now was mostly worried that Wendy's junkie boyfriend would make trouble for Peter. I also knew what that knotted stomach earlier in the day had told me. (I was sure now it had been a Micki knot, which made it no less my knot.) I talked volubly for me and rather passionately and articulately, I think; and if I was being an actress, I didn't know it. The words I was saying were prompted in part by the information Micki had given me, but they reflected my real and very strong feelings. I told Peter I wanted to see Wendy "again," and he said she wanted the meeting, too, and agreed to set it up. I was quite elated. I envisioned carrying out a series of cool moves that would leave Micki's life in even better shape than she'd left it.

Our fortune cookies were banal, but I saved the slips anyway. I paid for both of us, and Peter looked pleased. "You know how much I like it when you take me out," he said. "I do indeed," I said, and knew I liked it, too. We went home and read for a while, then went to Times Square so I could buy a cassette recorder for making notes, and came home again. We talked about the job Peter was starting the next day in the art department of a big record company. He'd be working part-time for no pay during the summer, and if they liked him, he'd be hired full time in the fall, so a lot seemed to be at stake. We talked about the drawing he used to do and might be able to do again and about his ambitions as a photographer. I teased him about becoming too visually oriented, but he said that living with Danny and me, there wasn't any danger. I couldn't stop myself. I drew on all my Nancy (and Micki) knowledge and started rattling away about the magnificence of Paul Klee, whose journals matched his plastic output in brilliance. Peter didn't draw back in shock, so I guess Micki likes Klee, at least has never disliked Klee out loud in front of Peter. We ate some blueberries and cherries.

Ted called and invited us over. When we got there, he had the TV tuned to the Watergate hearings, but he'd fooled around with the color and sound, so we had an abstract film set to rock. I thought of all the nights I'd forbidden T.M. to buy *The New York Times,* and I tossed him a little smile, wherever he was. I was dying to watch Watergate. Old Trig was getting his revenge.

We smoked marijuana and reminisced about the peyote trip "we" had taken the week before in Riverset. I had my head on Peter's knee, my knees propped against Ted's back, and there was a faintly sexual warmth to it all, but I felt sleepy and kind of bored. A half hour of grown-up worldly talk at Jimmy's would have gone down rather well just then. Nancy's boredom or Micki's? Peter and I went home. It was late, but no Danny. Was he staying away because of me? Peter and I said, "Good night, lover," to each other, kissed, turned our separate ways.

Wednesday, June 13

Woke up exhausted, though I'd slept very deeply. Peter woke up full of anxieties about his new job. I wanted to make him breakfast, but all he would eat was yogurt and blueberries. With his long ponytail and boots, he looked like a young pioneer as he headed off to his new life.

Danny came home. Wherever he'd spent the night, it looked like he'd had fun. We had coffee together and talked about Peter's need to leave the nest and his feelings of inadequacy. (My Micki vocabulary was up to par.) I had the feeling that Danny didn't quite trust me, wasn't sure if my concern for Peter was real, which it was, or play acting. He seemed hesitant about kissing me when I left, and I said, "Don't you love me anymore?" He embraced me warmly, but I knew I still had a distance to go with him.

Somehow I drove more or less directly to Hawthorne, though I was still mostly asleep. Carla had fresh iced coffee waiting for me, which was incredibly dear of her, but it did nothing for my eyelids. Part of my feeling of loginess came from being constipated. I'd survived the trauma of having Peter walk into the bathroom while I was peeing, but that was it.

I decided to work on these notes for a while instead of my Micki projects. There was obviously going to be neither time nor privacy enough to work on them at the apartment. I tried talking into my new cassette recorder but felt ridiculous, and writing by hand was torture. Decided to forfeit a bit of authenticity and asked Carla if there were a typewriter I could use. She asked Rich, the caretaker, to get one for me from an abandoned office, and then I was in business. Phone call from someone named Anne Upton. Didn't know who she was, but liked her name and voice, and agreed to meet her at her apartment Thursday for dinner.

Had another Riverset breakfast for lunch. More Slater. Back to the office. It was hot. I felt blah.

I wondered how Micki was doing. I decided I was mad at her for not having sent me her address book and the notes she was supposed to have done on her friends. I pulled out some names from her journals and her notations on my calendar and tried getting numbers from Carla and Information. Everyone I wanted to talk to was either unlisted or not home. I was sure that my blahness was the blahness Micki would have felt if she hadn't been able to make calls, had to wait for the phone to ring.

There was Ben to call, but I wanted to be in a good mood, a good Micki mood, when I talked to him. I started to read *Women and Madness*, look at it as I thought Micki would, but that wasn't so easy. The beginning of the book was full of references to Persephone, the mythic figure with whom Nancy most identifies and about whom she knows rather a bit; and it was impossible for me to concentrate on the political ramifications of the book, if there are any.

"Fuckadoodle," I said.

I heard the phone ring. A few minutes later Carla walked in.

"It's Nancy Weber," she said. "She needs to know the name of your banker."

"How does she sound?" I asked.

"Very busy, but very happy."

"My banker's name is in my notes—never mind, I'll tell her myself; it won't kill us." I picked up the phone.

Micki insisted that the name of my banker wasn't in my notes, which puzzled me, because I was sure it was. Oh, well. I gave her his name again. She said she'd received my letter and would send me the pills and would try to do the people notes that night and get them up to me. She did sound busy but happy. I hung up feeling good about how things were going at her end and forgave her about the address book.

I began to worry about how Peter was doing in his new job and wished he would call. Nancy realized a few minutes later that it was Micki who'd been worrying and wishing, and all of us felt better about how the day was going at this end. Had my favorite Seven-Up. Asked Carla to get my husband on the phone.

He was gentle and quiet and very friendly and sort of funny, and I couldn't wait to see him. I asked, as I was supposed to, how he felt about Peter coming down to Riverset for the weekend, and he hesitated and said he wasn't sure. I knew he liked being alone with Micki, and I was enchanted that he'd transferred the liking to me. Micki, Nancy, someone decided it would be nice to be alone with him.

I wanted to get a present for Peter to celebrate his new job (and maybe to make up for my hoping that he wouldn't want to come to Riverset). I walked over to the Hawthorne bookstore, looked in vain for Klee's journals or some other such perfect thing, ended up with Donald Allen's anthology, *New American Poetry*. I wrote "To Peter—to keep you a little verbal among the visual. Love and kisses, Micki," and had it gift wrapped.

Then I went into a phone booth and, putting on a crazy French accent so no one at the other end would recognize me, called Nick at his office in Hartford. It was a total violation of my rules but— hard to explain—an unquestionable necessity. It wasn't that I missed him, exactly; I just had an absolute compulsion, as I passed those phone booths, to hear his voice. And I wanted to know how he and Mother and Daddy were holding up now that the swap was under way, what he knew of Micki's feelings. (She'd sounded good, but she'd told me so little. Nick would know all.) By the time he picked up the phone, I'd convinced myself that not calling him would have been to pretend I was just another participant and horribly irresponsible.

Nick and I giggled and whispered like two terrible conspirators.

He said that he'd talked to Micki a couple of times, and she'd behaved a lot the way I would have and was coming up to Granby the next day to see him, and that he now thought the swap was an absolutely brilliant thing. He said that the Kids (our parents) were definitely going to meet her, maybe have dinner with her. I told him that everyone in Micki's life was being incredibly good to me and that some fantastic things had happened and that I hadn't yet had to drink Cold Duck. I said I loved him tons and would probably call on Friday to hear his silly voice and find out how Micki's visit home had gone.

I wondered guiltily as I walked back to my office if it wasn't only fair to tell Micki what I'd done, offer her equal time with one of her people. I felt guiltier toward T.M., who'd be furiously jealous if he found out that I'd called Nick and not him. I felt guiltiest toward Nick. Had I interfered with his ability to regard Micki as the one and only Tard? I discovered that I was paying dues for my transgressions. Nancy had started to sweat.

I decided to write off the afternoon. I picked up my copy of *Women and Madness* and told Carla I was leaving for the day. I talked into my cassette recorder all the way home from Brooklyn and nearly got killed several times. Felt that awful suicide thrill again as I drove down the curving ramp that I knew had pulled at Micki.

Danny was home, working on an historical paper he was to deliver to some Yale alumni. I asked him to add a note to the book I'd bought for Peter, but he said he didn't have anything to say, and besides it was really my present. He softened that a bit by telling me it was a good anthology, contained one of his favorite poems, Kenneth Koch's "Mending Sump." We read it, laughed together.

I'd brought home a copy of the woman-identified woman questionnaire I'd filled out on Tuesday. I thought it should have Peter's and Danny's okay on it before I sent it out in Micki's name, and I also wanted them both to know how much I understood and loved her. I gave it to Danny and told him what Carla had said about thinking real Micki had done the answers. He read it and said I could have fooled him, too. I hoped he meant it and would feel easier about me now. I knew Micki was important to him, though I wasn't sure exactly how, and I wanted to fill her space the best I could.

Gave him $5.25 for my share of the weekly groceries, tried some barbecued beans and rice he'd made, took my vitamin pills, decided to forgo my exercises (Micki cheated on them, too); rewrapped the book for Peter, showered and dressed. If things worked out the way my calendar said they were supposed to, Maisie and I would go dancing with some other gay women after dinner, and I paid more attention to my appearance than I had for Peter or Ted. (Micki or Nancy at work?)

There were several phone calls from friends of Micki's wanting to see me. Made a date with Cassie Davidson for the next day at the Riviera. She sounded confused about the rules of the game, a little shy. It was strange for me not to be the shy one. I was very glad she had called. I wasn't sure how close she and Micki were, but I knew she was an important feminist writer, and I loved the idea that I would be meeting her in the guise of a feminist, might even discover that Nancy was more of a feminist than I thought.

Peter came home exhilarated. I don't know if it was his mood, or my realization that I'd been genuinely Micki-mother-tense about his first day on the job, or the joint we smoked, or his quiet pleasure at getting the book of poetry, or everything together: I was flying again. He decided to come down to Mother Courage with me (that had been a question mark on the calendar), which got me a notch higher, cured me of whatever blues still lingered about his rushing off to see Wendy on Tuesday. I bought a bottle of Rhine wine at the liquor store around the corner, and we drove down to the Village.

Nancy immediately fell in love with Maisie Leonard. Cropped hair, pale skin, carnival face—she was Hermine from *Steppenwolf* sprung to life. I knew why she had told me she looked like a boy, but she seemed the very seed of femininity. I knew for absolutely sure that Micki was in love with her, too: how not to be? I also knew that Maisie would like Nancy a lot more than the Nancy-Micki she was having dinner with. Not that she'd like the real Nancy more than she liked the real Micki, but the hybrid just wasn't going to work for her in any important way; I could feel it. I grieved at the loss of her, then let her spectacular presence heal me. We talked about S and M, a lady with a dildo, and Wendy. I gathered that all "my" friends were just a little bit delighted that the Wendy-Peter thing had flapped my unflappable cool. I was happy that they were happy. Ate shrimp and drank a lot of wine.

Peter took the car home, and I followed Maisie to the Duchess, a gay women's bar near Sheridan Square. Nancy had never been in a gay bar, which is maybe why Micki took over and I felt right at home. My lover Pat Barry was there with her roommate Rachel Auer, and other friends of mine, and some strangers who seemed to know about me. I drank beer, and listened to the rock music, and watched the couples dancing, and talked, and enjoyed the rich golden bar light.

Rachel was the first to ask me to dance. She held me close, and our breasts all squished together. I loved her soft cheek against mine. She told me I was brave to be there—Nancy's reputation as a straight evidently had preceded me. I told her it wasn't brave at all, which was true. I had become Micki again, and doing this thing that she liked so much required no more courage than washing my hair with her shampoo.

Maisie asked me to dance and never looked in my eyes—an utterly heartbreaking creature, that one. I started to talk rather intimately to Pat Barry, but she looked scared, and I stopped. Rachel took me aside and said not to worry about Pat; she had lots of things on her mind. I wondered if she were comforting Nancy or Micki. I asked Rachel to dance. I had never felt so relaxed on a dance floor. The participant-observer snidely asked if that were because my Nancy indifference to women made my klutziness for once not matter. I told the p-o to mind her own business. In fact, my klutziness quotient was lower than usual.

Maisie left, and I decided to go home. Pat Barry was obviously sticking with Rachel, and it didn't seem to me that I'd further my understanding of Micki's bisexuality by picking up a stranger. I went to take care of the bill and found out that Maisie had paid it, which stung sweetly: I'd meant to pay for her. I walked across Sheridan Square to get a cab and ended up standing almost in front of the Lion's Head. I wondered if Micki and Abbe had gone there after dinner, were in there right now; then the Head and the thought wavered and receded. I settled into a cab, pulled out my tape recorder.

It's Wednesday, ten after twelve, and I've just left the Duchess, and I'm in a taxi heading home. God, there's so much in my head. It's incredible, but it didn't occur to me until this minute that there was some other home I might have gone to, the one two blocks from Sheridan Square. But the really extraordinary thing about tonight was that I could dance in a woman's arms and love it and love her. Was it because I was so much Micki or because that was always coming for Nancy? I feel incredibly high.

Peter and I made very passionate love. Maisie was there in the bed with us—Peter said he felt it, too. I missed her, but I wasn't really sorry I hadn't gone home with her. I would have missed Peter more. (Micki would have missed him? Nancy would have? In fact it was androgynous Micki, I think, who would have missed him more.)

Danny came home with someone named Allen, who had a California tan. They were both wearing white T-shirts and tight pants, and I thought they looked beautiful together. There we all were —a naked thirty-one-year-old woman and twenty-one-year-old man in bed, an older and a younger homosexual necking in the doorway—and it felt like the sweetest of family scenes, *was* the sweetest of family scenes. I dreamed about Maisie all night; she loved me and called me Micki.

Thursday, June 14

Micki, are you flipped back to childhood the way Nancy is when you wake to the smell of bacon frying?

Peter kissed me and was up and off to work. I had breakfast with Danny and Allen: some bacon Danny had saved for me, two eggs I fried myself, the half of an English muffin that Allen didn't eat, vitamin pills swallowed with unreal orange juice. Allen was talking a little bit about why he'd left California, what he wanted to do in New York (photography and psychology). I wondered if he knew about the swap, decided he didn't. He asked me where I grew up, and I said France; he asked me what I did professionally, and I told him about Hawthorne; and he seemed to take it all with perfect casualness. I liked him very much. Before the swap started, I'd been afraid, I don't know why, that despite my conscious acceptance of all things sexual, I'd discover some secret aversion to male homosexuals. If not aversion, at least some uneasiness around them. I was very much aware that Allen and Danny were gay (they talked about it a lot, for one thing), but to the degree that it mattered to me at all, I was actually positive about it. I knew that being positive (as opposed to neutral) was a Micki

word for a Micki feeling, but I knew that there was a genuine
Nancy gut-happy indifference, and I apologized to myself for having thought I'd be either horrified or liberal tolerant or some other
not-right thing.

My coffee tasted flat. I'd forgotten to put sugar in it.

Danny and Allen went to finish dressing. I cleaned up the
kitchen a bit and started to wash the dishes. Danny came in behind
me and massaged my shoulder muscles. My shoulders felt great,
and my heart sang. I felt as though I'd passed some major test.

End of constipation. I thought of Edna in *The Ewings,* who
experiences a similar triumph on the fourth day of her honey-
moon. It was nice to be synchronized with a John O'Hara heroine
this far from Gibbsville.

Carla had iced coffee waiting for me. I returned a call to someone in Connecticut named Mary Bell and agreed to have dinner
with her next Tuesday. I had no idea who she was, but her name
was down on my calendar as someone to call the following Monday, so I guessed she was reasonably important in my life. I wondered why I hadn't heard from Steffie Kahn, whom Micki's journals had described as being more like her than anyone in the
world. Carla had no number for her at work. Oh, well, I'd fill in
all those gaps next week.

Decided it was okay now to send off my answers to the woman-
identified woman questionnaire, and wrote a covering note to go
with them. It's interesting to write a note to someone you don't
know if you know or not. I reread the letter to Micki from the man
in prison, spent half an hour doing drafts of my first paragraph to
him, and gave up on it again. I picked up the copy of *New York*
magazine that had come in the mail. This week's competition had
to do with making up telegrams that were anagrams of people's
names, and I tried to work up something based on Gloria Steinem
and Bella Abzug. No luck. Micki's fault for being bad at anagrams,
of course.

Another unknown woman called from Princeton to find out if
Ben and I wanted to have dinner with her and a friend on Friday.
I checked with my sweet husband, who said not to get us overcom-
mitted. We were going to a party Saturday at Sig and Alice
Lewis's, and that was maybe enough. I realized that I'd never
discussed the weekend with Peter, and I called him at work to ask
him what his plans were. He said he was going to stay in town and

drive a cab because he owed Danny rent money. I wondered if he planned to see Wendy, whom he was seeing for dinner that night, but decided that would be less upsetting than not being alone with Ben.

Read a little more Phyllis Chesler. Tried to reach Sukie Sandler, with whom I was supposed to coauthor the review; she wasn't at home or the clinic where she worked. I felt very Nancy-hypochondriac looking all over for the doctor. Started banging away at my swap notes. Carla came in. She said she was going to the bank and then to the commissary for lunch, would I like her to bring back my favorite roast beef and American cheese on a roll? Nancy's stomach went "Ugh." "That would be great," enthused Micki.

From my notes:

How do I feel about it all after four days? I'm astonished (even though I wanted this) by the intensity of my connection with the people around me. My passion for Peter, my affection for Danny, my sexual delight in Ted the other night, the way I love and lean on Carla. Maybe I would have liked them all as Nancy, felt intimate with them if I'd been in such intimate circumstances with them. But what am I saying? How else could there have been such intimate circumstances? No, it wouldn't have been at all the same, being a guest in their lives. Admit it: Ted would have seemed boring and not at all a sexual magnet; Peter would have seemed young and a little bit weak and—despite the body Micki so responds to—not my idea of the world's most thrilling bedmate; and I might not have taken the trouble to work through Danny's reserve. Anybody would have to be crazy not to love Carla.

Would they all have liked me under other circumstances? Do they like me now? I think they do, but is it as Nancy or Micki or Micki's friend, or what? I want them to see me as Micki; I would like them at least to know that, however un-Micki I may act at times, I am full of Micki feelings for them. Do they see it? If they see it, can they believe it? If they believe it, are they right? I may not be as good as Micki is at loving them, but—some of the time, anyway—I'm just as inclined to love them; I'm sure of it.

I'm enjoying Micki's work. Obviously I'm not getting anything more than a dim taste of it; for certain it's infinitely tougher and more cerebral than this.

In this life I have a very distinct sense of having little to do with the real world (like Watergate). Or is that just a slightly abstracted state brought on by the act of swapping?

I wonder if the people meeting me now think I'm awful looking and don't care, or find me attractive, or just don't notice. And how they feel about Old Micki. It's incredible how naked I feel without lipstick, how much I hate the stubble on my legs. I bet if Micki were as hairy as I am (she often boasted to me about having almost no body hair), she'd feel differently about that whole thing.

I am dying to watch Micki make love.

It's terrific meeting people who've never met Micki, don't know about the swap.

Nothing I have done or seen feels alien.

Being casual in the gay bar because I was being Micki reminds me somehow of not succeeding in writing song lyrics until I began *Star Fever* and invented a character to write them for me.

I am amazed (though I'd hoped for this) about not feeling more competitive with Micki. Is that her sisterly serenity or mine?

I love Micki. In part because Micki loves Micki?

I miss Nick more than anyone. I miss my parents and T.M. and Magda and Susie, who became so close so quickly, and Gabriele Münter, but not in the way you miss people when you're on vacation. I honestly just don't think about them all that much. There really are enormous chunks of myself that I left down in the Village—hope New Nancy is taking good care of them.

I'm not particularly noticing my physical surroundings—because Micki isn't particularly visual?

I'm looking forward to the aftermath of all of this, to the big party I'm going to throw for everyone involved at both ends of it, to the rich new friendships. Still it seems incredible in a way that the swap itself will end next week.

Exactly who wrote these notes?

More Chesler. Was this hard-core feminism or a *National Lampoon* parody? Phone call from someone named Ben McCullen in Princeton who wanted my Ben and me to come to a party Saturday night. I explained that we already had a party in Princeton, would try to stop by his on the way. He called back five minutes later and asked for Nancy Weber's number so he could invite her, too. I said that I didn't know any such person, and he laughed and said okay.

I looked through some material on career choices for my feminist research meeting on Wednesday night. Looked at the long papers that needed working on and decided to get into that another time.

Gene Howard came in to tell me he'd had some small success in "communicating" with his wife. A student who was supposed to come talk about his term paper didn't. I wrote a letter of recommendation for a feminist sociologist and prayed that it wouldn't contradict anything she'd told Columbia University about herself. (Since Micki had put off writing the letter since April, I decided her career didn't hang on it.) I liked Mary Bell very much after writing about our long friendship and professional association and was glad we were scheduled to meet next Tuesday.

One of the tasks that had been left for me was to go to Altman's and arrange for engraving on the silver tray that the graduating students in the experimental program had given Carla. It wasn't my idea of kicks, but I was glad to have a hand in anything that would please Carla, and it made me feel less guilty about having stuck Micki with the job of presiding over the installation of my new telephone. I locked the tray in the trunk of the car and started for midtown Manhattan. Halfway there I realized I would never find parking, negotiate the engraving, and be even Micki-on-time to meet Cassie Davidson, so I went straight to the Village. I drove around and around then found a space right in front of the Riviera. I was suddenly very nervous. Why had I agreed to meet at a place that was a part of my Nancy life? Where I'd be sure to see people who knew me?

The meeting was a total disaster. From my tapes:

I'm riding up Eighth Avenue after an hour at the Riviera with Cassie Davidson and her friend Leona, and I am totally pissed off. They said right away that they weren't going to call me Micki, and they weren't going to try to relate to me as if I were Micki because the swap was only a game and their relationship with Micki was too serious, too important for them to play games about it. If that was so, I said, why didn't they honor Micki by going along with the swap the way she meant them to, by following the directions on the invitation she had sent them? No, no, no, they said, they and Micki always talked out of their most deeply felt experiences, and she wouldn't want them to play make-believe. What was my last name, and what had I written, and what was the theory behind the swap? I wanted to explode. If they couldn't go along with the rules of the game, why hadn't they waited until it was over to meet me? Didn't they realize how their stubbornness was fucking up my ability to look at them with Micki eyes? Right into the middle of all of which tension walked my old dear friend Victor Navasky. He said hello to me, and I smiled at him, and then we both realized we weren't supposed to know each other, and he said some patch-up thing like, "Aren't you Micki Wrangler?" and I said, "Who are you?" But it didn't work at all. He sat with us for a minute and then left to go to the Lion's Head, which made me feel worse. I was sure he was going to tell everyone that I'd looked glum and the swap wasn't jelling in the least. Cassie started in on how long it took her to trust anyone, and she and Leona both seemed so depressed that I decided I'd give in; what the hell, the hour was blown anyway. "I wrote a book called *Star*—" I started to say, but then I heard myself shouting "No!" They didn't have to treat me as Micki, but I wasn't going to pull out all my Nancy Weber identification marks, I just wasn't; half the point of the swap was to find out whether or not I was hooked on them, and no one was going to mess that up. We talked a little bit about some of the people in Micki's life and a trip to California Leona was about to take, and finally about why I wanted to do the swap, and then Cassie did the math on our check, divided it right down to the last penny. Should I call Vic and tell him not to judge the swap by what he saw, that it's been as different as could be? But I don't want to, too embarrassing, and Micki certainly wouldn't. Is all this anger Micki's? Fuck!!! Oh, where is my beautiful mood of a few hours ago? Hope dinner with Anne will put me back on the right track. And that I'll see Peter and Wendy later, and they'll pull me to someplace important.

Anne had told me I could bring dessert if I wanted. I picked up a pint of blueberries and a cheesecake. She'd reminded me that the last time I'd come to see her, my car had been towed, so I parked in a lot near Columbus Circle, walked over to her apartment, handed her the stuff for dessert, and begged her for consolation. She was incredible. An imp-angel:

On my way home from Anne's now. I felt better the minute I saw her. She's about five feet tall and looks like a tomboy. Could not believe it when she started to talk about her married daughters. I told her why I felt so foul-tempered. She gave me a soft couch to sit on, a glass of good white wine, and proceeded to talk to me as if I were a friend and colleague of long standing. The perfect antidote to Ms. Cassie Davidson.

I loved the way she criticized my performance, offered clues: She wanted me to be more Micki, not less. At one point we were talking about her love life, and she said I was supposed to tease her about her backward attitude toward sex with women. I did, in my best Micki vocabulary; I even got Micki aggressive and invited her to come dancing at the Duchess with me next Wednesday. She agreed and seemed delighted, and the whole thing felt as if it had everything to do with Micki and nothing with Nancy, and my mood jumped way up. I was also really pleased when she asked me if I could suggest any topics for a symposium of feminist therapists and seemed turned on by my suggestion that they discuss the possibilities of using yoga, meditation, and other such techniques to develop a kind of autonomic birth control. I don't know where that idea came from (Micki??), but Anne said she thought I was on to something important and that she'd been thinking along similar lines. My first success as a feminist therapist. She fed me marvelous lamb, and generally cheered me on with her impish presence. I just hope everyone in my Nancy life is being as good to its temporary occupant, giving her the clues she needs to carry off being me.

A young Canadian woman named Pam came over after dinner and was stilted and a bit hostile with me. Wish I'd had some idea about her relationship with Micki. I called Peter at the place where he was having dinner with Wendy, was told they were out taking a walk and that he'd call me back. He didn't and the phone was persistently busy after that, and I was sure it was off the hook —that without knowing it I'd somehow horribly offended him, maybe lost him forever to Wendy. I was a perfect half-and-half schizophrenic at that moment. Enough Micki to feel the kind of pain you feel when you think you're losing someone you've loved long and seriously, enough Nancy to panic that I'd failed Micki, that my presence in her life might cost her a lover. I've seen Micki in moments of need rifle through her phone book and dial one number after another until she got the comfort she needed, and I felt very bothered that I couldn't do that, too—not just so that I could be like Micki, but so I could have the comfort *I* needed. I had a wild temptation to call Trigger Mike, but I didn't want to remind him that there was another Nancy, jeopardize whatever was going on between him and Micki. I wondered if Micki had been tempted to call Peter or Ben or Ted. If she had, was it because she had to talk to them or because she'd found out how much I love to break rules if I think I'll get away with it and no one else will have to pay dues? But of course if she did call anyone, I would pay dues because I'd be that much less Micki to them, and they'd pay dues because whatever Micki reality I had for them would be diminished.

I dropped Pam off at her home on the East Side and headed home. Danny and Allen were asleep. Found a message asking me to call Peter at the number where I'd been trying him, and I did. He said he'd tried to call me back, but whoever had taken down Anne's number had got it wrong, and her phone was unlisted. I felt better, until he told me he was planning to spend the night with Wendy.

I got into our bed with Micki's copy of Cassie Davidson's novel and told myself I was glad to have a chance to read, to be by myself. Nobody was kidded for a moment. I wondered what Micki would do in this situation and bawled myself out for not having insisted on getting her phone book sooner, not having asked half as many questions as she had before the swap had got under way. Strange how I'd assumed that just because she was married and lived with somebody, her life was a more cohesive and accessible entity than mine and would require less preparing for. I began thinking it was quite the opposite, that there were a lot more contingency plans in my life precisely because I was my own home base.

I looked at the picture of Cassie on the back of her book. A serene face, with a kind of animal keenness to it, the face of someone I would have expected to like. I wondered what terrible things had happened to make her face as drawn as it was when we met, make her so unsporting. Was I asking something impossible of people? Dammit, no! I was making a demand, but I was offering a dip through time and space—more than fair return. I opened Cassie's book hoping to dislike it. Its longings overcame my longings and also my fatigue, and moved, unmoving, I read it straight through to the end.

Friday, June 15

Woke feeling unrested and lonely and hating the gray streets. I could hear Danny and Allen having at it in the other end of the apartment. There was Vaseline and sweat on the air. My stomach hurt.

Made coffee. Had some yogurt. Dutifully popped my vitamin pills. Wondered why my ten capsules and tablets a day weren't making me feel all zippy-doo-da energetic. Decided that fresh orange juice, rugola salads, and Irish whiskey did more for my metabolism than anything in a capsule.

Looked over the face and body I'd be bringing to my husband. A fine layer of bumps covered my cheeks and chin, grâce à marijuana, the face brush, and maybe being homesick for makeup. There was a nice coating of bristle on my legs and under my arms. I'd added a pound or two, it looked like—sugar and milk in my coffee, Seven-Up all day long at the office, no stairs to run up and down. About all that the physical plant had to recommend itself was ten magnificent fingernails. The vitamins might not be doing me much good, but the gelatin in the capsules was. I hoped Ben liked to close his eyes and have his back scratched.

Carla told me I looked nice when I walked into the office. Peter called and said he hoped I hadn't been upset the night before, and would I please bring back his *Whole Earth Catalog* and ask Ben for his camera, and could he do anything for me while I was gone? He could change the sheets, I told him; they'd been a bit too much company the night before.

Finally reached Sukie Sandler, and we agreed to talk again on Monday about getting together to work on our review. She had an enchanting voice, and I knew I would like her. Donna Holub and another student came in to show me a bird with a broken wing they were nursing, and we chatted for a while. "Just like Micki," Donna said as they were leaving. "Do nothing all day but sit around and shoot the shit."

Went over to the commissary to buy cassette tapes and a *New York Times*. Came back and found that Micki had called from Port Authority to talk to me about her address book.

"How did she sound?" I asked Carla.

"She says some of it's been heavy, but she saw Nancy Weber's family and liked them very much."

I tried to look surprised. That she'd seen my family, not that she'd liked them.

I gave her time to get to the Village, then called her. She sounded a little tired but full of beans. We decided to meet that afternoon so I could get my cue cards before I met the Princeton crowd.

A few minutes later Carla told me that a Mr. Finsterwald was on the phone for Dr. Wrangler, and did I know who he was, think it was a call I should take? "Yes, indeed," I said, trying hard not to grin. Mr. Finsterwald, never mind the first name, is one of Nick's noms de guerre.

He sounded miserable. He said Micki was being extraordinarily disloyal to me, that she'd cried all over poor Mother and Daddy, that she wasn't getting on very well with Trigger Mike, that she was going to bed with every man she met in my life, not just my lovers. He told me I was absolutely not to feel guilty about having talked with him a couple of times because she was breaking rules all over the place.

I was in shock. I didn't know what to say. I told Nick I wanted to talk to my father. My darling daddy sounded choked and peculiar. I felt guilty, horrible.

"Call me every day," Nick said, and asked how everything was going with me. "Still mostly terrific," I said and hung up.

I didn't know what to do. I longed to call Trig, see if he was okay; but he'd told me a lot of times before the swap not to worry about him—he'd have a good time out of it no matter what. There was really nothing to do except wait and see Micki.

I looked at my watch, one of the few times I remembered to do that. Twelve fifteen. Christ. Almost three hours.

Debbie Levitas called and said she wanted to take me to some feminist events. I said that would be great. I didn't say that I'd read some of her stuff on women and the law and couldn't believe she'd gone to Yale Law and studied with my brilliant friend Fred Rodell. We agreed to talk on Monday. It didn't occur to me, as I suppose it would have to anyone but a Tard, that I might not be behind the big oak desk on Monday, that my lovely adventure might be foundering.

A tall woman with a Memling forehead walked into my office and smiled at me. Clearly my colleague and lunch date, Karen Smith, and I greeted her by name with measured casualness.

We walked across a part of the campus I'd never seen to what I was told was my favorite place to have lunch. I ordered my favorite roast beef and American cheese on a roll, only to be informed that my favorite in this place was pastrami. Ah, well.

Karen couldn't have been nicer or more loyal to the rules of the swap, and lunch couldn't have been harder. It seems that the great bond between Karen and Micki is an interest in Haitian politics. Lemme tell you, it's a lot easier to be madly in love with a man you've met ten minutes before than it is to discuss Papa Doc when you don't know a thing about him. I tried to carry it off because I wanted nice Karen to experience the swap the way all our friends were supposed to, but I don't think it was exactly an exalted hour for her. I was dripping when we parted.

Walked around for a bit to settle down. The campus was lush, bright, airy. It was hard to believe we were in the middle of what T.M. calls the Republic of Brooklyn.

Went back to my desk. Carla and I had a long talk about how beautiful it would be down in Bucks County and how little she was delighted at the prospect of a weekend in town with her Canadian cousins. I considered inviting her to flee south with me, but the thought of being alone with Ben in the country was all that was keeping me sane.

I called Micki and asked her if we could meet earlier. She said she was working with George Warneke and wouldn't be through until three. I decided to take Carla's tray to Altman's to kill time and worries.

Drove to midtown. Decided I just couldn't hack Altman's and turned tail, headed down Fifth Avenue. Parked the car. Went into a small shop that looked like Micki and bought a blouse I thought she would enjoy and that went better with my pants than anything she owned.

Walked toward my apartment, saw George Warneke walking toward me. He stuck his nose up in the air, but couldn't stop a tiny grin. I felt better. I rang Nancy's bell.

Micki had never looked better. My apartment had never looked worse. I felt as though I was seeing something tender and green growing among ruins. She was wearing my second-best faded jeans and a blue Brooks shirt of Nick's and my jewelry, and she had a softness and womanliness and liveliness that I'd never seen in her face. There were papers scattered all over my apartment, clothes heaped in the middle of the floor, dead flowers in every vase. The flowers scared me.

"I know I know," she said as we embraced, "it hasn't usually been like this, I just got crazy today."

"The flowers," I said.

"I know I know I know, I'll go to your florist later, it's really been so crazy, you have a lot of friends, you know."

She started to tell about some of them. It was clear that she'd gone to bed with Aaron and Abbe and Henry as well as Trig, but her analytic posturing made it sound more like couch than bed events. She told me she hadn't had time to do any of my writing. I couldn't stand it. I wanted her to shut up and go back inside my life.

"I'm going to wash my hair," I said. I had washed my hair that morning. What I really wanted was to swim across miles of cold Connecticut lake. My water, my soap, my shampoo, my scrawny towels, my conditioner, my memorabilia-filled bathroom were absolutely delicious.

I washed my face and got out my Micki makeup kit. "I sometimes put cheek gel on my lips," she said.

"You do?" I tried it. Even sexier than my chopped liver lipstick.

"Maisie Leonard taught me that," she said.

"In case you don't know it, you're in love with Maisie Leonard."

"Oh, I know it."

I admired the new yellow bathroom phone. Micki told me that my unlisted number was a palindrome and that she hoped it was okay that she'd given it to T.M. and Nick and my parents. She said we were under strict instructions never to pick up the phone if we were in the bathtub—instant electrocution. The old number rang. She answered it. It was Trigger Mike.

"Stop trying to run my life, Trig," she said. I grinned. It was nice to know that he was being as persistently adoring as he was with me. She told him she was very, very, very tired and was going to go to sleep very, very, very early and would see him Saturday night. They talked awhile more. Something apparently made him think that she'd seen me or spoken to me because she told him that she hadn't.

Afterward she apologized to me for lying to him. "That's okay," I said lightly, "I sometimes lie to him, too. It wouldn't have been a good idea for me to talk to him."

Now I had a lead-in for all the questions I was and wasn't dying to put to her. How were she and Trig getting on, I asked. It was a little heavy sometimes, she said, but otherwise fine.

I was knocked out. There was no reconciling her words, her

tone, her looks with what Nick had reported. I was sure he hadn't exaggerated. I'd had the feeling when we talked that if anything he was pulling his punches; he knew the swap was going fine for me and didn't want to spoil that. What was I supposed to do? I didn't want her to know I'd talked to Nick. Being Nancy and not Micki at the moment, I was less interested in confronting her than in believing what she was telling me, that she was doing her best to fulfill our contract in every sense and was having a mostly fine time doing it.

I put on my new blouse and brushed my hair dry.

"There's cream rinse in Riverset," she said, watching me. "I don't buy it in New York because I don't feel like supplying Peter."

And suddenly she was crying and telling me that she always had to be the strong one with people, no one ever took care of her the way my family took care of me. I told her that I took care of a lot of people, too, and put my arms around her and got tears in my eyes and promised myself that I would take care of her. Anyone but a Tard would have known that the way to fulfill that promise was to pat her on the fanny, kiss her, and send her home, but I didn't get my name by accident. We both started to giggle, and I was more than ever sure that we could carry this thing off.

I went to the refrigerator. No fresh orange juice. "Let's go have a drink somewhere," I said. I wanted to get out of this place that was and wasn't my home, go somewhere I'd feel less pressure to be so absolutely Nancy.

She took her address book and the index cards she'd been making notes on, and we went down to O. Henry's. We drank iced coffee, and she gave me a short course on the people in her life. The card on Maisie said that she was very beautiful and was gay and that Micki loved her. So she did know. The cards on the people I would meet at Sig Lewis's talked mostly about what the men did (a lot of psychologists) and what the women looked like (a lot of them were beautiful) and who was gay. When she gave me the card on Ben, she had tears in her eyes. The card said that he didn't touch her enough and wasn't as happy as she would wish. She told me that she had never loved anyone as much as she had loved Ben Rothenberg. She made it sound like that intensity was a thing of the past, but the tears said something else.

She told me more and more about more and more people, and I jotted down as much as I could get of it on the cards. She told

me that some of the people in my life were pigs. I told her that
some of the people in her life weren't smart enough. She said that
my family and she had had a great time once they stopped letting
themselves be manipulated by me. I didn't know what manipulating I'd done, but she'd gone on to discussing the virtues of George,
and I let it go. I said nice things about Peter and Danny and Carla
and Ted. I told her what a downer Cassie had been and what
peculiar ideas she had about how to honor a friendship. She told
me she missed Peter a lot and asked if I had found him to be the
lover she'd said he was. I had, I said, though he was a little different
than described, more aggressive. It was a cheap shot, pure sexual
boasting. I don't know why I did it. Maybe the word "manipulated." Maybe the dead flowers.

She drew me a map for getting to Riverset (I'd lost the first one)
and reminded me to buy a new book of tunnel tickets and a new
roll of tokens for crossing the Delaware River. We went back to
the apartment so I could call Ben and tell him I was going to be
late. We hugged. She seemed very small and fragile and on the
verge of tears again. I told her to get some sleep. She told me to
have a good weekend in beautiful Riverset.

I got onto the New Jersey Turnpike and started to talk into my
tape recorder. All I could say was that I felt numb and blank and
speechless and mind-blown. I thought of all the things Micki and
I hadn't talked about, like how we really felt about each other and
whether or not the swap was what we had thought it would be.
I felt dislodged, a little terrified. I didn't know why. Maybe step-
ping back into the life that was and wasn't mine. I also felt very
high. Micki and I were both in new water, and our hair was wet,
and both of us might come close to drowning, but by God we were
finding something out.

I pulled off the highway at the first gas station. Called Micki and
told her that she was brave and wonderful and to hang in there.
She said Kylie Warneke was there with six-month-old Stephanie,
who was sucking on her fingers. Called home; it wasn't fair that I'd
talked to my father that day and not my mother. She was my best
friend as always but sounded—heavy. I talked to my father and to
Nick. I asked him if I had manipulated anyone lately. "What?" he
said. They all told me they loved me and to drive carefully. For
the first time that week I felt mortal, victim of all my usual death
fears. If I got killed on the highway, would Micki be stuck in my

life forever, like the classic science-fiction figure with a broken time machine?

I drove the turnpike as if it were the rally track up at Lime Rock. By the time I got to the Delaware River, I almost felt human again. Except that I was sneezing like crazy. I remembered a notation I'd seen on Micki's desk calendar: "Riverset allergy shots." Had she skipped her appointment?

There was a blue-black sky, the sky you sometimes see in Rome during the last ten minutes of twilight. The car seemed to fill with the serene dark air as I drove down River Road. River Road. Incredible that it hadn't occurred to me until now. In the novella about first love I'd written when I was seventeen, the hero lived in a house on River Road. I turned into the driveway and saw that it was the same house, Rod Dangerfield's house. The house in the Münter painting. My childhood house. My married-love house.

Micki had said I would understand everything about Ben Rothenberg when I saw him, and I did. I looked at the gaunt shy utterly open face and knew for sure I had loved him the most, and still did, and would. My husband of five years. I was suffused with him.

I also knew that he wasn't going to think I was Micki for a moment, but that he wasn't going to pull a Cassie and try to make me be Nancy. That he felt the bond I felt, had leapt into my limbo.

He was drinking a beer. He got one for me. We sat on the living room couch. I asked him if he was scared. He said he wasn't. I said neither was I. He took my hand. We were both trembling. Our shyness. The intensity of the moment. I wondered how I'd ever leave him.

I went upstairs and took a bath. Near the sink was a piece of wood with the Indian prayer that I'd seen at Ted's. "Great Spirit, Grant that I may not criticize my neighbor until I have walked a mile in his moccasins." Yes, yes, yes. I walked into the bedroom, naked, no towel, the way that Micki would have. There wouldn't be any pretending, but I still had to obey her details, wanted to obey them. Ben was lying on the bed, rolling a joint. We smoked. Didn't talk much. The moon outside the window was full, and the screen drew a cross over its face. The moon scared me. Ben's touch consoled me. I don't know if he made love to Micki or me, or if —as it felt, still feels—to neither of us. That night I understood tantric union. We were man and woman, god and goddess, celebrators of the sacred circle. It was all so uncluttered, so silent, the way I always knew it would be inside the Münter house.

He put on his pants, and I put on his shirt, and we went down to the kitchen. He ate yogurt, and I ate cheese and potato chips. He showed me around the house a bit. Books, Mexican hangings, lots and lots of plants, furniture that smelled like summer. I knew that Micki's heart was in this house, with this man. I felt very close to her. I wondered if she had looked so soft that afternoon because I was on my way down here, because she was.

Ben and I went back upstairs. We talked about his week and mine. There was much more silence between us than speech. I have never known such lovely silence. Such celebration. Such sleep.

Saturday, June 16

The understanding fell out of my head before I could write it down, but I woke up knowing that in my sleep I'd understood married love.

I wish I could describe the way Ben looked at me. With puzzlement and wonder and full recognition. Not the dark complex recognition Persephone used to dream of, though it had the same sexual center. Some spare and silent acceptance.

I put on a pair of old shorts and a blurred cotton shirt, the first of Micki's clothes I'd really liked. Ben asked me if I wanted to go into town for the paper with him. I said yes. We sat close in the car. I thought of Micki saying that they did everything together, and I knew why it was possible. He breathed only his own air. A totally present person who was totally unobtrusive. The words feel hyperbolic as I write them, but they're true.

We got *The New York Times* and some Allerest for my sneezing. Micki's ham-and-eggs drugstore was more modern than I'd expected but smelled airy and was otherwise pleasing. I liked the town, so wooden and white, and the drive along the river. I was glad to get home again.

I made a western for breakfast, and it came out looking peculiar. It's hard to make an imperfect western. I'd never done it before. Micki can't make westerns? I was going to have the same inexplicable problem cooking for Ben that I had cooking for Trigger Mike?

Ben showed me the garden. Snow peas, fat and bright: we decided to have them for dinner. Radishes. Baby lettuce. There was a cemetery across the field, but it didn't scare me.

We sat on the couch and read and looked and touched. His way of tugging my hair.

Silence. Space. Space without distance.

Ben told me that he was going to have to go back to Buffalo Sunday night instead of Monday morning—some sort of emergency meeting he couldn't miss. But he'd come down early next weekend to make up for it.

Next weekend. My heart tossed at the way he said it; then I wondered. Next weekend we might be altogether mortal.

We talked about taking acid together. For the first time I thought I could do it, wanted to do it. And thought it would be redundant.

We laughed a lot. I don't remember at what.

Micki called. She sounded frantic. She said my life had gotten too heavy for her. She had to take a few hours off, be herself, see Peter. Then she'd go back to the game.

I felt undone. I said I was inside the Münter house, and I wanted her to do whatever she had to do to feel that good. I said I broke rules anyway, so she could break the rules of the game for a bit and still be me. I said if she were in pain I was willing to bring the switch to a stop. She said no, she just needed those few hours. She told me to call her sister and ask her to tell their parents about the swap and to call on Sunday to wish her father a happy Father's Day.

I asked her if she was sure she wanted to go on. She said she did, and she loved me; she just needed a break. She told me to be Nancy with Ben.

She asked if she could talk with him. I went upstairs and turned on my tape recorder:

This bed, this bed. Downstairs Ben is talking to the real Micki, who called to tell me that she had to take the day off, play hooky. In a way I've been playing hooky ever since I walked into the house. Last night I brought all of Micki's love for Ben to this bed, but I was also fully myself, never more fully myself. I feel so many things. I'm crying. I mostly want Micki to be okay, but I guess I have to trust her that she meant it when she said she just needed a few hours. I feel so sad in a way. I guess I found what I did and didn't want to find, and I'm not going to want to leave this man or this house. A little while ago I went out and got a lot of tiny wild flowers and made a miniature garden in an eggcup the way I used to do in Ireland, and I was thinking of all the things like that which so far I've only been able to share with my parents and brother. It's all here for me in this house, the sweetness of family life, only now I'm one of the grown-ups. Oh, it's been grown-up and sweet and wild and deep with T.M., but never this feeling of home. I suppose this is what I meant the swap to be about, coming to this feeling, coming so hard up against it that I can't say no anymore. Micki, certify the beauty in my life, because it's time I created other beauty. Tell everyone how much I love T.M., because there's no way for me not to leave him. In this house we would hate each other, mock all the greatness that's been.

I heard Ben sort of shout that he couldn't always tell when I was being real. He got off the phone. I asked him if Micki was going to be okay, and he said she was. He touched me, and I believed him. I wanted him to know that I was always being real, but I didn't want to say it.

I called T.M. to balance things out and because Micki had asked me to tell him about her playing hooky. It felt all out of synch to call him, and he sounded very strained, which didn't help. I told him what Micki had said, and how hard I thought she was working at the swap, and that I wanted to give her 50 per cent of whatever money I made from writing about the swap. He made me promise not to do anything until the swap was over. He didn't sound very glad to be hearing from me. I asked him what was the matter. He said nothing, he was just in a hurry to get to the races. I didn't understand. I felt hurt.

Ben and I went to the supermarket to get some things to go with the snow peas. Still sitting close in the car. We went to the cleaners, then to buy some wine. None of the people we saw knew about the swap, and I felt like Ben's other woman, very illicit. I paid for the wine, though Ben insisted it was all the same money. Went into the jewelry store to pick up a ring of Micki's. It hadn't been repaired yet.

Home, and upstairs to smoke and play Scrabble. Ben won but said he thought he'd met his match, promised me a chance to retaliate. We lay down for a nap that turned into love. The world receded again. When we got up, I put a silver Mexican ring of Micki's on my wedding finger. Ben watched.

We steamed two baby bluefish and some mushrooms to go with the beautiful snow peas. It was supposed to taste Chinese, but it mostly tasted like fish. We drank a lot of wine. We got dressed for the Princeton parties.

He asked me on the way to Ben McMullen's who I was going to be. I said Micki, sort of, or maybe neither if that was okay with him. He said it was. I looked over my cue cards. He added some information.

We stood in the kitchen at the McMullens'. Drank beer. I kissed everyone whose name was on a card. Asked someone who didn't have children how her children were. Ben gave advice about houseplants to several people. I liked the way he did it. I felt very much a stranger.

At the Lewises' eight or nine couples in their young thirties were sitting in a circle waiting to pounce, but nicely. I wasn't told any names—I was supposed to know, and sometimes I did and rather astonished them.

I thought of a *New Yorker* short story we've all always loved in my family. A woman is a great hit as a hostess because she can ask ten people what they want to drink, bring back the drinks on a tray, and remember who gets what. Then someone discovers that she lines her guests' drinks up from left to right according to her assessment of their politics. Of course no one likes his place on the lineup. I think Jacqueline, who was so pleased that I knew her name, might have been less thrilled if she'd known that Micki's card on her said: "Blond hair. Bulging eyes."

I knew I was being too quiet to be either Micki or Nancy, but I didn't much want to talk. I guess I was pretty stoned. And though most of the people seemed warm, and quite happy, and smart and even funny, still none of them particularly drew me. I wondered if it weren't in this room, with this group, that Micki was most especially the participant-observer. Ben sat by my side much of the time. I wanted to make it easy for him and for Alice Lewis, who looked upset, but I didn't really know how. I suppose I could have said, "The hell with it, I'm Nancy tonight, let's take it from there, how about a game of categories?" But I had a sense of the crowd: They'd have been even less content with that than with this Micki manquée. Sig Lewis gave me a back rub. I liked him and thought he liked me, and I was sorry I was letting him down.

Ben seemed strained on the way home. I couldn't blame him. He took a backwoods route that he said was Micki's favorite. I felt he was underscoring my not being Micki. He drove quite fast and asked if I were frightened. I said I would have been before the swap, but my car fears had disappeared. He said that was funny because Micki often felt she was driving with death perched on her shoulder. I thought of the suicide sweep on the road between Hawthorne and her apartment and told him it was a different kind of fear.

We were in my car, and Ben asked if I had Delaware River tokens in the glove compartment, or should we take the old bridge. I was elated at the notion that he would go miles out of his way rather than pay fifteen cents. It was a perverse and complex elation but perhaps not hard to understand.

The moon was still crucified. Ben turned his back to me in bed, then told me to cuddle up. I dreamed of married death.

Sunday, June 17

We woke up restored to each other. Ben went shopping for bagels and lox and the *Times*, while I made coffee. We ended up drinking the wine left from dinner. We (mostly Ben) finished the crossword puzzle before we finished the lox.

Ben went out to work in the garden. I sat inside hating the thought of the weekend ending. I had no desire to see Peter. I could drive to Pittsburgh to see my lover Sue Ann, but Ben told me it would take five hours. I didn't like the idea of staying alone in the house. The bed would be desolate without my husband in it.

I wondered if Old Micki always found it so hard to leave. I pictured her in her New Nancy clothes at the Lion's Head. I could see the pepper mill on the table, the puzzle on her lap. I couldn't see her face. I decided to call her.

Strange, calling your favorite bar and paging yourself. Stranger still to be answered with a shriek.

"I'm not Nancy, I'll never be Nancy again, don't you call me that anymore, don't you dare call yourself Micki."

"Hey, hey, what's going on? I thought you were just taking a break, then getting back into it."

"No more of that, not ever again; I'm Micki Wrangler, and don't you ever dare call me anything else again."

"Okay, okay, take it easy. I just called to see how you were; don't jump on me like that. Do you want to call it all off?"

"No, I don't, but I can't talk now, I'm with Susie and Ken, and I'm going for a walk with Riff, there isn't time to talk."

"I'll talk to you later."

We hung up. I don't shake. I think I was shaking. I went outside. Ben was weeding. I offered to help, and he said later, and I lay down in the sun. Got up and picked wild flowers, made two more eggcup gardens.

"I have to talk to you," I finally said to him. He sat down on the grass with me, and I told him about the phone call. "Will she be okay?" I asked. "What do you think I should do?"

He said that Micki was as good at cooling off as she was at getting angry and was generally capable of taking care of herself, would be okay. He suggested we call her later. He was calm, but I knew he was worried.

I felt vague and dumb and lost. I didn't know what to do. I thought of Micki on Friday and Micki on the phone today, and I couldn't put it together.

I went upstairs and fell into the bathtub. After a while Ben came in and held out a joint. Then he was in the tub, and then we were in bed. I think we both knew that this was the one for the road. Ben, whenever you read this: I can feel you still.

He started to talk about Micki and how important she was and would be in his life, no matter how things worked out for them. Told me that he didn't mind about Peter, just minded Micki's efforts to make them be good friends. I had meant to carry those efforts forward for Micki; now I could only think of how I wanted to strengthen the bond between her and Ben.

T.M., Micki, everyone—do you understand that I didn't want more of Ben than I had, even though I hated the thought of leaving him? Never thought he wanted me beyond the limits of this joining?

Sweet thoughts, sweet talk, sweet smoke. We went downstairs to do something about dinner. The telephone rang.

Micki. I knew it was terrible. I went into the kitchen, out of hearing, then went back. "Let me speak to her," I said to Ben.

"She doesn't want to. She's very angry with you."

"Please. I have to."

I got on the phone. She was overcome with rage. She would start sentences and stop them and, when I would ask her to finish them, scream that I was manipulating her. She told me that I had no friends. She said everyone kept saying to her: Tell us who Nancy Weber is, we just come here to fuck her. She screamed that she had told Ben not to make love to me because I had monilia. She screamed that I had forced her to go to bed with men she hated. She screamed that she had left a love letter for me at her apartment and wouldn't talk to me another second, I was manipulating her by trying to stay on the phone, good-bye.

Why is it more manipulative to keep a conversation going than to end it?

I started to cry. Ben put his arms around me. If ever a man must have felt middled, it was Ben at that moment. He was perfect. He consoled me without making me feel that he was betraying Micki. I was still Micki enough so that was important to me.

"It's good for the book, at least," I sniffled. I didn't feel like being funny, but I didn't feel like crying, either. I don't remember a moment in my life with a smaller reality quotient.

We ate snow peas cooked with ham—every bit as successful as the fish and the western. I smoked three of Ben's cigarettes and left the sugar and milk out of my coffee.

We divided up the snow peas we hadn't cooked, got our things, went out to the cars. There wasn't much to say, to do. I couldn't tell Ben that I didn't have monilia. I couldn't tell him that I loved him. Neither of us could say we knew there would be no next weekend.

I talked into my cassette all the way to New York. The tape didn't come out, so I'll never know what I said. Bittersweet mumblings, I suspect. I bought a book of toll tickets when I got to the Lincoln Tunnel, then wondered why. Then wanted to scream.

Danny was asleep. No sign of Peter. There were beautiful pink roses in the bedroom, mixed yellow flowers in the kitchen. They made me really aware of just how ugly the apartment was. I also found this letter.

"A love/hate letter"

Dear Nancy—bitch—Machiavelli—Pollyanna—Barbie doll—girl—cunt—sex object—writer—woman—friend—sister (and last real-life flapper): I love you. You have put me through hell and I've

stuck to it out of some kind of sisterhood/masochism/compulsion/fascination/loyalty/duty/honesty/ and I don't break rules unless people understand that I do that. I try to be as honest as I can to people, I try not to oppress them, I talk too damn much all the time (which is why people haven't been talking too much because I usually ask questions, tell stories about my day, try to analyze what's going on, etc.).

Please Nancy don't be Micki any more (except with some of my office work if you like). Start trying to be Nancy (whoever that is). Don't play games with my people, because they're all freaked out and they've tried to make things easy for you by not challenging you. That's why they haven't been around much or have just played music so that you could watch and listen and learn. Try to flow. Apologize to everyone you've lied to. If you have monelia (thrush) in your vagina because your vaginal Ph is messed up by antibiotics get to the doctor quick and have them prescribe mycostatin, use a little baking soda when you douche, put plain yogurt in your vagina and eat a lot of yogurt whenever you take antibiotics. Do not fuck any more because this will only make it worse and hurt your poor sore cunt. Don't fuck my people or be fucked by them or fuck over them by lying or playing games. The only way for you to learn more about Micki (and Nancy) is to ask my friends questions like:

What is Micki like?
How are we different?
What are her values?

The only way you are going to be able to repay me for what I've gone through for you because you didn't know how to give me the right kinds of information (I'm not blaming you for this. I guess I thought you were more of a process person (sociologist) than you are and I didn't ask the right questions—but it has been hell because of misinformation or omissions) is to try to be as honest with my friends about what kinds of questions you want to have answered, why are you doing this, tell them what made you interested in it. Be real for goodness sake.

If Peter or Ted or Ben or I or anyone in my family/support gets monelia or any other disease you will have to pay for our medical expenses. That is such a no-no to me that it blows my mind.

Please don't fuck any more—make love if you want to and they want to and everyone knows who everyone is in mind and body. Stop putting yourself down, my friend, you're elegant, creative, kind, loving, and more than a bit crazy.

I am going to be Nancy only for some writing I want to try my hand at to see if I can gain something from this experience which will be useful. The places I have been in my mind warp/time warp have taken me back fifteen years to a place I thought I had left behind long ago. I hadn't realized how much of a masochist I was because you didn't tell me that you break rules and so I tried to carry through with our contract (which was and is ridiculous). I may decide to charge you for therapy to repay me for the bruises all over my body and mind, the tricks, cons, ripoffs you tried to pull on all of us. We still love you or some of us do. I am assuming that you are paying for the extravaganzas that I've done (not many) to try to be "you?" and for whatever medical care I am going to need to recover from this.

And just a few more things: I never order Peter to change the linen. We either change it together, or separately, but no one waits on anyone in this house.

I know this is scary as hell for you and I think you're very brave and it's going to be one helluva book if it can be written at all. Nothing will ever be the same for me again. I hope my relationship with my people has not changed so much because of my being freaked-out and messing with men because I was trying to come back to myself for the last seventy hours.

Thank goodness for Abbe and Jeff and George and Kylie (sp?) and Stephanie. And of course Riff! Why couldn't they have been the first in my life as you instead of Mike, and the boys in the bar, and Aaron and Mike and Mike, and Audrey, and oh, yes, marvelous Magda.

If you ever choreograph anything for me again—remember I love beauty (heads, bodies, flowers, love) and hate alcoholics, bars, male chauvenist pigs and fascists of all sorts and politicians and people with cocks in their ears, up their noses and in their eyes. And just one more thing—we don't like roaches either but they are all over New York including your bathroom, my elegant, lady friend. We all (here) love beauty, and nice things, but we are poor and our values are different and our priorities are different and we don't have daddies who give us money all the time now that we're grown up (although I don't blame you for this, your daddy likes doing that for you and that's cool with me) but don't be so fucking arrogant, Mlle. Weber, and try to "see" for the first time in your life (as Don Juan does in Castaneda's books).

Baby I know this is hard for you and you're very brave and terrific and I want you to be my friend (you can still wear perfume and be elegant and have panache and love clothes) etc. etc. and sister and I think you're coming along—rebirth is always hard, Nancy Weber, and that's what this book is all about. It's not at all about Micki Wrangler but about Nancy's rite of passage from fragmented to integrated. Your friends are ready to help and we love you. All right I've gotten it out of my system—I love you again. Will you please have a good time finding out about me and about you and try to go easy on my friends. No more games my love except! Nicki (GOD I LOVE YOUR BROTHER) type games and family games where every-one knows the real true Nancy (even Nancy) and no hustle-con is being done. Thank you for Abbe and Riff and your parents and NICCCKKIII and your agent and Louise and Audrey, and Jeff and I are about to have a love affair as friends for real not as Micki-Nancy or Nancy-Micki—but Micki-Jeff, and for George and Kylie and Stephanie. I forgive poor Trig—I know he can't help being the way he is—he just tries to patronize and father and fuck me—so it's fuck off for Trig as far as MW is concerned but I'll explain my own explainings so don't you worry—I'm always kind—but honest. And Magda didn't realize I was in culture shock.

Nuff said!

Enjoy the flowers you sweet thing you. Try to play hooky in the arboretum near Hawthorne.

Give my sisters and brothers my love, and if Cassie is willing to give you another chance be open & totally honest. Dig Sukie, she's my friend and will see through all your bullshit! and maybe help if you ask right. And call me if you need me but never call me anything but Micki unless I say it's OK or I'll smack you on the bare ass that Bob Rimmer loves so well.

I'm off to meet Susie. Can you tell that I love you you naughty girl.

Micki

I thought it was the most condescending and generally emetic piece of piggydoon that I'd ever seen in my life. I also liked it, liked Micki for having written it. I must have been totally out of my mind. I couldn't even remember what hotel T.M. was staying in that month, though I'd called him there the day before. Yes, yes, the Stanhope. He wasn't in, and nobody knew when he would be. At that moment I hated him as much, as absurdly as I liked Micki. I was utterly out of my mind.

I left Peter Ben's camera and a note saying I wouldn't be back that night. I drove down to the Lion's Head. Everyone asked me what I was doing there. I felt like an interloper, an actress. I wondered what had happened with tall blonde Audrey that had made such an impact on Micki, but I was too numb to ask her. I called Abbe and asked him if I could come over. He sounded funny but said of course.

"Hi," I said when I walked in, "don't talk to me, I have to write a letter."

He went into the other room. I sat down at his desk.

a love-hate reply

Dear Micki—mommy—camp director—grower of fabulous snow peas —Don Juana (Castaneda variety)—Hermine (Hesse variety)—yeah yeah yeah and woman, friend, sister: I love you, too. Loving you, I would not, for openers, think you dumb/cruel enough to fuck my friends/lovers/strangers if you had a communicable disease. I do not have monilia. I have a nontransferable upset which I am curing without eating the yogurt that would destroy what little skin your life has left me. If my doctor was wrong, I'll pay, of course. But my doctor is never wrong.

You, astonishingly (your astonishment mostly), sometimes are. You're also wonderful. When I told you on the phone before that I value your well-being as highly as my own, I wasn't kidding.

But I meant to take this from the top, it being mostly a reply to yours.

First, I am at Abbe's. I fled, I confess. Needing something familiar. Not being able to use your familiar, though I sort of did all weekend. That was the problem. Oh, God, Nancy, be coherent. You're supposed to be the writer in the *famiglia*. What I mean to say is: The weekend was so extraordinarily fine, except for worrying about you, and coming back to find your letter was so extraordinarily—I don't know—maybe so extraordinarily indusive to making me reply, and Danny was asleep, and I was anxious neither to see Peter nor to sleep in that bed alone, that I came to see Abbe. Picking, on purpose, someone whom we both like. Out of loyalty to you I would not have gone to T.M. tonight, even if I wanted to. Not because of conversation—I don't intend to share these letters or talk about much of what's going on. It just simply seemed that if I were going to cheat, it should be with someone whom you found sympathetic. Also, he has the same electric typewriter I do.

First, I haven't put you through hell. You've put you through hell. I gave you two tons of information, and even if it wasn't written in terms of sociological infrastructure, it was a lot of information. Mostly I gave you my journals; mostly I gave you knowing me. Where on earth, with all of that, particularly knowing me, did you think that you could get a glimmer of what my life was like the very great majority of the time without work? time carved out to be alone (we talked about that a lot)? arranging flowers? meditation (maybe you've done that)? reading? How on earth, knowing me, knowing yourself, did you think for a moment that I went through life saying yes to everything that was proffered me —particularly sexual? How, having read my journals, did you come up with the notion that I would go to bed with all those different people? Of course you came up not liking Trig. When I've been excessively chaotic, when I've had to lie to him, I haven't liked him either.

You do too break rules. Screaming at me, getting so mad, because I paged you as NW this morning, addressed you as Nancy. Yesterday you told me you were going to be Micki for the day. You didn't tell me, much less discuss with me, your decision that you couldn't for another moment use that name. I can understand the decision. But not your assumption that I was supposed to know about it without being told. That's not according to the Marquis of Q. Now that you've said what you have, I will of course use my own name. I use so many names— that part wasn't unsettling to me. But I'll gladly accede to you in that. *The worst rule breaking has been your insistence on remaining a sociologist. Try being a writer! Try being me! Stop observing!*

I have not played games with your people—except for *the* game, which we were all playing. And when someone (like Cassie) really needed (upfront) for me to stop, I did. But you see, I wasn't playing games with anyone anyway because everything I did that seemed to be grounded in feelings was grounded in feelings. Maybe he didn't think so, but I thought I brought your passion for Peter to bed with him, and it became my passion—just as in my conversations with him about

Wendy, it was indistinguishable to me what was your and what was my jealousy/coolness/confusion, etc. Maybe he couldn't believe that the transference could take place. But it did for me, and not just in my head. *I have lied to no one,* except to say things like (when asked): I grew up in France. No lies of feeling. Not one.

I don't agree with you that asking questions is the best way to learn about you or your people. If that were true, I would just have dropped in one evening and asked questions. If they have questions, of course I'll answer them later. But I think that's putting everything on a safe, dull level. My friends may have been heavy sometimes, but I think maybe there was a deeper acceptance of what was going on. *If you keep asking my friends questions, you may find out less about them/me than you knew at the start.*

Our contract wasn't/isn't ridiculous, my sister. And, simply, there were no tricks, cons, rips-off. With or without the contract. You can send your body bruises to the salon of your choice on me. The mind bruises I have to think, until I know more and different, come more from your not knowing yourself than not knowing me. And from your refusal/inability to fulfill our contract in the most important way: to try to *feel* like me in my life rather than superimpose your values, politics, on it. If I'd done that with yours, I wouldn't have got to first base.

Yes, a lot of people in my life don't know who I am. I am of many minds about that. It is also true of you/the people in your life.

I will pay for all the extravaganzas. (These two weeks should cost us equal in $.) Paying for them is part of the fun, especially when I don't have much money. Doesn't matter to me whether they're mine or yours. Yes, your doctor bills, too. Though maybe you should pay for my next five visits to Mario Badescu/Dr. Verde: fuck complexion brushes!

I didn't order Peter to change the linens! Jesus! Sometimes some of you are politicized right out of existence! Was I being "manipulated" when I took him to dinner? Or "slavish" when I got Ben more coffee this morning? Everyone waits on everyone in your house, which is why it is good, dummy. And I've done dishes/shopped/etc., so I don't think it was a big deal to ask that, which I did (I thought) gently and teasingly, when he asked if he could do anything for me over the weekend (right after he asked me to bring back his *Whole Earth Catalog,* Ben's camera, etc.).

We will talk about the people you've been let down by. I may fight you less than you think. They are of course the same people, mostly, who let me down; I wish they hadn't been so fucking authentic, okay?

But, as I did with Cassie, you may have judged too much by your own extremity of need. *But I still think a lot of the trouble with some of them, especially T.M., is that they were following the rules: trying to treat you like me.* Still, there are some people I will never forgive for their treatment of you, if it was as you say, and I'm sure it was at least some of the time. Any injury that's been done to you has been done to me. The good too.

We may have some different notions of what's beautiful. Your flowers are—*mucho gracias!*

What was the crack about roaches? I joked to Ben about it but never said a word in NY. It's Peter who goes around killing them like crazy: I just step around them. I've always had this theory that roaches in one's own apartment are less egregious than other people's, and I found myself thinking the other day that I regarded yours as my own. But you could get rid of some of them if you really wanted to. Admit they're a bit excessive. If I have more than an occasional roach visitor, call my exterminator—that's what I pay them for. But a couple are normal after his visit.

As for your rebirth line, Hermine, Don Juana: We'll have to go into that in the flesh. Yes, this is my rite of passage. Not the first or last. But yes, maybe the most important. If you look at my very first notes, which you have, I mention that, though in different words. But you, my sister, have not completed your journey either; you have a lot of things to reconcile too. Maybe you've dealt with a lot of things we're talking about in a way that to you is much more thorough, more upfront: but lemme tell you, we are sisters in schizophrenia.

I love you. I am glad you love my brother and parents and some other people. I love Ben so much that the feeling, especially now, overshadows how I feel about everyone else. Except you, whom I love all the more (and there was a lot to start with) for knowing your husband a bit. But I have so very much to say about Ben and you as two and as one & one that I better not even start.

Love and kisses,

Tard

I stress again—the more you try, in the ways that are important, to live my life as me (rather than worry about giving the proper sociological feedback to me), the happier by far you'll be and the more valuable feedback you'll give me. The point, *mon ange,* is not for me to come out of all of this with information that would let me reshape my life to your liking, or you to reshape yours, etc. Stop being so smug! You and your people talk too much about trust and flow—but I've seen too little, especially from you. And that, *ma soeur,* hurts.

I'm making copies of this and yours—will return a copy of yours with this.

The snow peas are from your garden. They are the best snow peas in history, I think. How the hell do you ever leave Riverset? How the hell do you ever leave Ben?

I read it over. I knew it was viciously inadequate about Trigger Mike and not quite honest (I was still hating him for not being at his hotel) and otherwise faultable, but I was too damn tired to do anything about it. I got into bed with Abbe. I am very fond of him and attracted to him and should not have made love to him for as many wrong reasons as I did that night. Abbe, I apologize. You were kind to me. I was barely human. Which is maybe what might be expected from a Machiavelli Barbie doll cunt.

Monday, June 18

Too impatient to stay for breakfast with Abbe. Down to the Village for coffee at Sutter's and another look at my letter, some emendations. Had photocopies made of it and Micki's letter to me. Went to my liquor store, explained that I was Nancy again even though, yes, I wasn't supposed to be; bought a bottle of vintage Piper-Heidsieck, Marxist Micki's favorite champagne, put my letter and some Riverset snow peas in the bag with it. I asked my vintner to keep calling my number until someone answered, for God's sake to address her as Micki, and to tell her that there was a package waiting for her.

I drove uptown, stopped off at Altman's and took care of the engraving on Carla's tray, bought a bunch of pink sweetheart roses, and went to Hawthorne. Gave Carla most of the roses, gave Rich, the caretaker, one for a buttonhole, and put what was left in a glass on my desk.

I wrote a letter:

Dear Ben:

It was all real for me, except losing at Scrabble, and I hope most of it was for you.

I still want my rematch. And a chance to prove that with a little hoisin I really can cook Chinese, damn it.

I love your wife. I think it was dumb and disloyal of her to have thought/said to you that I would make love to you or anyone if I had a communicable disease.

Thank you for the most serene hours I had all week, some of the most serene moments ever.

Nancy

I made a copy, stuck it in a drawer along with my other documents, and put the original in an envelope marked Airmail Special Delivery. I was going to give it to Carla, then decided I would take it to the post office. I wanted him to have it as close to that second as possible.

Debbie Levitas called to invite me to a party on Tuesday for Erica Jong's new book. I had to ask her who Erica Jong was, which shocked her, said I'd love to go. I talked to Sukie Sandler, and we decided to put off work on our review until later in the week, when she thought her patients might allow her a couple of hours off.

Called Alice Lewis in Princeton. Used my real name. Thanked her for the party and told her I hoped it hadn't been too awful and confusing. She said she'd been very tense. I said I would like to meet her and Sig as Nancy, and she said they'd like that, too.

Walked down to Hawthorne Avenue, had a piece of the pizza

I'd thought I'd be living on as Micki. Came back to find out that Herself had called.

"How did she sound?" I asked Carla.

"She says to tell you thank you for the champagne, and she isn't mad at you anymore."

How kind of you, Micki.

I called her up. She said I got ten points for the Piper-Heidsieck, and she was planning to have dinner with Peter.

I called T.M. We agreed to meet at Jimmy's at six.

I tried reading Phyllis Chesler for one last time, then drove into Manhattan. I went to the big post office on Eighth Avenue and Thirty-second Street and sent off my letter to Ben. I called Hartford. I had felt too crazy on Sunday to call for Father's Day, and today was my parents' anniversary. Why am I giving reasons? I just wanted to talk to them.

My mother asked me how everything was going. I said that my end of things was better than I could have hoped, but I thought Micki was going crazy.

There was a chunk of silence that finally made me understand the meaning of "heavy pause."

Then, reluctantly, telling me only because I had said what I had said, my mother said she knew all too well that Micki was going crazy. Because Micki had called her on Sunday and had hysterics and read her a poem of mine and said things about me that don't get said to one's mother and been quite unbearably awful.

"I'm going to kill her," I said.

"No, no, no, darling, don't do anything, please, just keep going with the thing. Promise you won't say a word, I don't want another one of those phone calls."

I promised. I could have torn buildings apart.

Nick got on. He said Micki was totally mad. I asked him if he thought she was going to slash my paintings, and we both had hysterical giggles. I asked him what poem Micki had read to my mother. He described it a bit, and I knew it was one of T.M.'s, the poem I'd left with his cigars. She'd read that poem to my mother, said it was mine? Oh, Micki, when I get ahold of you——

My father sounded the most shaken of all. I wished him a happy Daddy's Day and felt like the crummiest daughter who'd ever lived. What had I got them into?

I went to Jimmy's. Trigger Mike and I were terrible to each

other. I think we both felt betrayed and like betrayers.

Out of some impulse left over from reading too many English novels, I called Micki and asked her if she and Peter wanted to have dinner with T.M. and me.

"I don't ever want to see T.M. again," she said.

"Not even as my friend?"

"Especially not as your friend."

Trig and I decided to drive up to the country for dinner. I could hardly keep my eyes open, but I kept driving: The next place would be better, the next. We finally stopped in Nyack. I made a big thing out of having a Heineken on the rocks, but it tasted terrible; everything tasted terrible.

T.M. told me then that Micki had refused to see him after Tuesday, that she had made only small scattered efforts to be me, even at the beginning. I asked if anything had happened the way it was supposed to. One thing, he said. The first night at the Lion's Head, Audrey Evert had gone over to Micki and said, "Well, Nancy, do you dislike me as much as you always have?" And Micki had said the right and true thing: "I never disliked you." The two of them had gotten along, T.M. told me, so maybe Audrey and I could be friends now, something he knew I'd always wanted but didn't know how to make happen.

It was clear that T.M. hadn't exactly had a great time with surrogate Nancy. Insane as it sounds, I was less worried about what he'd gone through and was feeling than I was about Micki's state of being. While we were waiting for coffee, I telephoned Susie. "Will you see what you can do for Micki?" I asked. "I think she's having a very rough time of it, and she misses the company of women."

"Nancy," said Susie," are you out of your mind? You're worrying about her? Do you know what she's doing? She's calling up everyone you know and talking about how evil and schizophrenic you are and how you lied to her and set up traps for her. She's decided you don't know who your real friends are, and she's invited everyone she thinks is your friend to a meeting tonight. She's calling it the Nancy Weber support group, or something."

"Are you going?"

"No, I thought it was too obnoxious."

"Well, I'm going," I said.

I think it had finally got through to me just exactly what kind of things she must have said to my mother. I decided I didn't want her in my home, life, consciousness one minute more than had to be.

T.M. and I drove down to the Village. We went into the Lion's Head. I called Susie and asked her to call Micki and make sure the meeting was still on—I didn't want to barge in on her and Peter. Susie reported back that there were ten people or so at my place. I looked around the Head. Audrey Evert was there. I told her I thought Micki had done something nice for us. She smiled. I invited her and Roz and two guys I knew going back to my days on the *New York Post* to come along to the party. T.M. and I were still behaving peculiarly toward each other, but I felt incredibly merry. I knew Micki would fall over when we walked in the door. I knew she would leave. And I would have my beautiful life back.

We passed Abbe on the way over. He looked at us very strangely.

Through the courtyard and up the stairs.

"I never miss a party," I said as we all trooped into my apartment.

Micki looked as though she'd been slapped. I went over to her and tried to embrace her. "Stay away," she said, but I said, "Come on," and she relented.

I looked around to see who Micki had chosen as my support group. Fran and Bob. Riff. Ted Holzman. All giving me strange dark glances. Oh, what a lovely PR job she must have been doing.

Micki and T.M. started in at each other. I didn't want to hear it. I went into the bathroom and changed into my best faded blue jeans and a filmy English shirt and more Shalimar than I usually use in a week. Micki had given up on my jewels, and I put them on, too. I handed Micki her wristwatch and the silver Mexican ring.

I have a peculiar New England way of having a very good time when one might least expect it: my emergency appendectomy in Dijon when I was seventeen, my centerfold crash in an XK 140, this party. Everyone else seemed very tense. I could hardly understand why. The time for tension was over.

"How nice to give a party and not have to do the glasses," I said. Nobody laughed. Didn't they understand that in fact nothing could have seemed more appealing to me than the thought of washing my glasses in my sink? Taking the horrible pink peonies out of the Waring blender and putting them in the bathroom, where they belonged? Throwing out the wrinkled fruit and mango juice that Micki considered party fare and the enormous asparagus she apparently considered a brilliant visual joke? (Was buying asparagus in season her idea of my venal extravagance?) Turning out all the lights except the one over the Münter and tripping back inside that house?

Ted and I talked nicely about nothing much at all. Fran and I approached each other, but there was a wall between us, and little was said. I've asked her to report on the words that happened: There are holes in my head about that evening, particularly about what happened with her.

Peter came. He would barely say hello to me. Peter, who had called me lover.

Micki said she was going. I think she meant that to upset me. If only you knew, Micki. It did upset me that she wanted to take all my notes to her and a lot of other things in my file, but I trusted her, *malgré tout*, to return what should be returned, to let me have what I'd left behind in her office and home.

Fran and Bob and Riff went with her and Peter and Ted. I minded that because I knew it made her feel she'd won a round, but I knew they'd be back soon enough: They were all three real friends.

My companions from the Lion's Head drank and talked and laughed with me for a while; then they all went away. T.M. and I spent some quiet time together, then he left, too. I cleaned until four in the morning. I was just turning out the lights when Riff called. He spent an hour telling me that he loved me and was loyal to me and not to be upset or confused by his departure, and if I needed any strong-arming done to get my papers back. . . . I told him I loved him, too, and everything was okay, and I didn't like Micki having my papers but she'd return them, and I saw no reason why someone couldn't be friends with Micki and me both.

Then I was alone with Gabriele Münter and Tullamore Dew and the first shy daylight coming through the trees, as fine a support group as anyone could want of a Tuesday morning in June.

SORTING

My merriment lasted half a day. I was dizzy, out of step, in a haze all the rest of June.

Getting used to my life again wasn't the big problem, though some people and things once familiar looked foreign through the filter of my jet lag. What clobbered me was a steadily swelling awareness of the pain Micki had gone through and inflicted on others, pain I felt completely responsible for. My talks and meetings with Micki during the swap, even her letter to me on Sunday, had given me no real hint of the madness that had been.

A couple of days after Black Monday, Micki called and said I'd done a good job with her office work, and she was sorry for some of the things she'd written in that letter. She didn't specify which parts she withdrew. We met to exchange papers and other possessions, and we discussed different swap events that we still wanted to live out. She was going to tackle some of my writing; I wanted to go to her feminist research meeting. I don't think we were avoiding serious talk. We were saving our steam for the typewriter.

Some people said Micki would never give me her journals. I was sure she would. She wanted to tell her side of the story, and she wanted the money a book would bring.

Everyone else I knew was talking. There emerged a picture of a pathetic, paranoid creature who in return for the evil she believed I'd done her had tried to damage every important relationship I had, some that weren't even important.

She had bad-mouthed me to all. She had asked Kylie Warneke if she was really sure that George and I weren't lovers. What did my saying that we weren't mean, after all? She had told Jeff Bailey, my friend and sometimes lover for ten years, that I talked only about our sexual connection, not about his being a writer. Kylie is too smart and secure to have believed her, and Jeff found that I had made a point of leaving Micki his latest story—but still. She had accused me wholesale of giving her utterly inadequate information for dealing with my life. It turned out that she didn't read all the notes I had left for her until after the swap was over, but she had presented such a perfect victim's face that a couple of people wondered if I had a vicious side they'd never noticed. Will Jepson called and said that her tales had no more lasting effects on my friends than mosquito bites in early spring, and everyone kept talking about how terrific it was to have the real Nancy back; still, there were a few rough days. Part of the problem was that the perfect victim's face Micki had shown me was making me wonder how good some of my friends had been to her and therefore to me.

I realized pretty quickly that we had all been her victims. There was a new horror story every day. My friends' revelations were rivaling the Watergate hearings. Unlike the Watergate revelations, my friends' all jibed.

One incredibly painful discovery was that Micki had read many of the people in my life the notes I had written about them, without explaining what the notes were meant to be, without also reading them the more leisurely and sometimes warmer things I'd written in my journals. Of course without these things. Her object was blood, and she drew it.

My rage and guilt and sense of helplessness were compounded by my not being able to tell Micki what I thought of her; first I needed her notes on the swap. She called me right after I learned about one of her most egregious recitations, and it took so much effort not to tell Micki I wanted to kill her that I passed out for two hours after I hung up the phone.

I found out that she'd never shown up at my florist, never gone to see Mo at Balducci's, never done any of the big small things that have so much to do with why I like my life. Had she deliberately avoided all joy, all grace?

There were more cockroaches in my apartment than ever before.

I had dinner with two feminist psychologists, Serena Tisch and Liz Hibbert. They were goofy and otherwise endearing, and I began to have hopes for the research meeting they were taking me to. My hopes ended when all eight of the sociologists and psychologists at the meeting said, in answer to a question of mine, that no matter how much I thought I loved being a woman, I was oppressed, I was suffering. Ah, God, the predictable dumb dreariness of it. I started to spar a bit, but they were more interested in hearing about the swap. I said I'd rather talk about it with Micki there; why didn't we have a debate in front of the group? Enthusiasm. Serena called Micki and asked if she'd come to a special meeting with me next Wednesday. Micki said she was going to be away recuperating. I talked a tiny bit about my experiences, and Serena said something that surprised me, pleased me enormously. She told me that my feelings about Ben and our weekend paralleled Micki's feelings about him and their time together. When I had been least concerned about being Micki, I was being most like her.

I had my legs waxed and stopped taking the hateful pill.

I was astonished by the common reaction to the differences between Micki's and my experiences: Of course I'd had a mostly exhilarating time and Micki'd had a devastating time—hadn't I known it was going to end up that way? Hadn't I known that the life swap was my private dream? Hadn't I secretly hoped things would happen the way they did?

How could people ask me such questions? Why did everyone want me to deny my notion of the possible? Was what I'd set in motion all that outrageous? Ridiculous. Scary.

My fingernails stayed long. I wasn't much inclined to cook, and I found that I loved sometimes paying the check when Trigger Mike and I had dinner.

I couldn't meditate. My mantra tasted dirty. So Micki had tried meditating.

I dreamed twice about Ben. Once there were snow peas in the dream, once little gardens of wild flowers that I tried to sell to my florist—Micki stopped me.

I wrote to Ben and Peter and Danny and Ted and Cassie Davidson and Carla and Sig and Alice Lewis and asked them if they'd write about the swap for the book. I asked my family and some of my friends to write about it, too. This seemed the only way to arrive at truth, at least avoid arriving at untruth.

Fran and Susie and Magda went out of the country for the summer. I missed the company of women.

Logged a lot of hours at the Lion's Head. Al, one of the owners, said, "I saw the play; now I want to read the book."

The haze started to lift. Spent a weekend with my family, then got down to work. Wrote the first two chapters of the book, put my notes about the week of the swap in more or less coherent order. It was very tough at times. There was an extraordinary gap between the spirit in which I'd gotten the swap going and my mood of the moment. If I hadn't left a lot of notes behind, I might never have succeeded in sliding back into the rosy breathlessness of the spring. Writing healed me, helped me bring the rosiness into the present. I was no longer the least bit sorry there was a book to do.

I started to like my face very much. My cousins from Toledo came to town, sweet Danny and zany Ida; and Ida kept saying, not hiding her amazement: "You're lovely. You're beautiful. What happened? You were not a pretty child. I think it must be the writing."

Trigger Mike and I were rough on each other for a while, then better than we'd ever been. He was going through hard times with his work, but he was totally supportive of mine, incredibly flexible and generous. I couldn't have enough of kissing the ends of his ridiculous moustache. I fell madly in love with him.

Talked to Nick every hour, it seemed. Missed Bill and Katharine. Had sweet funny times with George and Kylie Warneke and baby Stephanie, with Riff and Aaron and the crew at the Head. Jack Barleycorn came back to town and called, and my toes still twitched, but I didn't want to see him. Nothing appealed to me but kindness. Would that last, or would my toes have their way?

Got reports that Micki was calling up a lot of my friends, explaining, explaining. She told several people that she'd helped my brother to work through his incest fantasies. (See Nick's notes.) She told someone that she was afraid I would use her hasty exit from my life as an excuse not to give her the money our contract called for. Oh, Micki.

Ben haunted my bed for a while. I didn't try to get in touch with him, apart from sending the letter asking him to write something for the book, and didn't expect him to get in touch with me. It was horrible thinking of what he must have been told about me, but it would have been more horrible to subject him to a tug of war for his soul. Someday he would read what I had to say, and I knew that meanwhile, no matter what he heard, he wouldn't put the lie to his days with me. A musician they both knew told Trig that Ben had thought I was marvelous. I wondered if I'd been meant to get that message. I suppose it's hard to believe, but I hoped that he and Micki were okay together.

I kept using cheek gel on my lips and thinking of Maisie Leonard.

Made dinner for Anne Upton. She told me that my mistake had been committing myself to Micki (or anyone) without asking her to submit to psychological tests like the ones they give Peace Corps applicants. We didn't go dancing. We talked about seeing each other again, but the intimacy I had felt (or imagined) was gone. Cassie Davidson agreed to do a piece for the book, pseudonymously, and we met a couple of times. I liked her more and more and more, was tempted to go back to my manuscript and delete my fury at her. I wanted us to be friends. How peculiar it all was.

Went to a party given by some friends of Danny's. Danny was neutral toward me. Allen was as warm and delightful and open as ever; I was sorry I wouldn't get to know him better. Peter was quite cold. I asked the three of them if I'd freaked them out. They all said no. Danny said if anything he'd been slightly bored. Micki spent most of the evening across the room from me, kissed me on the forehead when she left. Had lunch with Steffie Kahn, the woman Micki considered to be more like her than anyone else in the world. I didn't see the resemblance. Enjoyed our talk.

Ted Holzman came down to the Village, and we had dinner together. I didn't wear pink after all. He wanted to talk about the swap; I wanted to talk about anything but. I felt very strained. I had a notion of what Micki had been telling him about me and her adventures as me, and I was dying to counter and overcome what she'd said, but that seemed so incredibly sordid. I was afraid even to be charming. Ted had agreed to write a piece for me, and I didn't want him to think I was trying to influence him. He told me I seemed to be very much the same person I had been during the swap. I looked desirelessly at him and knew I wasn't the same person. Not in feelings. Not at all. I might never have been Micki to his Ted, but he had been Ted to my Micki, my neo-Micki, my un-Nancy.

I heard from Micki that Ben and Peter would probably write about their swap experiences and that Danny and Allen probably wouldn't. I wasn't sure about Peter, but I knew that Ben would never do a piece (just as I knew that my father, for very different reasons, would never do one). I talked to Peter on the phone, urged him to do something, but he didn't. Ben didn't either. The last week in July (she was late, as usual) I got Micki's own notes and found out what she thought had gone on with her, what she wanted the world to think had gone on.

FLINGING

Dear Nancy,

The only way I can describe what happened to me in your life is to start from the beginning and describe everything that happened to me as well as I can. I am not saying that my reality is the only reality, but just that what I have described below is the way I saw it and the way I experienced it. The week after I came back to my life, I read an interview that someone from the *New Yorker* had with Dubuffet, the artist. I think Dubuffet's words on reality express what I had in mind when I decided to take the plunge and what I thought you had in mind when you persuaded me to take the plunge.

For me, insanity is supersanity. The normal is psychotic—a collective psychosis. Normal means lack of imagination, lack of creativity. Creativity! *There* is a flowering, a bursting forth. What is called reality by everyone is something very conventional, an accepted interpretation of the world. I have always wanted to make my own translations, my own interpretations.... Instead of one reality, we can have billions of realities. Each person can legitimate his own reality. Is this not the negation of a surface approach to life, is this not *very* positive? . . . One must lose one's conviction of reality, dispense with the main food of one's life. One must conclude that all is accident, question what is real, what is false, reach a state where there is no north, no south, no compass.

I also read an article in *The New York Times* of June 25, 1973, which described to me what happened to me in your life when I went crazy.

A.M.A. SPEAKER DECLARES
MANIC PHASE HELPS GIFTED

The manic phase of the milder forms of manic-depression may be a positive energizer that drives some of the most creative and productive overachievers in current society, a psychiatrist told an American Medical Association symposium yesterday.

Dr. Ronald R. Fieve, of the New York State Psychiatric Institute, called depression "probably the most widespread of all psychic illness." He estimated that some six million Americans suffered "recurrent bouts" of manic-depression, "probably the most dramatic form."

"I have found that some of the most gifted individuals in our society suffer from this condition—including many outstanding writers, politicians, business executives and scientists—where tremendous amounts of manic energy and imagination have enabled them to achieve their heights of success," Dr. Fieve told the symposium, called "Depression: A Major Health Problem in America," held at the Coliseum.

Without proper treatment, he said, these persons "more often than not either go too 'high' or suddenly crash into a devastating depression that we only hear about after a successful suicide."

"Excessive telephoning and frequent buying sprees," Dr. Fieve said, might characterize the "moderately severe manic patient," along with "pressured speech," elation, hyperactivity and a decreased need for sleep.

I have decided that my name for purposes of this narrative will be Allison McCoy. I have chosen this name because it is unlike me as possible, because it is the name of a WASP and a number of people in your life said I was a "shiksa," and because I was the unreal McCoy in your life. My narrative is rough, it has dirty words in it, it is obscene in places; it may offend you, it may threaten you, it may hurt you, and it is full of dangling participles and inelegant phraseology. I hope you will leave much of it in its original form. Since no real name is being used except yours, I think I cannot be accused of slander, although some people in your life may find my observations to be cruel and unkind. The only way I could write it up and be true to myself was to write down everything I felt, thought, did as well as I can reconstruct it from voluminous but sometimes sketchy notes.

I first heard about the life swap when Sig Lewis saw the ad. He thought I should do it and gave it to me. He then answered it himself with the details (editorialized) of my life. Sig's motivation was vicarious pleasure and to write the winning letter, as he had been attempting to write the winning pun for *New York* magazine. He planned to have a friend call me and pretend to be the person who put the ad in the paper. You called first.

My motivation for doing it was: an interest in the effect of environment on personality, an interest in people's mind-sets, the challenge of changing you into a feminist, and the need for money so that Ben could go to horticulture school and I would not have to take a job that I did not like. For the last six months my life has been in a state of transition. I had been trying to figure out what I really wanted to do, get another academic job or drop out for a while and write, and I thought this would give me an opportunity to see if I liked writing. Also the thought of doing it was very scary to me, and therefore I knew that it was a test of something and that I should do it.

The days preceding the swap were very hectic. On Sunday, June 3, I had to drive to Baltimore to attend a symposium on women's studies programs in high schools and colleges. I drove back to New York City Monday night in time to attend a Charles Lloyd concert and drove back to Riverset Monday night. Tuesday, I took peyote with friends in Riverset. Wednesday I got the releases from Peter and Ben and me notarized and drove back to the city to get work done in my office. I went to dinner with Liz Hibbert downtown and went to your apartment to give you the releases. I met Peter and two other friends and went home to have a disagreeable evening with Peter after everyone went to bed. Thursday, I went to the office to work, met you at the Algonquin, had dinner with you, went to a research meeting, had a beer with one of the women in the research meeting, went home to apartment-clean and fight with Peter over whether or not he had lied to me. Friday I drove to school, did more work and drove to Riverset. I spent Saturday working in the garden, and I transplanted thirty coleus plants. I also addressed and mailed all the announcements. On Sunday I spent the day taking care of the Hawthorne loose ends, washed seven loads of wash so that all the linen and towels would be clean, and made a list of everyone I had sent an announcement to.

Monday, June 11, the hottest day of the year and the day of the exchange, I got up at five in the morning, did more work, packed, put labels on all my drawers so that you would not have trouble finding things. Put signs around the rest of the house to indicate things that could be done and things that shouldn't be done (leaving doors unlocked, or open, etc.). I wrote two letters: one authorizing the use of my car and the other to the Pennsylvania Motor Vehicles Bureau, telling them that they had sent me a license plate that did not match my registration. I then went to a notary to have these letters and copies notarized. Then I drove to New York. My first stop was my apartment. I left clean clothes there for you, made up with Peter, and drove to the office for more last-minute work. I wrote a number of entries into a calendar I was providing for you. I went through my answer/do folder and picked out things that you could do and might have fun doing.

I then did some more paper work and made some phone calls. Called you and told you I couldn't make it until two thirty. You said latest I should be was two fifteen because the Exchange closed. I rushed to get a cab—blazing hot! I got to Women's Exchange by two thirty. I expect that you will describe our interaction at the Women's Exchange and afterward, so I won't bother to do it. We left each other at five o'clock and I picked up your dry cleaning (seventeen dollars' worth) and went to your apartment. In your apartment I looked at the calendar you had prepared and found:

11 Monday

> Hi:
> Dinner with Trigger Mike—he'll call about where to meet him.
> Pants & dressyish top or blue & white dress maybe.
> Calls likely from Nick, Magda, and Susie.

12 Tuesday

> New phones coming between eight forty-five and twelve.
> This room gray—bathroom yellow. Nonjump auxiliary number. Second number goes only to the happy few.
> Call Mrs. Remington—370–XXXX—if any problems.
> Exterminator (Reggie) may come. Please give him ribboned package next to record player.

13 Wednesday

> 10:30: Yuric Lermentov coming (see Work). He has endless thirst for tonic and/or coffee. I always want to feed him. Jeans or khakis & bodyshirt probably.
>
> 7:30–8:00: Dinner at Abbe's, 30 St. Marks Place.
> (Gershon is name on bell). Khakis & dressier bodyshirt or maybe pink dress & sandals—no, pants are more likely.

17 Sunday

> Call Daddy.

18 Monday

> Call Mummy & Daddy—their anniversary. Sixish is good time to call.

23 Saturday

> Probably a Connecticut-Cambridge weekend—consult with Nick.

After looking through the other materials you had left me, speed-reading my way through them because I wanted to make up the cards on all the people in my life to give to you (I still hadn't had time to get that done), I called Magda, who'd called me. She wasn't home, and so I talked to Will. We had a brief conversation about the heat in New York City, about the possibility of my going to Martha's Vineyard, about Magda going to Hungary. He said Magda was having a drink with some friend in a bar and that he would have her call back as soon as she came in.

I had just hung up and was about to start on the notes on the people in my life when a man by the name of Phil Barnett called and asked if Mike was there and did I know where he was. I said no but that he was going to call around 7:30. Phil Barnett said to tell Mike to call him.

Went back to the desk and began working my way more slowly through your notes to me. Thought you had done an awful lot of work and that it was a real challenge to see how many of the things you had left me to do I could actually accomplish. Was particularly interested in the tantric sex thing. Did a second speed-reading of the incomplete swap novel. I had read it once before when you left me in the apartment alone and I was picking up things and reading them.

The phone rings. It's Mike, he asks how I am and what I've spent the day doing. Gave him a brief rundown, told him about Phil Barnett message. He said he'd call again around nine, that we would probably meet at Jimmy's. As soon as I hung up the phone rang again and it's Magda. We have a very strained conversation. She sort of starts in the middle of things, and between the fact that she has had a few drinks and she has a slight accent and I don't speak Hungarian and I'm feeling very anxious because I'm a stranger in a strange land and I really want to be as Nancy as I can be to Magda's Magda, the conversation did not go smoothly. As it was ending, I thanked her for calling back. That was totally the wrong thing to say, and she immediately told me that it was a stupid thing to do because I never thank her. So much for Magda.

I went into the bathroom, threw up the crab, the shrimp, the salad, and all the champagne I'd had for lunch. I washed my mouth out with peroxide, washed my face, splashed on some cucumber stuff because it was green and I thought it would make me feel better, and sat down to regain control. Started to meditate. Am just beginning to get the hang of your mantra when the phone rings. It's Aaron Tyman. While I am saying hello, I leaf quickly through the address book with the notes that you've left me and find out that Aaron Tyman is: "Old friend, through George Warneke. Is omnipresent—once you meet him, he's always there. Lovable. Lion's Head." Make arrangements to see him at 4:00 the next day for tea. Started working on notes to you. The phone rings. It's Riff. We have a mysterious conversation and he tells me he will call me tomorrow before noon. As we are talking, I look through cue book and find out about him enough to tell him that I'm having dinner with our mutual friend and to say "Good-bye, Comrade." I hang up and read your description of him: "This is someone intensely special to me. I've known him for years. He's an ex-con who does odd things around town. The red roses are from him. He cultivates mystery—no one knows where he lives. He is in the process of getting me some false identity papers—for no other reason than that I love such theater and he does, too. He needs to be fed and looked after and loved. We address each other as 'Comrade' and refer to Trig as 'our mutual friend.'" I look at the roses and look back at the notes you left for me and think how karmic it is that they are from Riverset, Pa., that Riff and I will probably become friends. I wonder why you use the term "ex-con" to describe him. It is a very strange term to use about someone who is very special to you. It also could lead anyone who reads the description down the stereotypic path of those who are categorized ex-cons. I wonder if he is getting you false papers because you both love theater or because he likes you and wants to do something for you and thinks you seriously want/need false identity papers.

Am still pondering this one when Mike calls and tells me to get up to Jimmy's in fifteen minutes. I tell him that I need a half hour to shower and dress and take a cab up there. He says I should be able to do it in fifteen minutes. I rush into clothes closet, pick out white dress with blue dots, rush through a one-minute shower. Slather myself with Shalimar, put on your makeup and the white sandals we had just bought at Charles Jourdan. Thought that I would probably break my neck trying to get to Mike on time. Rush out the door, try to find the keys to lock the door, have to rummage through purse because, as you, I cannot keep my purse in some kind of efficient order, and must always throw my keys in there. Finally find keys. They fall off key ring. I struggle to get door locked, am out on the street. Try to avoid the bizarro who tries to grab me by the arm because it is the bewitching hour on Eighth Street and Sixth, grab a cab, try to meditate in cab. Can't get into it. Look at New York sizzling by. It is still hot as hell. Three police cars whiz by. New York, you are indeed fun city. Speed-read what you said about Mike: "Hast heard of him? My Mike, my Trigger Mike, my T.M., my Trig, my Boyfriend, my Pal, my Oatmeal Head. Ask him about Willy Chilly. Or just say: 'Who's that ballplayer?' God, I love him. He loves to be gone down upon. Supersensitive nipples. Most erotic man in America. I constantly kiss the ends of his moustache, also in public. My lover, my pal."

The picture of Mike floats through my mind, and I feel like laughing, embarrassedly, and then I feel like throwing up again. We are at Jimmy's by this point. Chin up, through the doors, and there he is, the most erotic man in America. I kiss him. I order an Irish and I sit on a bar stool. The lady to the left of me tells me that I can't sit on that bar stool, she is saving it for someone. I move over to the next bar stool. Two men come up and take Mike aside. By the looks of them and the way they move their bodies and their mouths and smile only with their mouths, they are obviously politicians. I later learn from Mike that they are Badillo people.

Badillo will not get my vote. That is for sure. While Mike is talking in asides to them, a man sits on the bar stool to my left and asks me if that is all right with me. I said it was all right with me, but the lady sitting next to you is saving that seat for someone. The lady frowns at me and says it's okay for him to sit there, and then smiles. He turns and starts talking to me. Mike comes back. I excuse myself and turn to talk to him. A man by the name of Harry comes up and says hello to Mike. Mike does not know who he is. The man realizes this and explains that the last time he saw Mike he (Harry) made a terrible fool of himself. I thought to myself he's about to repeat the performance. Can I take a whole evening of this? Mike decides we should go eat at the Derby. We taxi downtown. He kisses me a number of times. It is still hot as hell. Can I get through the night without going bananas?

We arrive at the Derby. I order another Irish, a club steak, salad with Russian dressing while sitting at the bar. Mike begins to ask me questions about Ben. I told him that Ben is an idealistic radical and a great linguist who hates linguists and wants to become a horticulturist. Mike says he sounds like an interesting young man. I didn't tell Mike that he is exactly the kind of political person that Ben can't stand. While we are talking, another unctuous person comes by to say hello to Mike. We eat hurriedly and then head for the Lion's Head.

At the Lion's Head we run into a beautiful, tall woman by the name of Audrey. Mike introduces us and she informs me that I (Nancy) was not terribly friendly to her usually. I told her I didn't know why I wouldn't be friendly to her because she seemed nice enough and very beautiful. She told me that I (Nancy) was always ending conversations with her. I asked her to give me an example. She said that one time she commented about my blouse saying, "That's a nice blouse," and that I responded by saying, "I like it too." She thought my answer (your answer) was hostile. I thought to myself how far can one go with a conversation about a blouse. We got into a discussion of what she was doing these days. Living on Long Island, looking for work, being more honest with men about sex. I encouraged her to continue being more honest with men about sex. Mike asked what other plans I had for the week. I told him I was having tea with Aaron Tyman and seeing Abbe. He then said Abbe was sitting next to me at the bar. I got into a conversation with Abbe and a friend of his about Chinese cooking and Chinese restaurants. We exchanged the names of our favorite restaurants in Chinatown. I then had a short conversation with a man who was with Audrey. I think his name was Jay (sparse dark brown beard, about 5 feet 10 inches). He giggled a lot and I thought he was slightly uncomfortable with the situation, but that may have been a projection on my part. I certainly was uncomfortable with the situation and slightly drunk. I had a beer (without ice) and then Mike and I went home.

It was about one o'clock. We took a shower, opened your couch and then spent fifteen minutes trying to dim the lights. I was surprised that Mike wasn't more aware of how to turn the damn lights off. We never did get them all off. He proceeded to ball me. The regular missionary position. We did "it" this way, I think, twice. Then he wanted me to hold his testicles and jerk him off, which I did. Then he wanted to jerk himself off while I watched, which he did and I did. By now it was four o'clock in the morning and I was very tired of everything including telling Mike that he's all right and that everything is all right and assuring him that he is indeed very virile. I just wanted him to leave and I didn't particularly want to think about what he was doing or what I was letting him do to me. I remember at some point he got into grabbing and smacking my ass which was a bit bizarre. That and his ejaculation screams, I think, stand out in my mind most about that evening. Finally he left. I spent thirty minutes trying to get myself organized. I searched the apartment for thirty minutes more trying to find my keys and finally realized that Mike must have taken them home with him. I spent another fifteen minutes trying to get all the lights in the place off. It didn't really matter because by this time the sun was coming up. I covered myself with your sleeping bag, took one of your headache pills for the migraine I felt coming on, made a note to call Mike in the morning and to call my agent about getting some money from her and went to sleep.

Tuesday, June 12

Woke up at 9:30, showered, started to meditate, the doorbell rings. It's Reggie, the exterminator. We have a short conversation. I ask him if he would like something to drink. It must be ninety-eight degrees outside. He says he never drinks anything cold when it's hot, but that he would like something hot. I ask if he prefers tea or coffee. Oh no, he says, he prefers Johnnie Walker Black Label for the heat. I thought how unusual; would Nancy give him a shot? Then decided that you probably would and that I certainly would. He has shot, squirts the bathroom and the kitchen area. I give him the gift you've left him and he's off. I started to meditate again. George Warneke called and wanted to know the publishers for the three yoga books. I desperately try to find the books and can't find them. I told him that I would spend some time looking for them and would call him back. I call the answering service to find out what messages I've received from the evening before. No messages. What a relief. I called Nick. He wasn't in so I left a message that I had called (his sister). I called Riff's office and left him a message to call Mike about a job driving for Mrs. Badillo. I started trying to meditate again and Riff called and I gave him Mike's message. Riff said he would call me back in the afternoon. I was about to call my agent to ask her about sending me my check when she called and said that she would send me my check care of Nancy Weber. I start to meditate again and remember that I still have not found out the name of the publishers for George Warneke. I look in the case next to the bed/sofa and find them. I call George back. His answering service picks up, and I leave him the message. Mike calls to tell me he has my keys. Mike says he'll call back later and tell me what time and where I can pick up my keys from him. As soon as I hang up, Nick calls, and we have a pleasant conversation. He asks me if I want to come to Hartford on Thursday and spend the night. I said I thought that would be nice. Your father then gets on the phone and says hello. The conversation is a bit awkward, but both Nick and your father are very pleasant to me. As soon as I hang up the phone, Jim Cook calls, and I make an appointment to see him here at 2:30. As soon as I hung up, Mike called and said to meet him at Sardi's to pick up the keys at 1:30. George called back and told me to call Betty at Black Star and ask her to do a search for some pictures for the tantric sex book.

I rushed up to Sardi's in a cab, tried to meditate but couldn't get into it, made a note to buy a copy of the *Hackman's Guide and Chauffeur's Guide to New York City.* Had a short conversation with the taxicab driver about the heat and we were at Sardi's. I met Mike in the upstairs bar, where he was talking to a man by the name of Arthur Beckmann, who had gone to college with him. This man was quite interesting. He had lived in South Africa and just emigrated to Israel. He was unemployed, but had just passed the Israeli bar exam. We talked about Israeli politics, Watergate, Philip Roth's article on Nixon in the *N.Y. Review of Books* and Shana Alexander's article on Watergate. Alexander had suggested that just as Exxon had changed its name from Esso and hopefully its image, Nixon should change his name to Nixxon to see if that helped at all.

By this time it was two o'clock and I was about to leave, but Mike asked me to wait for him so that we could take a cab together downtown. I said I would wait; he had one more drink and then had to go to the bathroom. We rushed out of Sardi's and he suggested a subway as a faster method of getting downtown. I agreed and started for the subway and he ran into an old friend who was now living in Boston and they got into a conversation. By this time I was getting a little desperate because I knew that I was going to be late to meet Jim Cook. Finally, Mike said goodbye to the guy and we rushed to the subway. Mike put us on the local by mistake, so I was even more desperate. He said we'd probably go to Elaine's for dinner.

I arrived back at your apartment at two forty-five and found out that I had missed Jim. He called and said he would call me next week. I sat down to type my notes to you on the people in my life and the phone rang. It was the telephone company saying that they had been by at one-thirty to install the phone. I told them that I thought they were installing it between eight forty-five and twelve, and they said their order said between nine and five. I told them to come right over and install it. I sat down and started writing up the notes for you, and the bell rang. It was the phone man. I let him in and helped him discover where the trunk line came into your apartment. Then I called Black Star for George and found out that there was no Betty. The person I wanted was Irma and she was not there. The bell rang again. It was Aaron Tyman come for tea. Aaron seemed friendly enough and rather appealing in a pixieish way. We had a long conversation about how he was a creative stock analyst and how he might be a process person rather than a content person and how being a process person might help one to be a creative stock analyst. Then we discussed the money that one could make selling short, but that you had to know what you were doing.

The whole time Aaron is there, the phone man is there puttering about trying to put in the phone in the bathroom. Aaron is getting turned on, which is funny somehow because the telephone man is listening to our conversation and walking in and out of the room and Aaron is sitting on the sofa with an erection. The absurdity of the situation made me want to giggle. We were both quite giddy at this point, since we had drunk a bottle of champagne and I had had nothing to eat all day. Riff called while we were sitting there and said that he had some interesting dope deal to tell me about because I had (meaning you, Nancy) mentioned that I would like to buy some dope from him if he could score and that he was bringing me over a sample to try. I explained that I couldn't spend any time with him because I had a dinner engagement with our mutual friend. He said that was all right; he would just drop by a sample for me to try and if I liked it we would figure out how much I wanted to score. He arrived shortly and gave me a joint and a letter.

At this point Mike called and told me to meet him at Sardi's. Aaron helped me choose something to wear and I arranged to see him after dinner with Mike. I had already decided that I did not want to spend another evening in bed with Mike, and Aaron did seem "lovable," or at least preferable to Mike both physically and mentally. He also said some very funny things and made me laugh a lot. Also I guess we were involved in a conspiracy in that we both knew he had an erection and had to hide this fact from the telephone man. There was something else about Aaron that made me want to spend time with him, and that was that he mentioned the fact that he had spent most of the last few months celibately because he did not feel turned on to his own body or anyone else's. This may have been a ploy on his part to get my sympathy, but at the time I thought it was real and it did get my sympathy. I wanted to make him feel better about himself and about his body and I felt friendly toward him. Also I knew that he was in therapy and just beginning to open up. The champagne and the situation we were both in made me much more receptive than I would have been, or maybe when someone tells me that they've been in trouble or that they are insecure I tend to like them and want to help them. This may be a teacher-therapist-Pollyanna-mommy feature of my personality, but I have a feeling (or did) that it is a personality characteristic we both share.

I wore your wraparound blouse with small lilac flowers on it and your tan pants. I took a taxi up to Sardi's and did manage to meditate. Mike was in the upstairs bar at Sardi's when I arrived. He was in the midst of a group of men whom he introduced to me. I don't remember their names and meant to ask Mike at a later date who they were. I remember one was Evan. He was quite fat and had an elegant manner of speech. There was a smaller, darker weasellike man sitting next to him who was teasing him about his relationship to a group of Finnish airline stewardesses whom the owner of Sardi's persuades to frequent the place. It seems that Evan had tried to make time with one of these stewardesses and was unsuccessful. There were two other men present; one was a rather dandified out-of-work actor who came into town from Long Island to pick up his unemployment check, and the other was a man with long brown hair who seemed to be Evan's friend and continuously made sarcastic remarks. Mike was involved in a conversation with someone else at the bar. I ordered a club soda (I decided that I didn't want to drink too much because it did not have a very good effect on me and I had a headache from the champagne and no food all day) and I took one of your headache pills. The boys at the bar commented on my pill-popping and tee-totaling.

I then proceeded to watch this group of men very carefully. Weasel would not let up on Evan and his inability to make it with women. The comments he made were very derogatory and sarcastic but also funny and totally chauvinistic from my perspective. I felt very frustrated having to be you. Normally I would have called weasel on his male-chauvinist-pig attitudes and on his castrating behavior toward Evan (who I somehow liked because he had a great flair for speaking, beautiful hands that he used with great grace, and he held his own in the battle with extraordinary finesse). When weasel stopped getting on Evan's back, brown-hair started in. The out-of-work actor with his blue ascot (who wears a silk ascot in the midst of a New York heat spell, I ask you?) stood around and listened and made small talk with me. The weasel informed me in some subtle way that the actor did not know about the life swap, but the rest of them did. I felt that much of what was going on was some kind of a test or a performance for my benefit. I also felt depressed about the way these men interacted with one another. Instead of being supportive and loving (Evan and brown-hair obviously cared for one another; no one cared for weasel), they played this highly competitive word-dueling game. The object of the game was to nick the other person's ego and in that way to score points. If they were not funny, however, they lost points. I felt that they were all closet cases and that all of the sexual talk about women and their ability/disability with women was a camouflage for their homosexual feelings about one another.

I've been away from this type of men for a long time because I really dislike the way they relate to each other and to women, and it was really awful sitting there, not being able to speak out, knowing that they had all sorts of salacious thoughts about Mike and me. I felt very vulnerable because I did not have available any of my normal weapons: my tongue or my sense of humor and ability to be sarcastic. What's more, I wasn't even protected by my status as a sociologist, teacher, therapist, lecturer, or mean-mother (which I sometimes see myself as). To them, and I could see it in their faces, I was a somewhat attractive sex object who they could make up-tight by talking about what they would like to do to the Finnish stewardesses. I also felt at a disadvantage without my glasses, without my watch to remind me which hand is my right hand and too exposed in your clothing. They knew more about me as Nancy than I did about them or about myself as Nancy. I had no equity in the situation and felt totally exposed and helpless. A very uncomfortable place to be and one that I'm seldom in. At the same time I knew they were watching me very closely to see my reactions to them and to the situation and they were also trying to test my Nancyness, but I had no idea how well you knew them or in what capacity. Mike was oblivious to all of this and was having some self-aggrandizing conversation with someone who was quite elegant and elderly and who kept breaking into songs from *South Pacific.*

I finally turned away from the other group and rejoined Mike (who was standing next to me all along but a million miles away anyhow). The elegant gentleman was then introduced to me. I think he kissed me and made some sort of sexist comment. My memory of my interaction with him is rather vague. I think he said something about his age and when I responded sympathetically, he made a hostile remark.

On our way out, the head waiter at Sardi's talked to T.M. about some personal problem of his. On the way to Frankie and John- nie's, we met Tibor, a beautiful Hungarian who used to be a waiter at Sardi's and who now is the manager of a theater. Felt fairly good about Mike. I ordered lamb chops and asparagus while sitting at the bar. Mike introduced me to the bartender, and they got into a discussion of whether or not the individuals who were being questioned during the Watergate hearings could later claim that because of the press coverage of the hearings, it was impossible for them to get a fair trial anywhere in the United States and whether or not it was good that the hearings were being televised. They then told me the story of Nixon coming to Frankie and Johnnie's and encountering Jason Robards and how Nixon had put a twenty-dollar bill on the counter to pay for everyone's drink and then picked it up again. Doc, the manager of the restaurant, came over to talk to us too. I liked him immediately. He was having trouble with his wife and feeling rather down about his situation but also expressed his love for his son and the hope that things would go better for everyone concerned now that he and his wife were trying to be more honest with each other and were not living together anymore.

The lamb chops were ready, so we made our way to the part of the restaurant where the tables are. On our way we ran into Phil Barnett and a woman by the name of Mary Westergaard. Mike introduced me to both of them. Phil Barnett told me that he was an old friend of mine (yours) and I didn't put the name and face together with the person who had called the day before to ask if Mike was around. I liked Phil Barnett from the first moment I saw him. I liked his beautiful white hair and his light eyes and was glad that he was an old friend of mine (yours). Mary Westergaard asked me to repeat my name and I repeated "Nancy Weber." Then she asked did I go to Sarah Lawrence. I said, "Yes." She said, "I know Nancy Weber and I went to Sarah Lawrence and you're not the Nancy Weber that I know." So then she had to be let in on the secret.

Phil and Mary and Doc joined us at our table and we got into a discussion of the life swap, which was cheating, but anything else would have been ridiculous. She asked me about my life and I was fairly honest about my relationships and my sexual orientation. She told me that she was really quite amazed that I could be so open about who I was and what I was to a complete stranger. I explained that the only way people were going to be more open in general (I felt) was for those of us who could take small risks to take them, and let those who were still holding back and afraid see that lightning did not strike and that most people did not vomit or turn away from you when you were honest. I tried to explain that I felt we (all of us) were caught between trying to be open and honest and fearing the consequences of being honest, that our souls are the battlegrounds between the impulse to be honest and the paranoia of the consequences, our conscience does not want us to be cowards, and that I am a coward who wants to be a warrior.

Mary is very beautiful and seemed somewhat rigid, probably out of fear. She began to discuss a new children's book called *Willy and the Doll* and how she thought it was a good idea for boys to play with dolls and play baseball and that books like that were a move in the right direction. Doc said that he thought books like that were a good idea and that it would not upset him if his son wanted to play with a doll.

At this point Mike could not be quiet any longer. He said that he really hated the fascist women who sat at home writing books which forced boys to play with dolls. We said the book isn't about forcing anyone to do anything; it's about giving people options to be who they want to be without sex-role stereotypes forcing them into "masculine" and "feminine" molds. Mike could not be placated. He said, louder this time, that if any sons of his played with dolls he would kill them. I should say that Mike had had a bit too much to drink. Mary began to get mad at him and counter his arguments. Since I was playing you I felt that I could not argue with him but should try to stop him from making a bigger fool of himself than he already had. People at other tables in that small intimate restaurant were beginning to stare at our table. But Mike would not stop. He said he hated Christers and people who forced others to change and ideologues and the fascist women of women's liberation who wanted to put all children in state-controlled day-care centers. I told him that his arguments were getting a bit ridiculous and that I felt that since none of us had read the book in question, the whole discussion was academic.

To be totally honest, I wasn't angry at Mike for his attitudes. I just felt really sorry that he was making a fool of himself and that in the morning he would feel really lousy about making such an ass of himself in public. I should have just written him something on a napkin. If I had read Erica Jong's poem "Seventeen Warnings in Search of a Feminist Poem (for Aaron Ascher)," I would have written, "Beware of the man who denounces women writers; his penis is tiny and cannot spell." That might have stopped him long enough to rethink his position. But I didn't, and Mike kept on going.

Next he said that he hated the women that said he was threatened by women's liberation. What did he have to be threatened by. All they wanted was to make all men faggots. Then he said the trouble with faggots is that they've ruined the word gay. It used to be a good word, and now it had been ruined. I really began to see the ludicrousness of the situation and the Freudian interpretation potential. I could have said "methinks the gentleman protests too much," but I didn't. I just said, "Mike, you are really getting out there and when you realize the limb you are out on you are going to have a very hard time coming back to the tree trunk," or something like that. It didn't stop him. Doc, by this time, was close to tears. He kept saying to me, "Nancy, I don't know what's happened to him. I've known him for years and he's never acted this way before. I don't know what has gotten into him."

Finally Phil and Mary left. The restaurant had practically emptied out, either because of our table or because it isn't a late-night dinner place. Doc was still trying to discuss with Mike and at the same time count the money he had taken in that night. I excused myself and went to the bathroom and threw up and then took another headache pill. I wanted to take a taxi directly home and spend the rest of the evening having a good time with Aaron, but Mike very plaintively asked me to please have another drink with him so he could explain. I really felt sorry for the guy and didn't want him to feel any worse than he was already feeling, so I agreed to have one more drink with him at a bar that was down the street from Frankie and Johnnie's. He sort of apologized and tried to explain how he hated Christers and fascists of all types. And I said I didn't like fascists either, but that it was a mistake for him to categorize all feminists as fascists and that his arguments had not held together logically. He asked me if I was mad at him and I said that I wasn't, that I was just very tired and wanted to go home, and that I felt sorry that he had made a fool of himself. He tried to explain some more and I said I was really tired and just wanted to go home alone. I thought it would be adding insult to injury to tell him that I expected to see Aaron that evening, although by this time I thought that it was probably too late to see Aaron and that Aaron had probably given up on seeing me. I really just wanted to go home and sleep off the headache and the bad taste in my mouth. Mike acted as if I were punishing him for his bad behavior. I really just wanted to get away from him and the whole scene. I wasn't interested in telling him it was all right a few more times. Finally, he understood that I wanted to go home alone and he waited with me while I got a cab. On the way home the taxicab driver asked me if Mike were my boyfriend or my father. I said, "Neither, it's too complicated to explain." Why do taxicab drivers always talk to me?

By the time I got home, it was one in the morning. I called the answering service. Jack Barleycorn had called and left the message that he would call again tomorrow. Aaron had called. Susie had called, and a mystery person who didn't leave his name had called. I debated whether or not I should call Jack back. I knew from the journals that he was a night owl and probably would be awake but I decided that I really did not want any more heaviness in my life at the moment, and so a conversation with Jack was out. I called Aaron and he said that he had called twice. I apologized for calling so late and he said that it was OK and he would like to come over. So, feeling guilty about being late and not very enthusiastic about the prospects of a night with anyone, I told him to come over. I made a note to call Susie the next day and to get the notes for you typed the first thing in the morning.

Then I looked up Phil Barnett in the address book to see if you had said anything about him. Sure enough, under Phil Barnett you had written: *"New York Times* reporter. Is planning to cheat and try to seduce you, even though, as a good friend of T.M.'s, he always thought I was off bounds. If you need clips or such help, call him. A member of Sardi's upstairs bar." I was glad I hadn't read that description of him before I met him because I really felt very attracted to him but didn't particularly want him to "seduce" me. I debated calling him and decided that it was too late in the evening and that he might be in bed with Mary, and it wouldn't be cool of me to interrupt them. My feeling about him after reading the description was, so he thinks he's going to seduce me does he? We'll see about that. I decided that he would be a challenge. I mean, how could I get to bed with him and yet let him know that he wasn't seducing me, that I knew what I wanted and that there was no way for him to take advantage of me the way I felt Mike had done. I decided to call him the next day and confront him with the "seduction" bit.

At this point Aaron was buzzing, so I let him in. I then took a shower to wash off the boys in the bar at Sardi's, Mike's effects on me and the New York City pollution. Aaron and I were both very tired. We made very ordinary love. It was not particularly exciting for me. He seemed to have a good time. I was glad he was there because I was feeling rather down and exhausted and I felt that Aaron was okay as a person. After the boys in Sardi's and Mike, Aaron did indeed seem to be as lovable as you described him and not a male chauvinist pig at all.

Wednesday, June 13

I woke up at 8:30 and tried to go back to sleep. Aaron was sleeping and when I couldn't go back to sleep I decided to meditate and do a couple of yoga asanas to relax. Aaron woke up about 9:30 and we had tea and bread and cheese for breakfast. Then he told me about how he hadn't been to bed with you for a long time. I was surprised by that information, since my interpretation of your description of him was that you frequently went to bed with him, since he was omnipresent. He said he didn't go to bed with you because he couldn't stand Shalimar perfume and that the last time he had had any intimate contact with you, you were wearing your shaggy lamb coat and that it was a wet winter and the smell of the wet wool and the Shalimar made you smell like a sheep with Shalimar and he felt like vomiting. I asked him why he didn't ask you not to wear Shalimar and he said it would not have made any difference and that his relationship with you was not important enough for him to ask you not to wear a perfume you obviously cared so much about. I felt rather dismayed at this information. I mean, I had just spent the night with Aaron, and though it was not unpleasant, I doubt that left to my own devices I would normally choose Aaron as a bed companion. Certainly I wouldn't go to bed with him without knowing him a lot better and for a much longer period of time. I felt rather peeved at you for giving me an editorialized version of your life and not being totally honest about what your relationship with Aaron really was. And out of loyalty to you I felt that it was a bit crass of Aaron to tell me that the last time he was with you he felt like vomiting because you smelled like a wet sheep wearing Shalimar. The image was a very funny one but not particularly flattering to you, and I also thought that he had taken advantage of the fact that I didn't know that much about your relationship with him and that he had used me sexually. It is not as if he tried to rape me; in fact, I went along with his coming over and his going to bed with me, but I just felt that I hadn't been given enough information to make decisions and that I had slept with him on the assumption that you would have slept with him and that was a totally wrong assumption. In other words, I had been had.

As I was pondering this information, the buzzer rang, and the telephone man was back again for another bout with the trunk lines. He gave Aaron a knowing look and smiled and began to work. I told Aaron I had work to do and that Yuric Lermentov was coming over to talk to me about his movie and that I would prefer that he leave. As I was saying this, the bell rang, and Lermentov was there. Aaron let him in.

Yuric Lermentov seemed to me to be a very serious, very intense person. I hadn't had time to get the quinine water you had told me about in the journals and so I offered him coffee which was the other alternative that you had written about. I sat next to him on the sofa and listened very closely to the plot of his new movie. He wanted me to come up with a title for it. The title he had thought of in French had something to do with the trimestral accounting that French companies go through. The idea he conveyed to me was that the woman in the plot had looked at her life rather objectively and decided to stay with her husband even though he wasn't that exciting, but loved her, and to not run off with the gypsylike truck driver. He explained that when she looked at the accounts or the balance she made the rational decision to stay with her husband and that he felt that was the right decision because we must be responsible, and to run off with the truck driver would have been irresponsible and not the correct thing to do from a Political Polish Point of View.

He told me something about what his status was in Poland and that in Poland film makers are the conscience of the nation. We also discussed what his attitude was toward the United States. In many ways I thought he was rather ethnocentric and bigoted about the United States, but I agreed with many of his perceptions of the American Way of Life, having come to many of his conclusions myself from my own outsider perspective. The conversation was rather frustrating to me because I wanted to tell him that I had come to many of the same conclusions, but as Nancy I really couldn't legitimately tell him that I was brought up outside the United States and shared his dislike of the American Way of Life. I also realized that he was a bit uncomfortable with me or with the situation.

At the end of our interaction I asked him to give me feedback on my performance. He said that I was not at all like you. Although I knew that that had to be true, I felt very threatened by his saying that. He told me your clothes were all wrong for me and that I was too controlling and that I talked too much. Also that I sat too close to him and that I should have sat on the other side of the room if I were going to try to be you. I knew that I should have sat on the other side of the room, but then I wouldn't have been able to see him as well or hear him as well. I also knew that I had asked too many questions because I really wanted to know what he expected of me as a professional writer (that is, what he expected of you) and that since he kept saying that he had another appointment, I had felt it necessary to ask very specific questions about his film. Probably questions that you would not have had to ask because you knew what was expected of you. I thought he was very severe with me, but I was glad that he had given me what I thought was his honest feedback. He told me he would see me or call me on Monday, and I told him that I would work on a title for his film. The whole time that Lermentov was there, the telephone man was working away. I began to wonder what he thought about the situation, but he seemed too busy for me to ask him.

I started to work on the notes for you, and Riff called to say that he would call Saturday to see if I could take a walk through the Village with him so that he could show me some of his world. As soon as Riff hung up, Henry Blanck called and asked me if I would like to come over and visit. He sounded pleasant on the phone, and since he lived nearby, I told him that I could come over for a little while but that then I had some notes to type.

Before I left, I called Phil Barnett and asked him whether or not he had intended a seduction. He said that wasn't exactly what he had said to you. He said that he told you he wanted things left open so that he might sleep with me even though he does not sleep with you. I made an appointment to see him the next day at two. He said, "If I come over, we're going to fuck, aren't we?" I just laughed and thought to myself—well, here's an honest one at least.

I walked over to Henry Blanck's and we immediately got high. I looked him up in your notes to me while I was there and found the following: "Henry Blanck. Crazy writer friend. Talk about him in journals. A swinger—often calls to ask me if I want to go to an "org"; once I did. Might again in the right mood. I like him a lot. Also like his girl friend Celia, with whom he's sort of splitting— they're doing a book together, which I helped arrange."

I asked him how often he called me to go to an "org," and he said that the one time I had been to an "org" was with Mike and that we had both seemed rather uptight and left fairly soon. The way you described the situation, it sounded to me as if he was in the habit of calling you to ask you to go to swing with him; but his version of your interaction with him sounded as if you asked him about an orgy that you could go to with Mike. I wondered about this discrepancy in facts and also wondered whether or not you had actually gone to bed with him. From your description, it sounded like you had, but from his description, it sounded like he wasn't that interested in you sexually. I decided it would be impolite to ask him how many times we had been to bed together, since as Nancy I should know that information.

While we were talking, Celia came home from a shopping trip and seemed in a very manic mood. She was very mad at him and kept taking little verbal swipes at him, and he seemed really oblivious to her sarcasm and her anger. He had just bought a fish tank and had put some fish in it and was asking our advice on the decor of a fish tank. He placed a plastic cube in the tank and asked our opinion. We both thought it looked good. Celia got high too and decided to model the clothing she had just bought. We were standing in the kitchen area and she was undressing in the bedroom, but we could both see her undressing. I thought it was really nice that she did not feel uptight about undressing in front of a stranger and that it was too bad that things were going so badly for them because she really was nice and very beautiful. She sang me a song/poem that she had just written in the country. One of the lines had something to do with a time warp/space warp, and I thought that it was exactly what I was going through in the life swap—a time warp/space warp.

Celia was going shopping uptown and I really wanted to go with her, but she was meeting a friend and so I decided that it was not appropriate for me to tag along. I realized that one of the reasons that I wanted to be near Celia was that I missed talking to women, that since I had become you I had not talked to any women. Usually my life is full of talking and spending time with women or with gay men. I felt very alone and alienated in the land of the unabashed male heterosexual. Henry was going to walk Killer, his marvelously gentle ladylike Dalmatian. The thought of his calling his dog Killer really broke me up. I liked him a lot, even if he seemed very out of touch with his feelings about Celia. I mean it seemed strange that here they were ending a love affair and he was doing crazy things with a fish tank.

We walked through Washington Square, and Henry and Killer had many encounters with other dogs and dog owners. Killer is a wonderful dog. I have not had that many relationships with dogs in my life and I must say that Killer really left an impression on me. I can remember once having a dachshund named Harry who was very neurotic. One time my first husband wanted to mate Harry and so he advertised him for stud in the appropriate place in *The New York Times*. We received many strange telephone calls after this ad was placed, and I began to think that people thought we were advertising something else because they seemed surprised when they found out there was a dog involved. We finally did get a straight response. A woman wanted to mate Harry with her dog, Buttercup. We took Harry over to meet Buttercup, who was fat and obnoxious, and she took an immediate dislike to him. She would not let him mount her. We had to take Harry and Buttercup to the woman's vet who masturbated Harry and then artificially inseminated Buttercup. The whole business was very messy and humiliating for my first husband who seemed to be ego-involved with Harry's prowess as a stud. It exhausted poor Harry and probably made him more neurotic. It couldn't have given him a good feeling about sex. Anyway, I just thought I'd include the story about Harry and Buttercup so that you would know my experience with dogs has not been that great. Killer, however, definitely is a dog with a soul.

Henry walked me back to your apartment and came in with me. I had decided to make a pit stop in the apartment to get myself together, make a shopping list, make some phone calls, and decide whether I had time to go uptown and pick up a tape recorder. I called the answering service. Susie had called. I made a note to call her the next day. Henry Blanck asked me how things had been going in your life. I told him about Reggie the exterminator and described Reggie's behavior in your apartment. Henry said that a great pornographic script could be written about the exterminator and the middle-class housewife. The story line went something like this: The exterminator arrives and says, "All right lady, where are they?" She looks at him, he looks at her, he drops his spray can and they tumble into bed. I said we could call it *Deep Squirt.* I really liked Henry Blanck and was having a good time with him. He began to run his fingers up my back and at the same time make a strange buzzing sound. I said what is that. He said it's a new oriental technique he learned. I said, what is it called, the vibra-finger?

At this point George Warneke called and I made an appointment to see him on Friday at eleven o'clock to discuss the tantric sex book that you are both working on. I also told him that the information he had given me about the person to call at Black Star was the wrong information and that I would have to work on it the next day. The whole time I was talking to George, Henry was vibra-fingering my back, so that I was having a very hard time talking to George without laughing. George asked me what was going on and I told him Henry Blanck was there. George asked if Henry was presuming. I asked Henry if he was presuming. He said no. I told George no, he's just using the vibra-finger on me. I can imagine the image that George had in his mind about what was going on in your apartment, especially since he is a friend of Henry's and knows what a cutup Henry is and what a rake. I said goodbye to George because by that time, left to his own devices, Henry Blanck was "presuming." So, based on the assumption that you wouldn't mind his presuming and that he made me laugh, I let him presume, giggling hysterically all the time. He made some comment about having a giggler on his hands, which made me laugh all the more. The sex was ridiculous since it lasted exactly five minutes and we both had to keep appointments somewhere else. The whole time Henry was presuming, Killer was sucking on my toes.

We said goodbye and made arrangements to meet in front of the movie on Eighth Street that was showing *Memoirs of an Under-developed Nation* for the last show, and I called Abbe to tell him

I was going to be a bit late; and he said that I was right on time for you, since you are always about fifteen minutes late to your dinner appointments with him. I walked up to your florist to buy Abbe flowers, but they were closed, so I walked across the street to another florist and bought him five dollars worth of beautiful purple peonies because I decided that from what I knew of Abbe, peonies were appropriate. Don't ask me how I made this decision or came to this conclusion. It just seemed right. And in the light of later events, it turned out to be totally correct.

I took a cab up to Abbe's and looked him up in the cue notes. You had written: "Abbe Gershon. You know about him from the journals—will know more Wednesday night. We have had a lot of electricity between us, but for reasons I don't quite understand (because we're very fond of each other, and he's quite ardent), we've never been lovers, though I think will be, starting—? Violinist—I'm dying to hear him do the Tchaikovsky all the way through." I wondered what the evening was going to be like and was happy that I had somewhere else safe to be at 10:30.

Abbe opened the door and immediately French-kissed me in an extremely awkward way. I knew by the kiss that he was not ardent and that he had not had much experience kissing women. I was a little taken aback by his behavior, but when I saw what he was making for dinner—a beautiful risotto—I liked him tremendously. I also knew I had nothing to fear because Abbe was a very kind, sensitive, and shy person. I laughed to myself about your notes on him and how far from the reality of Abbe they seemed. I gave him the flowers and arranged them for him in two vases.

We sat down and had white wine. I realized that at the pace we were proceeding with dinner, there was no way I was going to be able to make a 10:30 movie with Henry Blanck and Celia. And that, in all fairness to Abbe's company and cooking, I couldn't leave that early. I then proceeded to try to phone Henry Blanck, but you had left out one of the numbers in his phone number, and when I called Information, I was told he had an unlisted number. I tried to figure out what the missing number might be, but after a few misses and a few strange conversations with the people at the other numbers, I decided that there were seven factorial possible combinations and that it would take me all night to try to hit on the right number using that method, so I gave up and called the movie house and persuaded them to take a message. I figured that if I weren't there on time it would be logical for Henry and Celia to ask the movie house if there was a message for them.

We drank a great deal of white wine and spent a lot of time talking. Talking was a bit awkward because, although Abbe and the real me have a great deal in common since we both grew up in foreign countries, you and Abbe don't have that in common, so it seemed illegitimate to talk about that. I really felt very frustrated by the ground rules you had laid down.

After dinner and much more wine, we moved into the bedroom. I don't know if either one of us wanted to move into the bedroom but we thought you expected it of us, since you had written, "We've never been lovers, though I think will be, starting—?" We made a very unsuccessful attempt at making love. Both of us felt very awkward. I felt very angry at you and at myself for getting myself in this situation, and I began to cry. I think I cried out of exhaustion and the feeling I had that I had been sexually used for the fourth time in a three-day period. I kept finding myself in bed with these men whom I wasn't particularly sexually turned on to because of what I thought would have been your behavior under the circumstances and because of the implicit messages in the things you wrote in your descriptions of people. I felt like a whore and I felt very paranoid. So far, none of your descriptions fit the reality that I saw, and I didn't know whether the descriptions fit an actual reality that you experienced or whether you had purposefully manipulated circumstances by writing the way you did, or whether you and I really see people in a very different way or whether people behave very differently when they are with you compared to the way they behave when they are with me, or all of the above, or none of the above.

I stopped crying because I didn't want Abbe's feelings to be hurt. I decided that he had been through enough humiliation just attempting to make love to me and that I didn't want to make it any worse for him. I asked him how it was that he had been able to go to bed with me when he had never been able to go to bed with you. He said it was because I was a bisexual and he was a bisexual and that you thought you would like to be bisexual but hadn't really come to grips with this feeling and that he felt more comfortable with me because he thought I had my bisexuality worked out in my head. I don't know how he came to this conclusion, but I assumed that you had given him information about me and that he had made assumptions based on your descriptions of me. His assumptions were not far from the truth. I decided that I had better find out what he meant by bisexual since everything in your life so far had not turned out to be what it was advertised as. I asked him if, when he said he was bisexual, that meant he was into men and women sexually. He said, "Oh, no, I'm not into men sexually. I like women. When I say I'm bisexual, I mean I'm a lesbian." I started to laugh, for this was the first time I had been in bed with a male lesbian! No wonder we had trouble.

We talked a bit more, and I said good night and went home and had hysterics. I decided that if I didn't call somebody real, immediately, I wouldn't be able to go on with your life. I couldn't call Peter, since you were in bed with him (or so I thought) and I didn't want you to know I was cheating on you. I couldn't call Ben since he was in Buffalo and it would upset him to know I was so hysterical, so I called Ted Holzman. Ted talked to me awhile and then said that it was too bad that because of the rules of the game he couldn't see me. I said fuck the rules of the game. I really need to spend some time with someone who knows me and likes the real me and I don't want to be alone in this apartment tonight. The Münter was beginning to give me the willies and I felt all the paintings closing in on me. So Ted came down and talked to me half the night and held me close, and I was able to sleep a couple of hours.

Thursday, June 14

I woke up at nine o'clock next to Ted with the phone ringing. It was Nicky. He called to give me the train information (2:10 to Hartford—must change in New Haven), and then he called again to remind me to bring a bathing suit (he told me which one—white bikini with red polka dots—and where to find it) and tennis shoes. He also told me we were having dinner with your parents so I should bring something to wear to dinner, and I should bring the Scrabble set, and did I play backgammon because we might be playing backgammon. I said no to this last query but said I could probably learn to play backgammon.

I didn't want to wake Ted up, so I went into the bathroom to shower and make phone calls on the new phone that the telephone person had just installed. Fully conscious of the fact that

I was increasing the chances of electrocution. I had a terrible headache and felt guilty as hell about Ted being there. I looked at my body. I had blemishes all over my face and big bruises on my legs. I had no idea when or where I had gotten the bruises. I called and made an appointment with your dermatologist Dr. Verde for Monday and asked the nurse to tell Fran Berman, whom I knew had an appointment with Verde that day, that I could not meet her as I had planned because I had to go to Hartford and that I would call her when I got back to town. I tried calling Irma at Black Star for the book you are writing with George Warneke. Irma wasn't in. Totally frustrated, I called your agent and told her about all the trouble I was having and my feelings about George and asked her how I should proceed. She was great. She told me not to worry about it; she would call Macmillan to find out what was available, that after all one had an agent to do this kind of thing and I had enough to worry about without this particular item. I thanked her profusely. If she had been present I would have kissed her. I called Phil Barnett to cancel our two o'clock appointment. There was no answer.

I found Henry Blanck's number in your other address book and apologized for not showing up. He said they hadn't waited very long, figuring that dinner had probably taken me longer than I had expected. It didn't occur to him that I might leave a message with the ticket seller. I told him about the Hartford trip and that I would be in touch on my return. I called Donna, Arno Karlen's secretary, and when she wasn't there, left a message for her to send the galleys of the Donleavy article to you.

I called the answering service and left messages for Mike, Phil Barnett, and Magda. Then Phil called and I told him that I was off to Hartford and couldn't keep our appointment and that I would get in touch with him when I came back. I then realized that I had just spent two and a half hours in your bathroom, crouched in the same position, and that my whole body was aching. I showered, woke Ted up, packed a bag to take to Hartford, made a note to myself to ask Mike who all the people at Sardi's were so that I could write about them in these journals, made a note to go shopping, buy flowers, take the clothing you left for me to the cleaners, and take the dirty laundry that you left to the Chinese laundry. I then put your birth-control pills in an envelope and addressed it to myself at Hawthorne. I had received this letter from you on Wednesday asking for your pills. I laughed at the part about how easy my work was. I guess you didn't realize all I had left you to do were the remnants of my work. School had ended for the students with graduation, and I had taken care of business before leaving.

Ted was ready to go by then, so we left. I stopped at the mailboxes and found the check that my agent had sent me and a letter from Robert Rimmer.

```
Dear Nancy:

What a delight to have your invitation.

I presume that if I visited the Village and
announced myself Micki would go to bed with me!
I'm really chuckling. You have a wonderful plot
for a novel and if you don't write it I will
spank your bare bottom. I'm delighted that you're
alive, kicking and still wondrous!

Cordially,

Bob
```

I made a mental note to answer the letter as soon as I had time. Ted and I had breakfast at Sutter's. I ordered quite a bit but could only manage to drink bouillon. I taxied to Penn Station in time to catch the 2:10 to Hartford.

On the train I tried to put some of my notes together and to get rid of the many little pieces of paper I had floating around in your purse. I wrote the following notes to myself about things I wanted to write about or think about at some later date (they give you some idea of how manic I was at this point): *Knots!* Peter's relationship to me as his mother. Guilt and what it does to you. Things

I want to write about: peyote, Peter's insensitivity and the difficulty of the Peter thing–Micki thing. What really happened after I left Abbe's. What happens in an open relationship. How difficult it is to get rid of old baggage (programs). The bargaining over my percentage of the book. Why I didn't use my real name. Trig. Riff. Nicky. Why I love Nancy Weber. What's fucked up about her life style. Why I keep wanting to go home. Why I needed, wanted, loved Ted. Why I don't trust weak men and women. Ben Rothenberg. Henry Blanck's and Celia's interaction. Call Mary Westergaard. Phil Barnett. Abbe, the lesbian. The life of a sex object. What it is like to be a cunt. Letters I have to/want to write: Aaron Tyman, Ben Rothenberg, Ben's sister Eve, Nancy Weber, my parents (the truth), Steffie Kahn, Pat Barry, Jack Barleycorn, Cassie Davidson, Trigger Mike. Why I like faggots. How I miss Danny. What Yuric Lermentov's feedback was and what it made me feel. Why I miss women. Machismo among writers. Why I cried at Abbe's. How I like wearing a watch. How a nonlinear person can be compulsive and organized. The switchboard of my brain. How and why Nancy lied. Projections, rejections, subjections, oppressions. Lies of omission and commission. I want to get back to my life! You can't get there from here. Books that have helped me. Reading lists for young men and women. How to be a sexual person. What's wrong? right? with swinging? Why there are some things I can't let go by. Abbe's cooking. Aaron's creative stock analysis. The script about the exterminator for a porno film, *Deep Squirt*. Henry's vibra-finger technique and far-out dope. The silliness of all this. Mike Kagan's strength, sensitivity, insensitivity, weakness, loneliness, pathos, bathos, alcoholism. Doc at Frankie and Johnnie's. The boys in the bar, Sardi's. George Warneke is a fake yadayadayada! Debbie Levitas. Anne Upton. Reggie the exterminator. The telephone man. *Willy and the Doll.* Fatness/thinness/body image/yoga/meditation. How I despise Shalimar. How Aaron despises Shalimar. Killer, the only dog I ever wanted to sleep with/Sex for the Technological Society. My life as a movie. All the stories to tell Danny and Ben and Ted and Peter? Descriptions of everyone! The train to Hartford. The shaving of body hair. *Growing Up Absurd.* Why Nancy doesn't use the last names of women!? (Donna? Celia?) The Audrey (Lion's Head) story (check with T.M.). The difficulty of being someone else. The difficulties of doing anything! The man with the green bodyshirt and dark glasses on the train to New Haven.

At this point I looked up and realized that people were staring at me, especially the man in the green bodyshirt, with the dark glasses, sitting next to me. He asked me if I was a writer. I said sort of. Are you keeping a diary? Sort of. He then offered me a Clark bar which I put away to give to Nicky. He had found the Clark bar in a paper bag left behind by some other passenger. I decided that a found Clark bar was the best kind of Clark bar and the only kind of Clark bar to give to Nicky. I asked him if I could borrow his newspaper. He gave it to me. I saw a very strange picture of Nixon which I cut out and decorated with the following: "This is what happens to you when you indulge in self-abuse and take too much Ex-Lax, relax, sexlax." I found a few other things in the paper to take to Nicky and I circled letters in the newspaper spelling out a message to Nicky. He may still have these items or he may have decided that I was/am totally crazy and thrown them away. For some reason I wanted to take Nicky presents and the pennies that I had found and was taking him just weren't enough and just weren't me.

I started worrying about what dinner with your parents would be like and whether Nicky would like me. The train from New Haven to Hartford was late, and Nicky was waiting at the station. He looked much younger than he appears in the picture on the back of your bathroom door. I liked him immediately. We went for a ride through Hartford, with his showing me all the sights I should be familiar with. (I have actually been to Hartford before and seen some of those sights.) Then we went to the country club and got a quick swim in before they closed the pool. He introduced me to someone he knew, not as Nancy Weber, but some other crazy name which made me laugh. I can't remember now what it was. I didn't keep my journals while swimming.

We then drove to your parents' house. The rambling roses were in bloom and looked beautiful. The house looked wonderful with all the paintings everywhere. Your parents are beautiful. I wondered to myself if being the plainest in a family of beautiful people didn't have something to do with your sex-object compulsion. Your parents commented on your clothing on me. Your mother had not seen you in the white dress with polka dots, and she thought it looked well on me. The scene was pleasant but awkward. I fell madly in love with your mother. She reminded me of my mother. Strong, athletic, articulate, sarcastic, a hard crust—but very tender and too sensitive on the inside. Her eyes were very intense and beautiful. Your father reminded me of my father, except that my father is not and never has been athletic. Your father is handsome, charming, a bit silly at times, very generous, not at ease with heavy topics of conversation, somewhat uneasy with emotional states, has trouble showing his feelings, very polite. I liked both of your parents very much and was rather irritated at what you might be putting them through to write a book. Nicky had mentioned that you always ask your mother for a pair of panty hose and some Shalimar. I didn't need any panty hose but I asked her for the Shalimar. Her reaction was predictable and I felt angry at myself for playing that game with her. We all sat around for a few minutes playing the game you had choreographed for us and feeling foolish. I admired your mother's art work and the Picasso stuff. I saw your room and Nicky's room. Your parents seemed pleased that I was wearing the jewelry that they had given you. And I knew then why you are such a fascist about your jewelry and about the Shalimar. Those tokens are the things that keep you connected to something real—to real people who love you and who know enough about you to not let you play games with them. Except that you do play games with them. They have no idea what your life is really like in New York City.

We went to dinner at their favorite restaurant. We had veal Holstein and the special potatoes they make. And crab fingers. I spilled some of the sauce on the dress and Nicky helped wipe it off and said that was a typical Nancy thing to do (it's not a typical Micki thing to do). Your father kept asking me questions about my life which I would answer as if I were Nancy talking about Micki's life. A really schizophrenic conversation to keep going. Then he would tell me I wasn't eating fast enough. I had a brandy after dinner. Your mother said that your father was getting restless and that we should go home soon. I said that I didn't know why Daddy should decide when we all should go home if some of us weren't finished yet. I realized that that was a rude thing to say and your father got a bit uptight about my saying it. Then we had a slight conversation about women's liberation. At some point, your mother corrected my grammar (my mother likes doing that too). It seems I made the heinous mistake of saying that Micki had just finished helping her students graduate, which we all know is the wrong usage of the word, but everyone uses it anyhow. I guess the visit was going well in that your parents were able to be sarcastic toward me and show anger at my comment about why did your father have to decide when we left the table. I came close to tears when I tried to explain that it took me so long to eat because he kept asking me questions that I had to respond to and I had been taught not to talk with my mouth full. At some point I really felt sorry for myself. I was tired and had already been through so much and I had to keep on with the ridiculous game. We went back to their house and then Nicky and I drove to Granby. It was a beautiful drive, and I was glad to be away from your parents' scrutiny and alone with Nicky.

There was a full moon and Nicky's place looked beautiful. We stood out in the yard listening to the brook and looking at the moon for a little while. Then I helped Nicky find the appropriate place in the living room for his new piece of sculpture. I'm afraid I was a bit too honest with Nicky about what my week had been like. I really trusted him and I treated him the way I would treat a brother whom I was close to. I made some comment about the men in your life taking advantage of the situation and using me sexually. I also said something about the fact that I hadn't seen a normal-sized cock all week, which I admit was a sexist thing to say, but it was true; the men I had slept with in your life all had less than average-sized penises. There was even an undescended testis. Now I don't particularly care about the size of a cock; it is the quality of the lovemaking (the versatility of the tongue) and not the quantity that counts for me. Unfortunately, the quality had not been very good either because I did not know the men well enough to trust them sexually, and without trust, sex is no good for me. Nicky made some embarrassed comment like, "That's a fine thing to say to a brother," and I realized that it was very insensitive of me to mention cock size to my "brother."

I stopped talking about things sexual and horrible and began to talk to Nicky about Nicky and what kinds of things he was interested in and what you were like growing up. We got ready for bed and cuddled a bit. The situation was too funny or too potentially threatening for Nick (and besides, he really wouldn't fuck his own sister) for anything much to come of it. We talked almost the entire night. We also played with ice cubes and his hair dryer and decided that that could be a new sexual experience that Johnson and Johnson could package and merchandise: cold wet sensations combined with warm air. I had a good time, even though I was exhausted.

Friday, June 15

After about two hours' sleep, we got up very early, had a breakfast which consisted of blueberries and ginseng tea, and he drove me to the bus station. On the way I thought of the experience of being with your parents, of being very tired, of memories of my own childhood, of your unreal life style and the things you put yourself through to be an attractive sex object: eyelash dyeing, pubic hair waxing, ridiculous unhealthy shoes, cortisone for blemishes, great attention to the surface and structure of things and not the meaning behind that surface and structure. I felt as if your life was just one fantasy after another. No close friends, no real love relationships, no intimacy other than superficial and contrived sex, no substance. The things you seemed to care about seem so shallow and meaningless. I felt sorry for you and sorry that I still had too much time left to play the part of Nancy. Your family seemed to be the only reality you still cling to. I guess Mike is sort of real in that he's been in your life a long time, but I think you delude yourself about him and sell yourself short. Mike is no way going to give up his professional restlessness to marry you or even live with you. Face it, you're Mike's piece, the booster of his male ego, the proof of his mach-studhood, which is why he always wants to be seen with you at places and have you page him all over hell's half acre instead of spending time alone with you in your apartment or somewhere else.

The best way I can describe what I felt about you at this point is to quote Erica Jong's poem "Alcestis on the Poetry Circuit" in *Half Lives:*

> The best slave
> does not need to be beaten.
> She beats herself.
>
> Not with a leather whip,
> or with sticks or twigs,
> not with a blackjack
> or a billyclub,
> but with the fine whip
> of her own tongue
> & the subtle beating
> of her mind
> against her mind.

For who can hate her half so well
as she hates herself?
& who can match the finesse
of her self-abuse?

Years of training
are required for this.
Twenty years
of subtle self-indulgence,
self-denial;
until the subject
thinks herself a queen
& yet a beggar—
both at the same time.
She must doubt herself
in everything but love.

She must choose passionately
& badly.
She must feel lost as a dog
without her master.
She must refer all moral questions
to her mirror.
She must fall in love with a cossack
or a poet.

She must never go out of the house
unless veiled in paint.
She must wear tight shoes
so she always remembers her bondage.
She must never forget
she is rooted in the ground.

Though she is quick to learn
& admittedly clever,
her natural doubt of herself
should make her so weak
that she dabbles brilliantly
in half a dozen talents
& thus embellishes
but does not change
our life.

If she's an artist
& comes close to genius,

the very fact of her gift
should cause her such pain
that she will take her own life
rather than best us.

& after she dies, we will cry
& make her a saint.

Thinking about all that had happened made me cry all the way to the bus station which was probably boring for Nicky. I tried to explain to him some of what I was feeling, but I don't think I managed to convey very much and I probably upset him because some of my feelings were negative feelings toward you or at least your life and Nicky is very loyal to you and loves you very much. He left me at the bus station and hurried off to work.

On the bus trip home from Hartford I worked like a fiend, writing notes, crying, writing a postcard to your parents for their anniversary, writing a postcard to my father and Ben's father for Father's Day, writing down all the names of the people in my life that I still hadn't given to you and writing short descriptions of them so that you would be prepared for next week. I felt very guilty about not having gotten you this information ahead of time and all week I tried to find the time to complete it but just couldn't find it because of the damn telephone. It is probably just as well that you didn't have all kinds of information because you were probably less biased by what I said about people and were more able to form your own opinions of them. I had to work my way through your editorialized descriptions of people and read oodles of material when I could have been doing some of your writing.

When I arrived at the Port Authority, I called Carla at Hawthorne to try to arrange some way of getting the notes to you and also to ask you to remind Ben to call his father for Father's Day on Sunday. I also needed the name of your banker, which I knew was in your notes to me but in my frenzy I couldn't find. You weren't in, and so I called the apartment to give Danny a message to give to you about the notes. Then I called the answering service to find out who had called and leave a message for George Warneke that I was on my way but would be a little late because I had to stop at the bank to cash the check so that I would have some more money to be you. Your father had cashed a check for twenty dollars, but I knew that wasn't going to go very far.

I found out from the service that Arno Karlen's office had called to say that they did not have galleys for the Donleavy piece yet. Mike had called, and George Warneke was arriving at the apartment at 11:30. In a rush I taxied to the bank, met Terry Verona, your banker, who cashed the check for me even though it was from another bank. I was incredibly paranoid walking out of the bank with $450 in the pockets of my jeans and knowing that I had to pass the cutthroat corner of Sixth Avenue and Eighth Street. I made it safely to your apartment, picked up the mail, and called the answering service again. Carla had called me and George from *Gentlemen's Quarterly* had called. As soon as I hung up, the phone rang and the bell rang at the same time. I answered the phone and told the man on the other end of it that I was putting him on hold so that I could answer the door. George Warneke had arrived and I forgot about the phone call on hold. When George had been there ten minutes the phone rang and it was Peter calling me from the office. He informed me that I had just put him on hold for ten minutes and forgotten him. I felt terrible, not only because I hadn't recognized Peter's voice, but also that I had put him on hold, and also (and at this moment worst of all) that I couldn't talk to him while George was there because I did not want George or anyone to know that I had dared to talk to someone from my own life while I was supposed to be you. I was still feeling guilty about Ted.

I had a short conversation with Peter and told him that I would call him later. Who is it, George wanted to know. A friend of mine, I say. A friend of yours or of Nancy's, he asks. A friend of Nancy's, I say. He said something that made me realize that he was very suspicious because I suppose I was too friendly and uptight while talking to Peter. I was prepared to dislike George Warneke because of everything I had gone through in trying to get information for him earlier in the week and because of the way he talked to me on the phone when he was with a patient. We sort of sparred for a while to see who was going to control the situation.

Finally I decided to level with him about the way I was feeling and fuck the way I should have been acting if I were you. Telling everything I felt really cleared the air and I was surprised that he responded in a very human un-uptight way. I told him about the trouble that I had been having and suggested that we get to work. He told me that generally your interactions consist of not much work getting done, but of a lot of sitting around and just talking. So we just talked. He asked me what you were like and what I thought your interactions with him were like and I showed him what I knew about him and told him that I knew that you liked him but did not have a sexual relationship with him. We talked about Henry Blanck and his relationship with Celia for a while and about Aaron. I told him I was really very manic and feeling very frenzied and chaotic in your life. He said that it sounded to him that I had a bad case of sexual indigestion and not enough sleep. I agreed. I told him that I still had to get some work done on the notes so that I could give them to you before you went to Riverset and met the Princeton crowd that weekend. We smoked a joint, and he tried to persuade me to play hooky and go to the movies with him. I loved him for that but was feeling too compulsive about the notes and my responsibility to you to be able to go and so I had to turn the attractive offer down. We discussed his relationship with Kylie for a while, and then he left asking me to tell Kylie if she called that he would be at Henry Blanck's later and told me to stop by there if I wanted to. I said I might do that or might have to go to sleep because I was really exhausted.

You called and said that you would come over and get the notes. I worked on them some more, and you arrived. You appeared more animated than I had ever seen you. I thought to myself that my life must be getting to you. I told you some of the things that happened to me, Mike, Aaron, Abbe, Nicky and told you that I was disturbed by some of what had happened. I also said that some of the people in your life really didn't know who you are. You said that there were some surprises for me in my life and that you had not gotten along very well with Cassie Davidson. I think you conveyed to me the idea that Cassie did not like me and that Peter was very aggressive. I thought to myself, What can be happening for her to think Peter, who is one of the most gentle and loving people I know, is aggressive. Your account of your interaction with Cassie did not lead me to believe Cassie didn't like me but that she liked me enough not to want to play any silly games with you.

You took a shower and while you were showering, Mike called and I told him that I wasn't going out with him that evening because I really needed to sleep for at least eighteen hours straight. I must have said something that led him to believe I had seen you or talked to you. He became very suspicious and asked me if I had seen you. I lied and said no because I didn't know whether or not you wanted to talk to him and I wanted to check that out with you first but I couldn't tell him that. There was a very pregnant pause and Mike became very paranoid. I said again that I really couldn't talk now and that I needed to rest. I was losing my voice and it must have sounded manic and at least a few decibels higher than its usual squeak. He said that I sounded upset and that he would talk to me later.

We went to O. Henry's and had iced coffee and I verbally communicated to you all the information that I hadn't given you on the note cards and gave you the note cards. I also explained who you might be running into that weekend and what their relationship was to me. The rest of the people at O. Henry's were staring at us, probably because of the topic of our conversation, all the little pieces of paper I kept handing you, and the speed with which I was talking. You came back to your apartment, took my address books and called Ben to tell him you'd be late. Finally you left.

There was silence for exactly ten minutes and I remembered that I had promised to call Peter back before five and it was now 6:30. I called him at the apartment and apologized for not calling him before. He said he wanted to see me and that he was coming over. I felt guilty about it but I really wanted to see him, so I agreed. I hung up the phone and tried to do a shoulder stand to relax. I was feeling awful. More bruises were showing and my head felt very hot. You called up from the New Jersey Turnpike to tell me I was terrific and that I was doing a good job and to have a good time. I thought that was very kind of you, but it made me feel even more guilty because I was cheating.

The doorbell rang and it was Kylie with Stephanie. She had been carting Stephanie all over Manhattan looking for George. I gave her George's message and offered her some Perrier water with a lime in it. She was like a cool breath of fresh air. There was something so calming about her. I explained that I was very glad to meet her, that I had heard she was very beautiful and that Stephanie was a beautiful baby. She breast-fed Stephanie, which was nice, and she changed Stephanie with my assistance. I told her that I hoped I would see her another time when I wasn't so crazy and feeling so hassled. I also told her that my lover was coming over and please not to tell you. I think she was confused by me but she took everything very much in stride. We discussed what it was like being a foreigner in the United States and whether or not she was jealous of George's relationship to you. She said no, that she wasn't jealous of you because she knew George loved her and that, besides, he didn't have a sexual relationship with you which might make her jealous. She asked if I was jealous of you spending time with Ben and Peter. I said no, because both of them loved me and I knew it and felt secure in their love. George called and Kylie made arrangements to meet him at Henry Blanck's in forty-five minutes.

Peter arrived, and I introduced him to Kylie. She left shortly thereafter. I was really glad to see Peter and wanted to make love to him immediately, but he said he was too hungry to make love. So we went to Mother Courage and I ran into some feminist friends and told people that I was playing hooky from your life. It felt so good to be back among my people. At the restaurant Peter told me what it had been like the first night he met you and how you came in the door, said "Hi, lover," and within ten minutes you were in bed with one another and how unusual that was because whenever he and I see each other at the end of the day, I ask him how his day was, tell him how my day was, hug him, touch him, kiss him, and about two hours later, go to bed and make love. He told me of your telling him to be gentle with you because you were a little sensitive down there and when he asked what was wrong you told him that you had been taking antibiotics and that your flora and fauna were unbalanced but that with the cream everything would be all right. He asked me what I supposed you meant by saying something was wrong with your flora and fauna. I said, Oh shit, she probably has monilia or trich because the damn antibiotics upset your vaginal balance and now you probably have it too and I'm going to get it. Peter said he didn't want to talk about it at dinner, so I shut up about that.

We came home and he said he was very tired. I needed to talk and kept talking and talking until finally he said that he couldn't listen anymore. I felt very rejected and felt that he was tired from making love to you and to Wendy who he had been seeing that week and that he had no love left for me. I decided to let it go and I rubbed his back and he went to sleep. I couldn't sleep. All night, fantasies and images kept running through my mind. I felt very guilty about Peter being there and thought that the only solution was to call T.M.'s sister and explain to her what the situation was and ask her to please call you and tell you that I was going crazy. The fact that I thought that was a solution will tell you how insane I was. Mike called two or three times to ask if I was sleeping. I told him that I was and hung up. The last time he said, "Are you sleeping? I'm at the Lion's Head," hinting broadly that he would like to come over. I said I was asleep and hung up and thought to myself, What a pig! He must know that this has been an exhausting week and here he wants to come over and fuck me some more. What an insensitive asshole. Peter kept talking in his sleep, saying, "It wasn't that difficult for me. I just had to be myself." I finally said, "It's all right, Peter," and he stopped talking.

I felt feverish. I began to think in images. Peter and I had discussed the book *Scented Garden for the Blind* when he saw a copy of it in your apartment and said that you and he had discussed the scented garden for the blind in the Brooklyn Botanic Gardens where he had been with Wendy. I thought to myself that it was interesting how everything seemed to come together and make sense. And that the book was a clue to how I should communicate to you since you didn't seem to understand the way I talked or how I thought; that since you were a writer and dealt in images I should tell you how I felt by describing the situation in images. The image that came to mind was the picture of Dorian Gray. I felt like the picture of Dorian Gray. All the evil in your life and in your apartment was flowing into my body and that's why I was having migraine headaches and had bruises all over and was breaking out in pimples. I thought about your telling me that afternoon that the way you dealt with Mike was by lying to him and thought that you should have written that into the script or program you fed to my computer because then I would not have put up with as much of Mike as I did.

I started to go over in my mind all the distortion and discrepancies between the way you described your life and my perception of it. How everything seemed like such a fantasy. How you had no friends. I worried about how I would tell you that I had cheated and decided that I would tell you that I just had to be me in your life so that I could do some of the work that you had left me to do, that I couldn't be you and see any more people because it didn't give me enough time to write. I thought about the fact that when you described your sexual interactions with people, you told me what you did to them and what they liked but that you had given me no information about what you liked. I had no idea of what turned you on or what you liked or whether you were orgasmic, except that in your journals you do mention lovely love-making, so that I assumed you were orgasmic and you did like sex. I thought that I had regressed to the age of seventeen, when I couldn't say no to men, and I lied about enjoying their lovemaking because I thought I had no rights of my own. I felt like a whore who had gotten herself into this for money but not even enough money to make it to call-girl status. I thought about Szasz's concepts of the psychology of helplessness and how helpless and insecure I had felt at Sardi's. I also thought of Szasz's concept of the to-lose-is-to-win strategy of game playing and thought that was the game you were playing. Everyone who used you and abused you, you were attracted to. The worse they were to you, the better you liked them. I thought of your having intercourse with Peter, which must have been painful for you if your vagina was sore from the imbalance of your "flora and fauna" (what a prude you are way down deep) and also because his cock is very large. Your maso-chism began to make me sick to my stomach, and then I thought of my own masochistic behavior and how I had gone to bed with men I wasn't attracted to, not told them what I wanted. I thought again of your calling Peter aggressive and got angry at your calling him that and at your lying to him about your own sexual pleasure. I hate women or men who lie in bed. It is such a destructive, unproductive thing to do. I hate the fact that you lied to Peter. That you didn't understand the least thing about being me if you didn't realize that I don't lie or try not to if I can help it and know that that is what I am doing. I thought about how you had lied to me with your editorialized version of the people in your life.

Saturday, June 16

Finally, it was morning. I went into the bathroom and called the answering service and found out that Riff had called. I called you in Riverset and told you that I was really going crazy and that I wanted to be me for a while. You told me that was fine. I said, "But that's breaking the rules." And you said you always break rules, you like breaking rules. I thought to myself that it was something else you should have told me from the get because it is an impor-tant difference in our personalities.

Riff called and we talked from 10:30 to 12:00. I was still sitting in the bathroom because I didn't want to disturb Peter. We had a very chaotic conversation, mostly about Mike. I made arrangements to meet Riff Sunday at two after my breakfast appointment with Susie and her husband at the Lion's Head, which I had made earlier in the week.

By this time Peter was awake and we decided to go have breakfast. Before we left, Jeff Bailey called collect, and I accepted the call. I told him that if he was calling me to lay me, he should forget it, but that if he wanted to see me as Micki and not as Nancy, I would talk to him. He laughed nervously and said that he would like to see me as Micki to talk and that he was on his way to NYC and would stop by. I told him that Peter and I were going out to have brunch and he could join us for that, but that then I wanted to spend the day getting a tape recorder and talking to Peter, so that I couldn't spend much time with him. He arrived shortly, and I thought he was very attractive and certainly not at all the way you had described him in the notes. I also felt mad that you hadn't written in the notes where I would see it immediately that he had written two stories, one of which had to do with his daughter Sally and was directly related to the socialization of women, which I would be interested in. I later looked in the journals you had written me and realized that you had mentioned them there. He had brought a joint with him and we smoked it and went to eat at Sutter's. Then he left and Peter and I discussed what we might do for the rest of the day.

I decided that I didn't really want to go uptown to buy a tape recorder so we returned to the apartment to make love. But somehow we got into a terrible fight about Wendy and his not being able to listen to me the night before. We started to make love and I could not get into it, so I said I thought I would take a bath to relax me. While I was bathing, Jeff called again and asked if I wanted to have coffee with him. I decided that it would probably be a good idea to leave the apartment for a while and so I went with him. We had a pleasant time over a beer and I felt there were many vibrations of attraction between us. I returned to the apartment and Peter told me that he had been screaming "Let me out of here," and that he called Wendy and now he felt better. I felt like hell. We tried to make love again, and he said his penis was a bit tender. We gave up on that, and we had oral sex. I finally had an orgasm which lasted about fifteen minutes. I felt much better because all along I knew that if I could only have an orgasm, I would be back in my own body again and centered. We went to The Bagel for dinner and I had a very large sirloin with two poached eggs on top of it. We came back to your apartment and Peter said he would prefer to go home for the night because your apartment was giving him the willies. Ted called as we were packing up and said that since he was driving a cab he would come pick us up and drive us home. I took some of the flowers to give to Ted and to leave at the apartment for you and we waited for Ted about fifteen minutes in front of your apartment.

Peter was very rude to Ted on the way home and when we got there Ted left immediately. Danny had left Peter a note telling him to please sleep in the single bed because he was sleeping with Allen in the double bed. Peter and I went to bed in the single bed. It was hot as hell and Peter was in a lousy mood. I felt awful. Finally, Danny came home with Allen and I hugged him and told him I hated men and that I loved faggots and thank God he was a faggot. He hugged me and kissed me and listened to all the disastrous adventures that I had had. Allen offered to sleep in the single bed with Danny so that Peter and I could have the double bed, and I accepted his offer gratefully. I walked Peter half-asleep to bed. I think I probably slept a total of two hours.

Sunday, June 17

I got up at ten and wrote you the long love/hate letter. Then I taxied to Ted's to get his phone number because, since you had his number in my address book, I didn't have it. I then taxied downtown in time to meet Susie and her husband. I called the answering service and left a message for Riff to come at 2:30. I went to the Lion's Head with Susie and Ken and told them about the terrible time I was having and that I thought you were schizophrenic and needed help and had chosen me to be you for a reason. They must have thought I was crazy because I was so frantic and I'm sure that much of what I said to them made them uncomfortable since they were supposed to be your friends. They were a bit standoffish toward me but we arranged a meeting for the next day and I said I'd call Susie about what time we were meeting. I ran back to the apartment and met Riff and we spent a lovely afternoon walking around the Village and talking like maniacs.

Then I came back to the apartment and called your father for Father's Day. I called Ben at Riverset to tell him not to sleep with you if he hadn't already because of your flora and fauna. Asked Ben to give me my father's telephone number. He couldn't find it right away and said you wanted to talk to me. I told him that I didn't want to talk to you, that I was very mad at you and that I would talk to you some other time. He insisted on my talking to you and we had a very nasty conversation which you insisted on prolonging when I told you I was too angry to talk. I felt you were very manipulative and I got angrier by the minute at you. Finally I hung up on you and called my father to wish him a happy Father's Day. Then I called Ted and told him I was coming over because I was going crazy in your apartment. I called the answering service and left his number. Riff during this period was going through your files to find everything connected with the life swap because I wanted to do some work at Ted's. He found this poem, which I had probably seen before but had forgotten:

> To tell the truth
> And get paid for it
> Has that ever happened?
> To tell the truth
> I don't recall
> And I know something about history
> To tell the truth
> And be modest
> Is crazy
> Is the only self-destruction
> Is Socrates therefore my brother?
> But I never sucked a cock
> To tell the truth
> I kid a lot
> And I know what happens to a smart-ass
> To tell the truth
> And kid a lot
> Is crazy
> "Miserable merchants of unwanted
> Ideas"
> They may be
> But even they

> Mr. Justice Douglas
> Doubtless make the rent
> To tell the truth
> And be self-pitying
> Is crazy
> To tell the truth
> It's time to work.

I was sure you had written the poem and that it was the key to the whole thing. That you really did think it was time to work and that you somehow wanted me to help you become real. This was very arrogant on my part but I don't think I could have justified having spent so much painful time in your life if I hadn't thought that there were some deeper meaning to it all. It came as a great surprise on Tuesday morning (when I was back in my own life) to discover that Mike had written the poem. I felt even sorrier for Mike and the fact that he would miss the most important moment of his life by stopping off in a bar to have a drink on his way to it. When I talked to your parents, I told your mother that I was very distressed by many things in your life and that I wanted to see her later on in the week to talk about it. I read her the poem and asked her if she thought it was significant. She said that she thought it was just a poem and that I shouldn't be so upset just because we had very different life-styles. She was very nice to me and tried to calm me down, but I was crazy mad at you and crazy sad for you and really did think that my mission was to help you be reborn.

I went up to Ted's and talked and talked and talked to him. I called Jeff Bailey. He was asleep and so I told his wife what was going on. I called Fran Berman and told her that I thought you would be very upset by my note and would need a friend when you came back to your own life and that I would call her the next day to get together with her. I called Yuric Lermentov and he invited me to a screening Tuesday night. I asked him to come over tomorrow night and he said he couldn't because he had another screening. I told him that I had come up with a name for his movie. *Balance Brought Forward.* I explained to him what that meant, and he said he'd think about it for a while and see if he liked it. I called Danny and told him to tell you that I was less angry.

Peter called and came over and we came back to your apartment to spend the night since we thought you would be coming back from Riverset. Things were still not very pleasant between us. I tried to go to sleep but only got about an hour of sleep all night.

Monday, June 18

I woke up early and started menstruating which explained a lot to me about my madness. I also took it as a sign that the end was in sight! I went into the bathroom (what had become my office) and started calling people to come to a meeting. I called Henry Blanck who said he would come and that he would ask George Warneke for me. I called Abbe and there was no answer. I called Susie and she said she would try to come. I called Jeff Bailey and talked to him for a while. I made a note to call Mel Green, who had called and who I had told I would call back. I made another note to call George of *GQ* about the ideas I had on the "right" time to do things, which we had talked about the week before. I called Abbe again and asked him to come over and bring some food which I would pay him for. I called Ted and asked him to come over that evening. Abbe called back and asked me what was going on and said that he didn't want to bring food and that I could order the stuff myself from Balducci's. I said that's OK, I would do it myself. I woke Peter up and we left the apartment. He convinced me not to see Dr. Verde because it was setting up a new dependency. We ran into Henry Blanck and had breakfast with him at Sutter's where he picked up a very attractive woman who was living with a guy who sold wool.

We left Sutter's and I ran into three people I knew. I called the answering service because I knew that you had probably called and left me a message. Sure enough you had, telling me to go get a package and letter from the liquor store. I called you up and talked to you. You said that you did not have a communicable disease and I asked you what did you have. You said that you didn't ask the doctor. She had said that it was something going around. I thought to myself this is really crazy. She doesn't even care enough about her body to find out what is wrong with her. And if it's not communicable, how is it going around, by spontaneous generation or electricity? I decided right then and there that there was no way you and I could communicate with each other and that it was crazy to try and set up a support group for you. That I didn't feel positive toward you and that there is no way for one person to set up a support group for another and that in any case it was very arrogant of me to try to do anything like that. I decided that I would try to call everyone back and tell them that I was just going to have a party and that it would make me feel better. I picked up your letter and read it at Henry Blanck's. I decided not to show it to him, although I am sure he was very curious, but because you had asked me not to show it to anyone, I decided that it would not be fair to you to show it to him.

I left Henry's after having a very awful interaction with Celia who was in a foul mood and not able to understand anything I said. Their fights were getting worse and I felt that I should not stick around anymore. It made me too sad.

When I got back to the apartment, I called the answering service and found out that Phil Barnett had called. I called him back and asked him to stop by that evening if he could. He said he couldn't come that evening, but he would come over immediately. He came over and I cried hysterically and told him everything that happened and he listened and said, "Oh, my God, oh, my God," and patted me and left.

Abbe had called too. I called Susie and she said that she didn't know whether she could come. I called Will Jepson and told him about my paranoia about you and he told me that you weren't crazy, that most writers are voyeurs and not to worry about the people in my life, that they would understand, and to just cut my losses.

By then it was ten o'clock. Fran Berman and Bob arrived. I asked them to apartment-sit for me while I went out and bought goodies for the party. I went to the greengrocer's and bought fruits and fruit drinks; the thought of liquor made me want to throw up. I also bought some enormous asparagus because they were so phallic. I came back and the rest of the people started arriving. Riff came. I introduced people to one another and started putting out the fruit. I made a sculpture arrangement of the asparagus and placed it next to your typewriter so that I could look at it and laugh. Fran saw it and started laughing. I said, how do you like my asparagi, and she said, is it asparagi like penii? I said, exactly.

Henry Blanck had come with an old girl friend who asked if the woman whose apartment it was was an actress. I laughed hysterically and said, "Of sorts." Henry found the book *Deep Wood*, and we both started to think of a porno script based on either a carpenter or the kindling man. I took that book and *Scented Garden for the Blind* and placed them under my asparagus so that my sculpture had a name and had symbolic meaning for me. The asparagus were penises, and they were large penises, therefore *Deep Wood.* And you needed me to talk in images, which brought me back to the scented gardens for the blind because that is an alternate way for the blind to see flowers, by touching them and smelling. The message was a message to you about your blindness when it came to men and your life. I admit that it is a very complicated message and had many levels of meaning, but I was very pleased with myself, and it made a lot of sense to me and probably to no one else.

Susie called and told Fran that she didn't know if she was coming. Ted sat at the typewriter and wrote me a note.

sometime in june
no memory for dates, but the night of the strange
  gathering in the year of the grand experiment

dear micki

some things in my head
(parenthetically—it seems strange that a writer
  should not have a better typewriter.)
on paper
because ive wanted to write you a letter for some
  time
and this seems a good opportunity because it
  doesnt seem
an opportune moment for the spoken word
and some of this is fairly fresh
—a virtue?

i dont feel all that strongly about the views that
  follow mostly
because of the limitations of my input on this
  whole situation.

to begin, perhaps to finish:

it occurs to me that you are perhaps in the
  process of violating
an agreement that you made in good faith with
  nancy—i.e., to live
her life for a period of two weeks and to allow
  her to live yours for that same period.
it seems to me that this violation takes two
  fundamental forms:
1. by seeing people from micki's life you are
   interfering with nancy's ability to live your
   life during this period.
2. by overtly refusing to live nancy's life as
   nancy for the most part.

i realize that you feel justified in these
   violations (and incidentally i feel that you are
   justified in these violations) by (1) your
   inability to physically and mentally tolerate
   living nancy's life and (2) the mis- and obtuse
   information provided to you by nancy (here i
   feel that you are less justified, since nancy
   probably didnt know that you wouldnt have an
   opportunity to read the materials in "the box"
   before Mike moved in for the kill.)

anyway, all this you will probably grant. the
   point is, that since you have decided that you
   cant/wont live nancy's life, i feel that you
   shouldnt go ahead with constructing any sort of
   new and/or altered trip without renegotiating
   the whole thing with nancy. if you dont want to
   do that, then maybe you should call the whole
   thing off.

i realize that this letter doesnt sound all that
   supportive, but it is in a less narrow (better?)
   sense of the word. anyway, as i said to Robert
   Hacker this evening: my child, seek the answer
   under the wheels of a moving school bus.

   love

   ted

Fran and I began to play this word game. If Nancy is Micki and Micki is Micki, then where is Nancy? Just then you walked in with Mike, whom I had told you I did not want to see again. You had called earlier in the evening and asked if Peter was coming over and did Peter and I want to have dinner with Mike and you. I had said that I thought that was crazy. I didn't want to see Mike again. You asked, "Not even as my friend?" I answered, "Especially as your friend." You said, "All right."

I thought to myself, what an insensitive bitch. After I've told her that I didn't want to see Mike, she still wants a confrontation so that she can add that to the book. And how unfeeling can she be about Mike's feelings. As much as he denies it, he really is very insecure and jealous. How is he going to feel when he meets Peter who is beautiful and young and has a nice body, and he knows that not only do I have Peter as a comparison with him but that also Nancy has been sleeping with Peter. I thought you were disgustingly insensitive to Mike's feelings and even though I really don't like Mike, I think he has some rights as a human being and can empathize with his pain.

Anyhow, you walked in and I was outwardly very angry but inwardly thought the whole scene was hysterically funny. Especially since you brought four people from the Lion's Head with you who really did not have a candle at this funeral and although you may have thought of them as your friends, I knew they would be Fair Witnesses in this situation. I decided that it would only make everybody very uncomfortable for me to be angry, so I decided to be gracious. I knew that this was so much a violation of trust that I could legitimately leave and end the thing and not even feel guilty about it. I also knew that Peter was coming at one o'clock and that I could not leave until then. You seemed oblivious. Mike said something about not understanding why I was angry with him. I said that he knew why I was angry and that I would discuss it some other time but that I thought it would not be a good time to discuss it now. He said he did not know what I was talking about. I told him that I would drop it if I were he because I could be very nasty, and things would not go well for him if I told why I was angry at him. I knew that I had the ultimate weapon if Mike really got nasty because I could be totally honest about what his behavior had been to me.

You kept walking around the apartment, and I thought you put on Shalimar because the smell of Shalimar began to waft through the room. At some point you noticed the asparagus but not the books and said, "They sure are big." I said, "That's the way I like them." Then you said, "They're the largest I've ever seen." And I said, "That's for sure." I was being very catty, very obscene, and somewhat funny, but the remarks went right by you. I didn't know if you were purposely not understanding my meaning or if you really did not understand. At some point, you made a comment about this being the first party you had given where you wouldn't have to do the dishes. I smiled inwardly and thought, that's what you think, sister. I began to get ready to go. I packed up your files that I still had not looked at and my clothes. You looked upset about my taking the files but couldn't legitimately stop me, so you offered to Xerox anything I wanted. I didn't know what I wanted, so I told you I would look through them and give you the things I wanted Xeroxed. You also told me to please send you your notes which were in my office desk. It was such a freaky situation. I had all the power. I had not only your files but your notes.

There was no way you could stop me from leaving. There was nothing Mike could do to me. I must have said "Fuck off" to Mike eight times in a row. The people from the Lion's Head were witness to everything, and I knew the gossip would be all over the place the next day. They were amused by what was going on but couldn't really laugh since they didn't know what exactly their role should be.

Finally Peter arrived and I left with everyone, leaving you alone with Mike and those four people and all the dirty dishes! There must have been an awkward silence for a long time after we left.

When we got to Ted's house, I noticed that Mike's sketchbook was in the car and I tried to call you on the unlisted number, and there was no answer. (I later found out that the telephone man had not connected the bells to the phone—he was probably too rattled by the whole apartment scene.)

I spent the next two hours getting high and dancing all my blues away.

I have never appreciated my life and my friends and everything about me more that I did that night and ever since.

Thank you, Nancy Weber, for making me realize that I am very lucky to be me!

Yours truly,

Allison the un-real McCoy

Dear Micki,

At first I wasn't going to answer your letter; not really. I wrote these rather lumpy lines:

Vitriol
should always be answered
with poems.
So I waive the fearful right
to wear the enemy's face
into battle.
She claims I have no friends;
it was enemies I was missing
until I invited her in.
I had sweeter things in mind
when I sent that invitation,
but it was time, I suppose,
to see who the enemy was,
to learn the look of the face
never to wear.
The face has many scars.
I will not name them here—
names can veil.
Vitriol flung in the dark
only burns who flings it.
Such scars
should be left unveiled
as a warning to children.

Not as good as Erica Jong, I'm afraid, but much more about me than the poems in your letter. I do feel that in trying to destroy others, you only indicted yourself. Do believe that if I borrow your methods to strike back, you'll have succeeded in doing me yet more harm than you meant me. Yes, it's tempting to make that bad poem my only answer, walk away with all my nose in the air.

I'm not quite that sanctimonious, though. I don't want to cut you up so badly that you spend the next ten years regretting that you said yes to my invitation, but I just as strongly don't want you to spend another five seconds thinking that you fucked around with me and got away with it, came out looking good.

No question. I could spend a hundred pages answering your lies with truth, underscoring your contradictions, mocking your mockery, spurning your innuendos, and otherwise showing your letter for what it is, and some people would still think you came out looking good: those who love you, your sisters and brothers in ideology, and the grim few who have always been allergic to me, always will be. I'm concerned about the happy many, about people like the kind woman who read your letter and wanted to know if I'd been devastated by it. I was somewhat devastated by the vigor of your bitterness toward me—I've never before been the target of such strong dark feelings. I'm not devastated by your explanation of that bitterness. Your letter is not about what I am or did but about your own constricted, destructive vision and where it's led you. I owe it to the happy many to let them know that I'm okay, and why. And, as I said, I'd like to wipe the smug smile off your face.

I have to tell you first that I think your letter is a damn good piece of prose. Maybe living in a writer's apartment, even with the wrong-color flowers, did have some impact: I can hardly believe that tough, punchy, witty, engaging document was written by the author of the ponderous academic papers you gave me to read in the spring. You're admirably honest about your pain (though not about what caused it), and there are sympathetic sprinklings of self-criticism. All that makes your small and big lies even more sordid and demanding of being answered with something other than bad verse. So a point or two.

About the telephone, which you make one of the villains of the piece: Telephones can be turned off. Telephones must be turned off if one is going to write, meditate, read, make love, breathe. Half the point of having an answering service is that you can turn the phone off without worrying that you're missing the call of your life.

About your feeling "too exposed" in my clothing that lovely hour at Sardi's: You note often, before the swap, that I have an absurdly large wardrobe. Instead of wearing one of a dozen bodyshirts that are opaque, nonclinging, and can be buttoned up to the neck, or one of three smocks, or one of many mother-bought man-tailored shirts, why did you wear the one blouse with so low a neck that I never put it on without a pin to make it less exposing? (I'm the girl you called a prude way deep down. Would I let it all hang out at Sardi's?)

About my flora and fauna: That's what my doctor called it. (Maybe she's a prude way deep down.) Would I have understood more about it if I could have chatted with it in Latin? I know you've read a lot of books aimed at putting you in touch with your body and eliminating the need for all those killer gynecologists; did you speed-read the parts that talk about why some disturbances are popular even though they're noncommunicable? I haven't received any medical bills from you or yours, so I guess you know by now that there are such disturbances. Of course you knew it to begin with. If you really thought I had trichomoniasis or monilia, you would, I hope, have warned Ben on Friday when Peter first told you about my affliction, not waited until the very end of our weekend together. You didn't want to warn him. You wanted to slug him in the gut for having liked me.

About my friends calling you a "shiksa" and making "sexist remarks" to you: My friends (including the non-Jewish ones) sometimes call me a shiksa, too. I'm not exactly sure why, since they all know I like being Jewish. I guess my New England upbringing occasionally overpowers my Galitziano horse-thief blood. As for the sexist remark made to you by that very fine elegant elderly gentleman at Sardi's, it was probably, "You look lovely tonight, my dear."

About your desperately needing the comfort of women: Is that why you put off seeing Susie day after day after day, even though you knew she was a feminist, had wanted to do the swap, and had many other reasons to be sympathetic to you? Gave up on Magda after one phone call, simply because—as my notes had told you she would—she played the game strictly according to the rules? Didn't call wonderful Katharine in Florida, or sweet Barbara in New Jersey, or great childhood friend Prue on Bleecker Street, or passionate Ruthie in Cambridge, or—until it was too late—compassionate Fran in Queens? Alienated gentle and beautiful Kylie by trying to make her a coconspirator, and Henry's Celia—whom you liked so much—by blithering at her until she wanted to hide under the couch? Because you needed the comfort of women?

There's sadly much more on that level. I've answered a lot of it elsewhere, and a lot of it is too obviously what it is to need to be answered at all. So on to more serious matters. Trigger Mike Kagan, for openers.

I remember so well the three of us sitting at a table at Jimmy's before the swap. I remember that you were tense and I was edgy and that T.M. wasn't at his best either. He'd just been interviewed on television (something about the impact of political cartoons on the national mood), and he was sweaty and rumpled and irritated because the show hadn't been very good and was also a little bit looped.

And you liked him. You liked him very much. Meeting him convinced you finally and forever that you wanted to do the swap. That's what you told me on the phone the next day, and you never told me any different. Can you explain how in God's name you got from that unqualified enchantment with him to writing about your first cab trip as Nancy up to Jimmy's: "The picture of Mike floats through my mind, and I feel like laughing, embarrassedly, and then I feel like throwing up again."

Okay. Your queasiness came partly from nerves, heat, all that champagne. Fair enough. I think it mostly came from knowing that you had no business being in that cab because you had no intention of being me, no inclination to love Mike. I think you'd disliked him from the start, not because he sometimes drinks too much, sometimes gets carried away, isn't a beautiful boy, but because you knew that his free mind, his great spirit, his crazy humor, his fantastic sense of style, his grown-up charm, and his deep loyalty to me and the swap were the antithesis of everything you were and had and felt. You'd never seen him as anything but a sparring partner, a target for your hatred of men. And now you had to approach him as his pal and lover. I think it's terrific that you didn't vomit all over the cab.

I have a theory, doctor, about why you were willing to put yourself through the tortures of such a charade. Hang in there. Some other things first.

"And I knew then why you are such a fascist about your jewelry and about the Shalimar. Those tokens are the things that keep you connected to something real, to real people who love you and who know enough about you to not let you play games with them. Except that you do play games with them. They have no idea what your life is really like in New York City."

The small end of that first. I wear Shalimar because I like the smell of it on me, and so do most of the people whose noses I care about. Since my mother and I have the same coloring and similar body chemistry, it's not amazing that we wear the same perfume, and I think it's fun that we do. Period and end of sentence, as George Frazier likes to say. I wear my pearls and the garnet pendant because I think they're beautiful and because I think they become me. I'm glad they were gifts from my parents. I would be as much of a fascist about wearing them if, like the rings I almost never take off, they came from T.M. or if I'd bought them myself or found them in an oyster. Sometimes the surface and structure of things *is* the meaning behind that surface and structure.

Now for the big end. Nick knows more about my life in New York than anyone. My parents know as much as they want to know, which happens, nicely, to be as much as I think they should know. This will shock you. In my family we all believe that privacy and grace and particularly kindness are as important as honesty, sometimes more important. I remember once, many years back, starting to tell my parents something or other about my sexual life (some happiness I thought would make them happy for me), and my father stopping me and saying: "The blunt truth can be a blunt weapon." How right he was.

When I was younger, I thought not being able to tell my parents everything I was doing and thinking was a limitation on our relationship. I grew to realize, and I do mean grew, that this restraint assured the separateness which necessarily precedes all exciting closeness, that it was a major ingredient of real adulthood, genuine freedom. I know that must sound very peculiar to you. You believe in a kind of psychological communism in which everyone's soul and psyche is public property. You practice a compulsive laying-it-on-the-line that you mistake for living in truth.

Real truth, I think, is the kind that prevails in my family. It's the truth of our love and respect for one another, feelings so grounded in honest affections that we don't have to be exactly like one another, or share all our values, or know every inch of each other's lives in order to go on believing in one another. But my parents know infinitely more about my life than you do, Micki. If you think they don't know about hours and days such as you spent here, you're right. There are no such hours and days in my life.

T.M. and I, who have been soul-honest with each other since the day we met, also make a point of avoiding the blunt-truth-weapon syndrome with each other. (It was Trig who told me that great line of Bill O'Dwyer's: "If you can't lie to your friends, who can you lie to?") But, like you, I have a great distaste for sexual lies. They make you contemptuous of the person you're lying to, are—as John Fowles said in *The Magus*— the real infidelity. And here T.M. and I have now and then been in conflict. He mostly doesn't want to know about other men in my life; I mostly don't want to lie about them. So we've been left on this middle ground (described in detail in the journals I gave you in April), and I've sometimes told the truth to suit myself, sometimes lied to suit him. But as I said in my letter to you the Sunday of the swap, I've always hated him when I've had to lie to him about such things (hated him, convolutedly enough, for making me contemptuous of him), and so I've rather more played it the other way. When I consoled you that Friday by telling you not to worry about having lied to him because I sometimes did, I didn't know that you had already lied to him more and in a vastly worse way in five days than I had in six years.

As for lying to you—I never did it; to do so would have been utterly self-defeating. True, the more or less alphabetized notes on my people were thin and hasty and lopsided. I told you that when I gave them to you. And, as I wrote in my letter to you during the swap, you had those thirty single-spaced pages of journal notes to ponder for three months, you had knowing me. Part of the problem may have been your being a process person and my being a content person—whatever you meant when you described us that way. The heart of the problem was you.

You decided to interpret the words "omnipresent" and "lovable" as meaning that Aaron and I were lovers because you wanted to go to bed with him. You wrote condescendingly about him and tried to make trouble between him and me because he never called you again after your night together. I have always known how Aaron feels about Shalimar. I remember the wet-sheep night.

(Actually, it was Mongolian lamb.) I sort of wanted to throw up myself. That was three years and many coats ago, and Aaron and I have often been in close proximity since (though not in bed), with nobody retching. He's a good friend, and the reason he came over here when you called him at two in the morning and said you wanted to make love with him is in large part because if I made such a phone call, sounded as full of need as he says you did, he would respond as kindly, would even be rather pleased. I'm sure he also found you attractive. I know he never dreamed that you would describe your episode as a triumph over Guerlain, Revillon, and me.

You decided to interpret what I said about Abbe as meaning that you were supposed to go to bed with him because you wanted to go to bed with him. Yes, I thought it would be fantastic if the attraction Abbe and I had for each other really jelled when you were being me. What in the world did that have to do with your being lovers without the attraction really jelling? And what combination of insecurity and megalomania compelled you to make it sound as though Abbe never really wanted me until there was you?

You decided to interpret what I said about Henry as meaning that I "wouldn't mind his presuming" on you because he made you laugh and made you want him to presume. It's true that T.M. and I once went to one of his "orgs" and left, not because we were uptight but because we found the company less than grand. It's also true—and I can't believe that Henry, who's so upfront about all things sexual, lied about this—that he has since asked me three or four different times to swing with him, and I've for various reasons always refused. I wrote that I might say yes in the right mood because it's so. You'd expressed curiosity about group sex, and I thought you'd like to know that this right mood could happen to you and still belong to me. Henry is no more achingly attracted to me than I to him, but he has been the aggressor, if you can call it that, in our sexual exchanges. You, the great celebrator of sisterhood who told me so contentedly that your lover Sue Ann had been lovers with both Ben and Peter, had to suggest to yourself and the world that Henry was only eager to presume on my bed when you were lying on it. When Killer went down on your toes, did she bark that she liked them better than mine?

Why did you choose to interpret my notes the way you did?

Where did you get the insane notion that it was somehow your duty to go to bed with every important man in my life except my father and my dry cleaner? Did you think that I'd done "an awful lot of work" in lining up writing assignments for you because I expected you'd only be using my desk as a place to toss your panties?

Here's my theory, kid. Let's see if I've learned as much about shrinking as you have about writing. You went to bed with everyone you did because (1) you thought that since you were such a sex expert the best place to compete with me for my friends' affections was in bed; (2) the only way to obviate your pain at my being lovers with your lovers was to score more often with more people; (3) you wanted to have the wherewithal to hate me because (4) you wanted to be able to turn against me in my life and in my book and otherwise destroy my project and make me repent of having conceived it.

The last part of that long sentence explains a hell of a lot else. It explains your dealings with T.M. It explains your very successful attempt to make me suffer by making my family suffer. It explains your vicious use of my notes to wound friends of mine and make them think I'd betrayed them. It explains your efforts to poison Peter and Ted and Danny and Ben against me while the swap was still going on. (Did you ever think how unfair that was to them?) It explains your decision not to experience my life but to analyze what you thought it was, even though you knew I consider uninvited analysis to be the great intruder of the twentieth century. It explains all the agony you wished on yourself.

The reason behind the reason is as simple as can be. You have always been, as you often told me, the initiator of most of the events and "interactions" in your life. In taking me up on my invitation to swap lives, you were, for once, not the initiator but the respondent, and the respondent to whom? An antifeminist! A nonscientist! A Jewish princess who's invited to charge clothes to her parents at Bonwit's! Someone who doesn't have to drop out to be a writer because she is a writer! A capitalist who drinks alcohol! Someone with friends so loyal to the rules of her game that they were willing to put up with the Mad Talker! A woman who wants too much but knows who she is and more or less where she's going and likes what she sees! In short, darlin', the enemy. Someone whom you had to sabotage no matter the cost to yourself.

I like to think that somewhere way back you dealt with me in good faith. (I don't exactly get high marks this semester on character judgment, but I hate to think I failed altogether.) I want to believe that you really did decide to do the swap because you had scientific curiosity and wanted to test yourself and wanted Ben to be able to go to horticulture school. I especially want to believe that last part. Everyone keeps telling me how your bad behavior and bitchy writing are going to boost the sales of the book. It's nice to know that the blood money you'll be raking in (I hope) will be doing something good for one of the best men I've ever met.

I don't know when your ego got out of control, what made all your insecurities bubble to the surface. You offer this elegant explanation about, on the one hand, the manic phase of the gifted, and, on the other, premenstrual stress. I'd call it identity crisis: simple panic at not having your own name, clothes, and credentials to carry you along. I'd call it not knowing yourself. I'd call it ideology up the ass. And, as I said, I'd call it a total inability to be sporting about an idea that came to life in other than your head.

Which talk about other hands and heads brings me to the parts of your letter that made me want to call up Riff and ask him how much it would cost to have your legs broken. Those are the parts where you told me how bad you felt for my parents about what I was subjecting them to and how upset you were at my disgusting insensitivity to Trigger Mike's feelings in bringing him to your Monday soirée manquée. I almost don't have to say it, do I? My parents never liked the idea of the swap, but the right person could have turned that around. I'm convinced of it. The only place I let them down was in choosing you to share this adventure with me. I picture Susie or Barbara eating *rösti* with my parents and Nick at the Edelweiss, and I see only warmth and laughter. No tears. No talkathon. No hysterical phone calls full of misplaced recriminations and misattributed poetry. My only offense to Trigger Mike was asking him to love someone who, I should have known, was utterly incapable of delighting in that love, returning it. For inflicting you on them: Mother and Daddy and Nick, I'm sorry. T.M., I'm sorry. Everyone, I'm sorry.

I apologize to you, too. It was no kindness to you to let you into a situation you couldn't begin to handle. I don't agree with George Warneke and Anne Upton that I should have subjected you to psychological testing before I signed the contract with you (and that if I'd done so I wouldn't have signed the contract). But I should have looked at you harder, differently. I knew you'd done an enormous amount of self-analysis, with and without professional help, and I thought I could accept your words about yourself as having more than a casual connection with the truth. I believed you when I read in your notes that you used Ivory Soap in New York and pine-tar soap in Riverset. I believed the description that goes: "I am a rather silly person and like to frolic and detour. I'm fairly strong and quite tolerant of individual differences."

That's it, I guess. I've flung my vitriol, too. It had to be done, and I think I did it according to the good Marquis, but my stomach hurts, and I have a miserable taste in my mouth.

I suppose it's my ultimate Pollyanna act, but do we have to leave things like this? I don't deny that we're enemies. Our politics, our aesthetics, our styles, all our orderings of things are totally at odds. And I'm not saying I forgive you the injury you've done me and a lot of people I like and love or that I expect you to forgive me the pain you endured during the swap, whatever caused that pain. Still, we're like two fighters in the ring. We may be doing our best to knock out each other's brains, but we're linked in our distance from all who merely look on, whichever side they take.

You maybe think I'm trying to out-nice you or am trafficking in fantasy again, and maybe I am. Maybe I'm not. We'll probably meet again. Can't it be as friendly enemies?

Here's looking at you, whoever you are, whoever's doing the looking.

Nancy

VIEWING

A Word from Trigger Mike

I encouraged Webs to do the swap. It was one of the few original ideas I had ever come across. If it seemed incredible that people could go around changing skins, my girl's track record made her the Vegas choice to change our ideas about possibilities. But I had no illusions about the swapee, whoever she might be. Webs, I was all but certain, was the only normal person in the world who would have the desire and the nerve to try something so bold. The other party was bound to be crazy or certifiably insecure or a mind engineer or G. Gordon Liddy's kid sister.

None of which bothered me, although I was slated to do more time with swapee than anyone else in the kid's life. It figured to be interesting, no matter what; and even if it were terrible, it wouldn't be too bad, since it meant no more than six or seven nights and maybe a couple of lunches out of my life. Hardly a lot to give up for a girl I had loved on a straight line since I watched her sit a bar stool one morning six years ago. We had kept it alive through what the novelists call everything. I had no concern that the swap would change things between us. A couple of weeks, a few new lovers couldn't shake what we had. Looking at it from every angle, I couldn't fault the proposition. Even after I got the word that Micki would be the swapee.

Webs briefed me on this one as she had on the previous contenders. She was trying to make her out to be terrific, but off her curriculum vitae Micki sounded to me like a commandant at Bergen-Belsen. She was a sociologist and therapist, a radical feminist, and a proud bisexual. She never shaved her legs, she eschewed deodorants, and she dressed in a style that could best be described as early Golda Meir. All in all my fifth of Black Label.

Still, when Webs brought her over to Jimmy's on the eve of the swap, my hopes moved up considerably. She couldn't carry my girl's lipstick in the looks department, but there was no dog in the face. Not a bad figure, either, and I quickly began imagining her as she might look as Webs. She'd be wearing the kid's clothes, which meant an immediate forty-point spot, the kid being one of the great dressers. She'd wear the Shalimar, she'd spritz under the arms, she'd take a Wilkinson to the legs, maybe it would work. On top of which she was rather pleasant, even laughed some. Maybe you can't tell a girl by her résumé, or so I decided to think. Considering what I was expecting, this preseason night was aces up.

I felt even better when Micki dropped a demand that would have made her a virtual censor over Webs's book. She appeared to be acting very reasonably, giving my girl less and less difficulty as the big day approached. Webs was happy, as high as I'd ever seen her, and that pleased me. I was determined to be as good as I could be to anyone who was putting so much hope into the kid's eyes. I began to believe that it would work on both ends, that Micki would actually act the part of Nancy Weber and maybe even think like her, perhaps *become* her for a while.

It took two drinks to bring that one down to earth; within twenty-four hours it was shattered.

The plot called for doing the same things with Micki as I would with Webs. On the first night she met me for cocktails at Jimmy's; she came in nice and larky, looking fine in the kid's clothes. She kissed me on the ends of my moustache, called me "Trig," and ordered Irish neat in a wine glass. Perfect.

The bartenders (primed) called her "Nancy," I called her "Webs," and we were off. And then clang! The first thing she said was that she didn't like Irish whiskey. I had understood that she didn't drink, but she had understood that Webs did, and it was everybody's understanding that this was one kind of thing the swaperoony was about.

"But Webs," I said, "you always drink Irish; don't you remember, kid?"

"Well, I'll try, but no guarantees," she said.

I told her nobody wanted her to get sick, but why not finish the quick one before deciding, okay?

And then she began talking about the swap. She wanted me to know how tough it was going to be, how her life-style was so different, etc., etc.

"But that stuff was settled in the exhibitions," I said. "We're not supposed to talk about any of that. You're Nancy Weber, this is the championship season, we're in it now, this is it."

The warning lasted a few silent moments, and then it was back to her life, Micki's, and granted it would be an adventure, but would she be able to pull it off, could she really be Nancy.

I tried to put the best face on it.

"Look, kid," I said. "I'll let you play this tonight, I guess it's understandable that the first day is just too exciting, too crazy to be able to sink right into someone else. You need to talk about it, we'll do it for a while. But after tonight you've got to get off this, you've got to be Webs, or the thing is dead. It's only going to last two weeks, which is short enough, so we can't afford to lose much time. Nancy wouldn't want me to give you tonight, but I'm a sport, so okay. But not after tonight, right?"

"Right," said Micki-Webs.

She made the most of the night. At dinner she talked about Micki and what the problems of the swap were likely to be. Then we stopped at the Lion's Head, where it seemed like the whole place was lying in wait to quiz her. It made sense that this would be a problem, that people who had heard of the swap would not be able to resist a little cross-examination. I had warned Micki of this, telling her to try and cool this stuff down or it would never end. Instead she positively warmed to it. It must have darkened me, despite my efforts to believe that she was just getting it out of her system. A friend confirms that at the Lion's Head that first night I told her that the thing looked bad, that Micki was making no effort to be Webs, and that I doubted she ever would.

When we got to Webs's apartment my hopes came back a bit. She stopped talking about the damn thing, and I believe she made an attempt to act like the kid. Not immediately, since she hopped into the shower with me, something I told her Webs didn't do. But I must admit I didn't fight it.

In bed she did try. The kid had obviously prepped her on what made me happy. I played it as if she were Webs, and for a spell she actually looked like her to me. It was the only time it would happen, but it surely deserves to be mentioned if only to show that the possibilities were there. The sex was excellent. We made it at least four times, and I don't think we slept much that night. She claimed two orgasms, and if she was lying, she gets the Emmy.

When we got to the apartment that night, she gave me the keys, the way Chicago hookers do (and radical feminists?), and the result was that they were still in my pocket the next morning. I had a lunch appointment at Sardi's, and we arranged to meet there for the transfer back, else Old Micki would not be able to get back in for afternoon appointments. My lunch was with a South African whom I had known in law school, a guy now living in Israel. A nice-enough fellow but strange in the manner of most South African Jews, whose psyches seemed to be mixed like an extra-dry martini, or ten paranoias to one ambivalence. We were at the upstairs bar when Micki came in, and of course I introduced her as Nancy Weber. Since this guy didn't know anything about the swap and had never met Webs, it came off like a charm. I think he took her number when I went to the john, which would have been quite like my girl if you can forget that she would have had better taste.

At cocktail time we met again at Sardi's, but this time the old crowd was there, most of whom had received invitations to the swap. It was once again to Niagara, and this time she really took the falls. She was passing herself around to them like a touch football in the stadium bleachers. She kept saying "heavy," a word that ranked with "far-out" on Webs's egregious list. I had tried to stomp it gently out of her on opening night, but like everything else, it was no dice. She was turned on, animated, hither and yon, to and fro, filling every casual acquaintance of ours with stories of how difficult it all was, how heavy. The only saving grace was the one glass of beer she had with ice, though watching her sip it made me all the more upset. I was gnawed with guilt that I wasn't controlling her, that I just wasn't doing right by Webs, and the goddam beer made it worse.

The only way to end it was to get her the hell out of there, which wasn't that easy, as she seemed unable to cut the buttonholing of the entire bar. On the way through Shubert Alley, I told her that this would be the very last time she could pull the outpour, that from now on, this second, she had to cease and desist.

"Right," said Micki-Webs.

Five minutes later she was at it again. We were in the little bar at Frankie and Johnnie's, a mistake to begin with, since there is in attendance at my favorite steak house a certain maître d' name of Doc who likes nothing better than to sit with customers and delve into his (and their) "interpersonal relationships." But I had to go there because Webs and I would have gone there on such a night when I desperately needed a steak and she would be craving the nice fat lambie chops. (I made Micki order that, I wasn't going to let everything go to hell.)

Well, if it wasn't for bad luck, I wouldn't have no luck at all. Who should turn up but Mr. Phil Barnett of *The New York Times* and his lady friend Miss Mary Westergaard. Now Phil is an old and dear pal of both of us, me and Webs. And Mary Westergaard turned out to be a person who went to Sarah Lawrence with Nancy Weber. But it was a time when a fellow didn't need a friend. The combination of Phil and Mary and good old reliable Doc (who joined us at table, natch) was to Micki the irresistible force meeting the movable object.

A brief scenario feels necessary here.

PHIL: It's just great; it's wonderful, Trigger Mike. How do you do it? Everything else and now this. You're sensational; you're the Michelangelo of life. Oh, my God, it's great!

MARY: Well, ah, ah, shall I call you Nancy? Nancy—it's hard to say it 'cause I know the real Nancy—how do you manage to do it?

MICKI: Well, let me tell you, it's very heavy. You know it was a very scary thing to enter into, just taking over someone's life, someone's lovers; it was not easy; it was scary.

MARY *(interrupting):*   You bet! I couldn't do it in a million years, not for a million dollars.

DOC: Do you really feel like you're Nancy, is it possible—maybe it is, I don't want to say it isn't, don't get me wrong, I'm only asking—is it really possible to do a thing like that? I'm just interested, don't get me wrong. Trigger laughs at me; he thinks I'm trying to put you on, but I'm interested, really.

MICKI: No, you're not putting me on. It's a good question. Let me tell you, it's heavy. It's very interesting——

I broke in a couple of times to remind the fans that they were talking to Webs, and this conversation was out of bounds. It stopped them for one breath, a kind of hah-hah pause, and in again to the perils of being swapee.

But this wasn't a mere bar scene; this was leisurely, which gave Micki an opportunity to talk about her life. And so we were treated to everything from her vigorous bisexuality (Doc: "Does that mean that Nancy will be with your, ah, your female lovers? I'm not kidding, I'm interested, really.") to her radical feminism. It was on those shoals that I chose to crack out, and so herein a few lines about Trigger Mike and the libbers.

Webs is my idea of a liberated person. She goes where she likes and does what she pleases. She punches no clock and takes no punches, at least not from anyone who can do anything for her. If she has a glass jaw it's the best kind, made of innocence and a warm heart. Which is to say that only a powder puff can damage her. She can handle a shark for lunch. And she does it all without fanfare, with New England grace. She's a woman to the small intestine, but she could never be a feminist. Just as she could never be a Communist or a Democrat or a Fascist or a Republican. My kid is precisely what Women's Lib should be striving for: the iconoclast, the one-pillow gal who will never kiss an ism, the free woman with a cant-detector as sensitive as Secretariat's nose. And Women's Lib hates everything she is. I love what she is, and that ought to say what I think of the movement.

We are back at Frankie and Johnnie's, and I forget the line that brought it on, but I said something about a book featured that week on *The New York Times* family/style page, a thing called *Willie and the Doll*. It's a book dedicated to making little boys like dolls, so that when they become daddies they can wash diapers while Moms goes to the liberation meeting.

"If any little City College monarchist broad tried to teach that crap to my kids, I'd have her legs broken," I said.

Micki cringed, held her head, and then shook it, kept shaking it as if she were in the presence of every blasphemy promised by every tract in the maddest-lesbian-strike-'em-dead-they're-all-pigfucks part of the liberation.

I warmed to it, laid it in about the mind engineers, the totalitarian bastards who would turn every Huckleberry Finn into a faggot; Christ, I couldn't stop.

They were aghast, all of 'em, even Phil. Doc was shocked out of his clichés. He became quietly elegant, it was impressive, it was interesting, really.

"I never knew you before," Doc said. "I never would have believed how deeply sick you are. I thought I knew you. But this— this——"

I never liked him as much.

It sure did break up the party. Phil and Mary, both a little pale, suddenly found it was getting late. Micki had a headache. When we got outside, she wanted to go to bed—alone, she said. That was fine with me, except that I was afraid that I had ruined the swap, failed my lovely Webs just when I had no right to.

"Micki, look, you can go home alone, it's okay, but just let's have a drink, I've got to explain, just one, please don't argue."

She was game, in fact she was very sweet about it all, even ordered a brandy at the Theatre Bar.

I came on as if I were defending a Murder One case to a jury. I told her how deeply I believed in the liberation of women, how I was for everything substantive they yearned for, how long I had been preaching it, that my only argument was over some of the excesses of some of the extremists in the movement, those people who were only setting things back. I must have sounded like Chaim Weizmann explaining the Stern Gang to Churchill.

"It's okay, honey, I understand, I'm not mad," Micki said. "I don't like the fascists in the movement, believe me, I don't. Honey, look, let's both get a good night's sleep; we've been through a lot, we need it. I'll talk to you tomorrow. Please don't worry, I understand."

What I didn't understand was that she was late for a date with Aaron Tyman, an old friend of Nancy's (not a lover) and a guy I like a lot. A few days later Aaron told me about how she called him when she got home, apologized for the hour, and insisted that he come over as they had arranged that afternoon. Aaron told it to me in all innocence, not knowing that she had never let on to it. He went through the shower scene with her, and she complained to him that I had kept her up the entire night before with my sex demands.

It turned out to be the last time I would see Micki during the swap. She was busy the next night, and Thursday she went to Connecticut to visit Webs's family. I was supposed to see her on Friday night, but she begged off; she was too exhausted. I tried her a couple of times late Friday from the Lion's Head. I was pretty shot myself. I remember saying to someone at the bar who gave me change for the phone, "I've got to keep calling her because I'd keep calling Nancy, but I hope she keeps saying don't come over."

We agreed to meet for dinner on Saturday night. On Saturday afternoon I was surprised by a phone call from Webs, who was spending the weekend with Micki's husband in Bucks County.

Since the call was a severe breach of the rules set down by Webs, I asked what was up. She sounded serene, entirely happy, and explained that Micki needed a few hours off and had called her and talked to Ben, so now she thought it all right to call me. I did not know how to respond. Webs has since told me that I sounded distracted, disturbed, and I was. I knew how badly things were going on this end, and she was so obviously happy on her side that I couldn't put myself together enough to con her. I went off to the race track plenty confused but feeling better. Tonight was another night, and maybe it was going to work out after all.

Back from a winning day at the races, I called Micki from Gallagher's.

"Baby, how are you," I said.

"I'm not your baby tonight," Micki answered. "Tonight I'm Micki; I'm not Nancy; didn't she tell you?"

"She told me you were taking a few hours off, that you called her; but I mentioned to her that we were going out tonight, and she said fine. So, no, she didn't tell me you were not my baby tonight, no."

"Well I'm not, Trigger; tonight I'm Micki."

"Okay, kid, but don't you think you could have let me know? It *is* seven o'clock, and maybe I could have made other plans, did that occur to you?"

"Well, I'm exhausted, I can't take it; it's been fucking heavy, and I can't go on with it right now, you just have to understand. Call me tomorrow."

"Okay, kid, tomorrow."

"No. Change that. Don't call me. When I feel like I'm ready again, I'll call you. Maybe it'll be tomorrow, maybe not."

"Bullshit. I'm not playing that game. You better call Nancy if you want it that way. I'm not going to wait around for calls, and I'm not going to be afraid to call you. I think you're killing this deal, and you owe it to Webs to tell her."

"Well, all right, call me tomorrow, but no guarantees."

"All right, kid, good-bye."

I passed the next day; I wouldn't call her, the hell with it. On Monday, Webs called; she was at Micki's office. I told her a smidgeon of the troubles, and we agreed to meet at Jimmy's for cocktails.

The kid looked great to me, even wearing Micki's *shmatas*. I filled her in; I felt lousy about the whole thing; I knew I had failed her. She told me a few messy stories about Micki's act, particularly in Connecticut with her family. We drove out to the country for dinner. I wasn't very nice to the kid; I don't know why. While we were waiting for coffee, Webs called a friend who told her that Micki was having a meeting at Webs's apartment for some of Webs's friends. I hadn't been invited and neither had Webs. She wanted to go; I was petulant, said the hell with it, but after a few drinks at the Lion's Head, we were off to it, together with a few pals from the bar.

The party has been reported by others, I'm told, so no point to labor it. My girl was superb, as she always is in difficult circumstances. I bothered to cut with Micki for a while. She was easy, but it was a dumb move. No matter. I didn't like it that a great lady was hurt by a powder puff with long teeth. I resented that. I know it matters little because Webs has survived it without breathing hard. But I still don't like it. It's not in me to forgive a two-dollar mind engineer who grants herself the right to preside in judgment over a girl who can sit a bar stool like that.

Ted Holzman: dear nancy

1973 the late august

dear nancy

with each thought it grows/shrinks increasingly difficult to express meaning in a language of thriving ambiguity. at one point in time (behold the exemplary phrase of official deception), these thoughts were entitled "the eclectic marmalade placid mess (with apologies to mr wolfe)." this title grew out of a somewhat para-noid fantasy of a world in which "literary intellectuals" create life situations in order to write about them—each one more fantastic and bizarre than the tradition. each writer striving to manipulate the world into configurations more novel than those of his/her contemporaries. all well and good, perhaps, except that in my paranoid vision life becomes subordinate to or subsumed in the written word; life is manipulated to make journalism. in the end, the word becomes these lives rather than these lives being ex-pressed and joyfully shared through the word, if you see the differ-ence. it is my prejudice to prefer the latter. i hope i have cause to discount the former, but i offer the perspective to you because it is *part* of my experience of the life swap.

although these visions of poisoned sugarplums indeed raced through my head, they did not prevail. as i awaited your arrival on that first evening i was excited about meeting nancy *comme* micki and enthused about the prospect of turning you on to my place in micki's life. those were the rules, and i felt good about playing the game.

immediately upon seeing you dressed so typically in micki's clothes and hearing you say micki's words, the evening was injected with a delightful humor. this humor was generated by the game and was sort of outside the game. you see, the clothes were definitely not nancy's style, but it was delightful to see nancy so full of bravado plunging ahead at being micki. this was the first of many, many gaps in nancy's micki act, and each time one was exposed, it tickled the sense of delight. it seemed to me that we shared that sense, and at times we would delicately negotiate about these gaps—like, did you know that you spoke french, and if you knew, could you, and if you didnt, could you anyway, and if you could, did you know you could—delightful. at the same time that whole process of gaps in nancy's micki act generated some tension for me. the delight was in danger of becoming tedious and trite if i allowed myself to indulge in it. furthermore, it really existed outside of the game and was detracting from the purpose of the whole situation—turning nancy on to micki. the act gaps were really making that process difficult. we were to have dinner together, which for micki and me is a relaxed, unsophisticated event full of endless chatter about the day and the next days and everything in the world. nancy was not the talker that micki was, and the dinner got a little sticky (marmalade). nancy *comme* micki wasnt talking about things she didnt know to talk about (?) or just wasnt a talker (?) or (?)

by the time we came back to the apartment to listen to some music and maybe get into our bodies, the process of turning nancy on to micki was becoming a definite strain for me. conversation was difficult, nancy wasnt responding to the music, and we were both generally tired from the day and evening. at one point i had to take quite a bit of initiative to get nancy to stay awhile longer.

it seems to me that only when we began touching each other did we begin to become freely responsive to one another in a way that rivaled the initial delight. it was a tremendous release from a verbal encumberment within which we were so out of phase.

when i saw you with peter the next evening, you were again unresponsive. it was very easy for me to act toward you as i do toward micki, but apparently very difficult for you to respond as she does. the process required an integration of our responses which was no doubt handicapped by the brevity of our contact. a true measure of the experiment cannot be taken from such a brief experience.

in short, id have felt better if i felt you were more into experiencing and less into attending—if id felt more resonance. this is not to say that you were into it in that way, only that i experienced you so.

anyway
id love to turn you on.
affectionately,

ted

Notes from an Overground Mother

Nancy phoned tonight. I knew she had something special on her mind. Her voice took on a quiet, rather breathless quality. She sounded a bit bored with my usual chatter: family news, politics, her clothes, my clothes, her social life. She asked, Mummy, do you think people can swap lives? Can you get into someone else's skin? Actually almost become someone different? I tried to be patient. Was this another bit of her whimsy? Like the time she wanted to be a private detective and ended up working for a day as a spy on shoplifters at Bloomingdale's? We discussed. Oh, how we two can discuss. Perhaps, Nancy, I equivocated. Why couldn't I be more forthright about how I feel? It's ridiculous. We agreed to talk more.

Another breathless call. Mummy, I placed an ad in *The Voice*. She reads me the copy. Very funny. Oh, God. Perhaps this is the ultimate extension of the fear she used to express as a child that maybe she was adopted. I'm not going to worry. No one will answer the ad. No one who does answer will go through with the deal. No publisher will buy the idea. Meanwhile, I try mildly to express my disagreement. I moan to Saul, no, no. It's crazy, let's bribe, it's so risky.

Can I accept this on face value? Does she truly have a statement she wants to make? Or is she bored with her own life; is she unhappy with herself, dissatisfied with her relationships, hoping this can serve as a break? Could this wonderful girl want to be someone else? And yet haven't we all had fantasies about what other kind of a person we'd like to be? Maybe I'd like to swap lives with a senator, a conductor of a symphony orchestra, the owner-cook of an all-night diner.

I reassure myself. Saul and I keep reassuring ourselves.

Nancy and I have another long phone chat tonight. I can't believe how many idiots replied to that ad. I feel much better about the whole frightening plan; obviously all the "applicants" will or have already turned out to be nuts. One thing I must say. Nancy is being very sane, level-headed, careful. I'm sure she'll get a new exciting assignment or meet some glamorous guy, and the whole swap idea will be scrapped.

Big phone call. We cover a lot of ground—new hair styles, a holiday trip, a dinner party menu. Then, I can't believe it—there's a candidate for the swap whom Nancy has met. A REAL PERSON. Nancy chooses her words carefully. She has always sensed what I am thinking. She keeps reassuring me: Everything will be carefully worked out so that there is no jeopardy of any kind. And Mom, it's really going to be terrific.

No—no—no—Something, someone will prevent this idiocy from happening, I whimper to Saul. Why isn't Nancy just working on a regular job, just writing poetry; her verses are so lovely.

And still another phone call. She has met with Micki several times. I make the standard family offer—by now a routine joke—would Nancy consider a Maserati, a trip to the French Riviera?

But for the first time, I sense that this nightmare is likely to become a reality. I desperately try to hide my lack of enthusiasm, my deep hostility. I listen to long descriptions of Micki.

How stupid the whole idea is. We are what we are.

The worst phone call comes on a night when Saul is out; I have no one to cry to. Publishers are actually fighting for the book. Thousands of dollars are being offered to my little girl to record her reactions to a ridiculous set of events.

After I put the phone down, I think: Have I been narrow in my reaction, provincial, overly protective? Is there something here that I have missed?

I don't think so. The publishing industry has made many mistakes, turned away many brilliant authors, printed more junk than good stuff in the past twenty years. So what if it does like Nancy's crazy idea? But it's my kid; I've got to go along, and deep down inside, I know that I am incapable of an objective reaction. Nancy always manages to land on her feet; she has an innate honesty, a loving-ness that everyone involved in this project will sense and appreci-ate. I know, because she's Nancy.

A couple of weeks go by. Lots of meetings with Micki and—that marvelously reassuring word—lawyers.

Then that rather scary final phone call. Well, Mummy, we're off. I get that choking sensation—nothing more I can do. We engage in some of our usual light bantering. The silly stuff: her hair style; will she cheat and ever drink good wine instead of Cold Duck; what if she needs a dentist? But behind all this, I sense that she needs some small sign of support from us. Saul and I have already talked over this aspect. He has naturally discussed the whole thing endlessly with Nancy. I tell her—with what I hope is some grace —that if and when Micki visits Nick in Hartford, we will meet her, have cocktails with her. Obviously, Nance is pleased. She realizes our reservations, knows this is an indication of our underlying loyalty and support always.

What a day that was, the day of the swap. I played miserable golf, snarled at my friends, inwardly cursed the Muse, the literary tradi-tion, permissive society. Why did that phrase "Get thee to a nun-nery" keep filtering through my mind?

It was Thursday, I remember. Talked to Nick, hysterically planned with Saul. We would meet at our house when Micki got off the train, have drinks, and then, Saul and I decided after much discus-sion, unless we were too uncomfortable, we would all have dinner together.

Micki walked in the door with Nick. Strange, strange. Yelling as did her alter ego, I'm home, I'm home. I look at her. She's wearing one of Nancy's thirties dresses and around her neck, my daughter's pearls and pendant.

I kiss her—one of those ladylike kisses, not the big-hug kind.

Nick makes drinks while she rushes up to "her" bedroom—always the pattern. As she flies up the stairs, she calls down, Mom, I'm out of Shalimar. I clutch; this is forever Nancy's opening line. Supplying my daughter with Shalimar could be a full-time occupation for a *very* rich man. I follow her up. I ponder this request: How ethical do I have to be? Nuts—it's enough. I go to my dressing table and, without explaining, give Micki some Shalimar cologne. Nancy of course only wants perfume from me and knows the difference immediately by color. Poor Micki accepts the scented water, thinking it's the real thing, thanks me, and I feel much better; in this small way I sort of feel as though I've gotten back at both of them. After all, who is this strange creature who wants some of my special scent? I'd gladly give my own daughter the last drop, but not the phony one.

Saul arrives, tired, harried—he is marvelous in forcing himself to play this game. We sit in the living room and drink. Micki tries— oh, yes, she tries—she calls us Mom and Dad. But her trying doesn't make it happen. She knows what to ask: How's my painting, how is our golf, how are things at Saul's office? What's new with our friends? But she doesn't listen, just talks. She attempts desperately to convince us of her brilliance, that she is smarter than Nancy. No way she can persuade us. She talks too much.

We go to Edelweiss for dinner. A favorite family spot for a simple undressed meal when I'm either tired or lazy. She keeps talking.

Her knowledge of us is awesome; her knowledge of Nancy's interests, habits, attitudes is tremendous. But she is Micki all the way.

In the restaurant, she orders à la carte extras. It's an old family gag —we don't do that sort of thing unless there's a special reason. After dinner, she asks for brandy. Edelweiss just isn't a place where one sits around sipping brandy, particularly since we have much better stuff at home. How different from our real daughter. Every so often, she says that now she is going to be herself, not Nancy, and she then launches into some pretentious critique of an aspect of Nancy's life, a critique full of that illiterate jargon of pseudopsychiatry.

We return to our house for a short while—more of the same.

Do I like Micki? Do I *have* to like Micki? Is this a fair way to judge? Perhaps if I met her under other circumstances—but could I possibly enjoy another girl in Nancy clothes, wearing Nancy's jewelry, living in Nancy's apartment? No way. Most important, she is making snap judgments about too many facets of Nancy's life. In spite of her professional training, she cannot do this effectively; no one could. And I still don't know her motivation in going into the swap. Nancy after all has a statement she wants to make. But Micki—why?

We finally say good night. Micki cries as she leaves, hugs us both. Why does she cry? What does that mean about her emotional stability? She must see us again after this swap is over, she says. Maybe, I think.

She goes to Nick's place with him. The next morning we compare notes, he and I—very similar reactions.

Oh, it was a bad night. How did my darling daughter get into this? There's no way she could ever truly swap lives with Micki—no way.

We talk and talk, Saul and I. Let this whole thing be over with . . . let the book come out . . . let Nancy finish the actual swap experience unscathed. That's all.

Perhaps we can meet Micki again, just talk with her as we have with many of Nancy's friends. She's smart, and we like smart people. But, listen, girl, stay out of my daughter's life. You can't swap with Nance. There's only one Nance: She's the one who knows the real from the imitation—she knows the difference between cologne and perfume.

Sig Lewis: Oh, Pooey

Sometimes I study *The Village Voice* public notices compulsively; other times I skim the ads or skip them completely. This time I was skimming when LET'S SWAP LIVES caught my eye. It seemed like an interesting idea, but who—?

Micki and Ben dropped over that evening, and suddenly I knew who. She was right in spirit, but size 8 wardrobe? She said yes. Could I answer the ad in her behalf? Again, yes.

A couple of weeks later Micki called. "You did it. I'm doing it."

March 9. It was getting serious, and I noted the date. Ben was concerned because he didn't know how to act toward Nancy. Micki told him to act as if Nancy *were* Micki. He said he couldn't. I said Nancy wouldn't know the difference, so why care?

March 16. Micki said Nancy was getting a better deal in terms of a "body count," Micki's many versus Nancy's six-year-old lover. No, a lover of six years' standing. No, a lover who—We were too stoned to rephrase it correctly.

June 16. I knew that Micki and Nancy had swapped a few days ago and that Ben was with Nancy in Riverset. Ben called me. We talked about other things for a while. Then I asked, "How's Micki?"
BEN: Hard to answer. There are really two answers. Do you want to talk to her?
ME *(nervous):* Okay. Hello, Micki.
NANCY: Hello. Are you the son of a bitch that got me into this thing?
ME: I guess I am. How are you?
NANCY: Okay.
ME: It's good to talk to you.
NANCY: It's been a while.
ME (flirtatious?): Well, we'll make up for it later. See you.
NANCY: Good-bye.

I had spoken to Her. I was shaking. She had swapped lives, and I had spoken to her. I once won an honorable mention in a *New York* magazine competition but never actually got to *speak* to Mary Ann Madden.

June 17. Alice and I had a party for Nancy and Ben. Eight people came who knew Micki, and two who didn't. All knew about the swap.

Nancy and Ben were the last to arrive. Nancy hugged Alice and me when she came in. For a moment or two the noise of the other people masked the general awkwardness of the situation. Then the noise died down. Nancy greeted several people by name. I wondered how Micki had described them to her. And how had she described me?

Nancy walked boldly into the living room. Had she been given a floor plan, too?

Boldness over, awkwardness resumed. I took her arm. "Come on, Micki, why don't you sit in your favorite spot on the floor?"

There were some others sitting nearby on the floor. Nancy initiated several short conversations—with Alice, about teaching; with Ed, about his latest film project—but they fizzled out. Nancy asked me a few questions in whispers. "Who's that? Do I know him?" Sometimes the questions were more in the spirit of the game. "In the red slacks. I've forgotten what she does?"

I tried some lines of conversation that would make sense to the real Micki, but they went dead. Nancy tried hard. She was actually quite clever in handling my remarks in an ambiguous way. I wasn't trying to defeat her in this game but to play along, to cooperate. Why was it so difficult?

Ben tried to help. Some others came in for a line or two. The New York mayoral race was touched upon, and Nancy launched into a long story about Badillo. It killed time. No one looked comfortable. Micki might discuss radical politics, especially if there were an interesting sexual angle, but never liberal politics.

People moved around the room, danced. Nancy remained sitting on the floor. Micki would have been dancing.

Ben looked uncomfortable, bored. Micki would have put her arm around him and said comfortingly, "Oh, Pooey."

Why was I continuously comparing this Micki to the real Micki? What did I expect? Why were we all doing this? The game was wearisome. I was thankful I only had to play for hours, not weeks.

Nancy and Ben were leaving. Alice and I walked them to the door. In the flurry of good-byes Ben mumbled something about "kicking my ass." I didn't hear exactly what he said. Nancy snuggled against him and said, "Oh, Pooey."

Francine Berman Rosen:
Micki's Meeting / Meeting Nancy

Bob and I are the first to get there Monday night.

"You're Fran," Micki says at the door, though we haven't yet met, just had some wild phone calls. "Come on in."

It's too easy to walk in and sit down. It's not easy with Nancy. The apartment is Nancy's. Micki's in it, but Nancy's with it. The room doesn't feel the same. Who is this woman living in it, and why have I answered her summons to a meeting for Nancy's "support group"?

"I'm so glad you came. Make yourself at home," Micki says, then launches into a discourse on how distraught she's been and brings out evidence.

"Here, I found this poem that Nancy wrote. She just wasn't straight about leaving me clues. She wanted me to get rid of Mike for her."

I don't want to know all of this about Nancy and Mike. It's none of my business. I don't want to read Nancy's poetry. I read. I joke, "And she has the nerve to criticize my poetry." Say anything, Fran, to relieve your tension.

I never sucked a cock
To tell the truth

Micki's talking on about Nancy's "clues." Micki explains how she understands the poem but that she wishes she'd found it sooner. How it's too late now.

The doorbell rings, and an older man, Riff, walks in. He's carrying a bottle of sangría. Someone named Abbe arrives. He has curly hair. He sits down and takes out a book of cartoons in French. Bob attempts to discuss it with him.

Micki's friend Ted is at the desk, typing. I don't know where he came from. A man named Henry comes and goes. I'm chain-smoking and can't fit into place. Bob askes me if I want to leave. "Nothing's going to happen. Let's face it." "Something's going to happen. I can feel it," I assure him.

Micki sits down next to Bob and me, and the three of us start to discuss the swap. We realize that if Micki's being Micki, and Nancy's being Micki, there is no Nancy. Has Nancy truly disintegrated? Micki starts talking about Nancy's habits. How Micki always wears a watch and Nancy doesn't, how Micki always keeps a neat purse and Nancy doesn't, how Nancy always carries a pepper mill in her purse. That strikes me extremely funny. She speaks about Trigger Mike, and as she does, I begin to break out in welts. Micki touches them gently. While talking, she pushes my hair from my face. They feel like nice gestures.

"Hey, Bob," I say, "should we ask all of our questions now?"

"Like what?" Micki asks.

"Like who's King Sylvester in *Star Fever?*"

"Well, Nancy left me a list of people." Micki hands me a bunch of papers. "Maybe you'll find him in here."

I thumb through the pages.

Micki points as my eyes glance at it. "There's you."

"Yeah, I see."

It strikes me that I shouldn't be reading this, but how can I not? I'm not even sure if I want to read it; I'm afraid to read it. I've never known what Nancy thinks of me. I'm insecure about Nancy. How can she feel anything, anyway?

Her note says that I'm about twenty, we met when I went for an interview for a secretary job, I'm a writer, I'm prone to her advice, we have a mystical connection and one night I picked up her panic, I think she's a witch, I'm engaged to a really nice guy Bob, and that she feels protective toward me and likes me a lot.

My eyes have become attached to that last line: "I feel protective toward her and like her a lot." It's ironic and scary. Ironic because Nancy, of all people, helped me realize that it's not necessary to look for someone to be protective. I've been able to relate to her in the present tense, unobsessively. It's scary because I've always been scared of Nancy and know that if I explore it, I'll finally know why. But I can't. I have to digest that last line.

The doorbell rings.

Micki turns to me, "We really shouldn't let anyone see that paper. Of course it's all right if you see it."

Am I special? Why can I see it?

I hand the papers back to Micki.

I know that I shouldn't have seen those notes at all. I feel suddenly obligated and responsible and try desperately to place my feelings.

The door opens, and Nancy charges in with some people.

My initial reaction is to hide. How can she be here; how can she catch me intruding?

Vibrations start flying through the room. I know that this isn't going to be right. I immediately light up a cigarette, and Bob points out that I'm shaking. I'm not even sure that I exist.

Micki looks at Nancy, "I'm very unhappy that you're here."

"Well," Nancy says, "if this is for the support of Nancy Weber, I'm one of her greatest supporters."

A confrontation is in progress. I turn my head so I can hear but don't have to see.

"At least I didn't go around telling all your friends that you're schizoid," Nancy shouts to Micki.

I know I won't be able to handle this.

Someone calls "Mike." Bob and I both turn around and for the first time see him. We both pick up strange and dangerous vibrations from him.

At one point, I find Nancy sitting next to me. Who is Nancy? Bob explains the no-Nancy theory. She's drinking Irish whiskey, and Micki walks over and says, "Why not ask Nancy who King Sylvester is?"

Dramatically, Nancy gets up and says, "King Sylvester is—King Sylvester," and walks away.

I get up and go over to Micki. I can't relate to Nancy and feel a strong hostility. If she hadn't shown up, maybe I could've survived. I can't relate to her at all and know she doesn't understand why Bob and I are there.

"Micki? Where did you hide our jackets?"

Micki turns around, looks at me pleadingly, and puts her arms around me. What is this subplot in the insanity? Why comfort Micki and not Nancy? I put my arms around Micki and actually feel who she is. I'm into the rawness of all the emotion. I've never seen Nancy so stripped of protectiveness and exposed and harsh and fighting. I feel hostile; I can almost believe that I hate her.

Touching Micki and comforting her is a comfort to me.

"Please don't leave me now. Now is when I need you," Micki pleads.

"If you want us to stay, we will."

"Just until Peter, my lover, comes. Then we can all leave together."

"All right."

I feel this growing bond with Micki.

There's nothing, less than nothing, going on between Nancy and me. I'm tripping on it. I hope that with Bob's strength and Micki's new comfort, I'll be able to retain my sanity until the night is over.

Nancy's in the john changing her clothes. There are vibes: I must go in there.

"Hi, Nancy."

"Hi."

"I'm supposed to say something to you."

"Like what?"

"I don't know."

"Who sent you in here?"

"I did."

Nancy turns around and touches my shoulder. I make it a point to touch hers. At this point I know she's not a witch. I feel an emptiness knowing that. But I still know the vibrations between us exist. I haven't yet digested what she wrote about me, and at this moment, it's even harder to take.

"Did you get to know Micki at all?" she says.

"A little. She called me in the middle of the night."

"Did you take care of each other?"

"I think so."

"That's good." She walks out, and I follow her.

"She called right after vibes and welts," I say.

"Oh, Fran."

"I know it's only a coincidence but don't think you believe I believe that."

Unconvincingly, "I believe you."

Micki's sitting on the floor, and Nancy takes a silver wedding band off her finger and hands it to her. Micki puts it in her pocket. It's over. I want to cry. It's too dramatic. I turn my head.

Lover Peter comes. He's so young. Why does anything surprise me at this point? Hurry, Micki, please. I have to get out of here.

I feel filled with guilt about leaving with Micki. But something's going on. I'm getting a hunch. Looking at Nancy is making me feel awful, but I can't believe she'd give a shit if she knew. It doesn't seem to matter to her that I'm there. I try never to take silence from my friends as indifference, but I feel that Nancy's less than indifferent. Let me leave with Micki. I know there will be warmth.

Micki, Peter, Ted, Riff, Bob, and I walked out. Down in the courtyard Micki suggests we all go celebrate. I'm physically and emotionally exhausted, and I want to run, but I'm still into something with Micki. I look at Bob and know he just wants to go home. I have to let some of that bridge-playing communication he's taught me come through. I squeeze his hand and tell Micki we'll come along. "A hunch," I whisper to him.

Bob and Ted head off to get our car. The rest of us walk toward Grove Street, where Nancy's left Micki's car. After a block or two, Micki's walking by my side. I try not to think of my confusion and pain with Nancy. I'm not ready to admit, just yet, my feelings for Nancy. I decide instead to collect as much data as I can.

Micki and I cross the street, and a car comes. I reach out for her arm and tell her to be careful. I realize that Micki and I are having a spiritual affair. I find it good for my soul at that moment, a comfort. Like the rest of the evening, it's all so totally raw and real. I'm not afraid; I'm eager. But I don't know for what.

We get to the car. I wonder where I'll sit. Peter says he'll drive, and Riff suggests to Micki that she get in next to him.

"I can always sit with Peter," Micki answers. "I want to sit with Fran."

She smiles at me. We're sitting exceptionally close to one another, and I feel good about it. Micki talks on about how Nancy is a lying cunt, how awful Mike is.

I look at Micki and say, "There's one part mostly when I felt strange tonight."

"When was that?"

"Remember that list of people you showed me?"

"Yes, I have it with me; you can look at it when we get to Ted's." That makes the guilt return.

"You know what Nancy wrote about me?"

"Yes."

"Well, I never knew she felt that way about me."

Micki puts her hand on my knee. "I know."

"How did you know?"

She smiles.

Micki talks some more about the evening. My mind switches back on the scene with the wedding band. At one point I mention that I seemed to have been the only one there tonight with only one lover. She says that's not really true because we're all lovers. Pointing to Peter and Riff in the front seat, Micki says, "We're all lovers. They're your lovers, and I'm your lover." It's a real feel-good statement.

We go to Ted's apartment. Bob is there. I kiss him and tell him I've missed him and give him a look. I know he knows what I'm saying. We all sit down and someone begins to pass around two joints. Riff keeps one, and the other one goes around. Bob doesn't take any. After a while we explain that we'd love to stay, but we have to be up in three hours.

Micki walks over to me and kisses me on the cheek. We put our arms around one another, and I want to cry. I hug her hard, and she answers back. It's as if no one else is there.

Bob and I go into the elevator, and I fall against the wall mumbling, "What a hug."

"Hug?" Bob says. "That was an embrace."

Wednesday I wake up scratching my body and hear voices shouting, "Micki, Nancy, Nancy, Micki," on and on.

That evening I decide to call Nancy. I don't know what I'll say, but I can't bear it any longer. She's not in. I'm relieved. I ask her service to say that I've called. Bob and I end up seeing a porno movie. It wasn't our intention, but we misread the ads. I almost cry at the lesbian scene.

We come home, and I run to the message pad. Nancy hasn't

called. I decide to get straight with myself. I matter-of-factly speak to Bob of the possibility of my loving Nancy. I know I do and have been afraid to admit it. I know that when I walked into the bathroom, I wanted to tell her. I know that what scares me about it is the responsibility and obligation I tend to feel on admitting love. But I also know the torment that goes along with suppressing it.

Bob hollers, "You don't love her." It sounds so threatening, like "don't you dare."

I want him to understand the transactions with Micki and the confusion and suppression of my feelings for Nancy. I explain the differences between physical and emotional bisexuality and then relate it to the spiritual affair with Micki and how unthreatening it was. He understands it all, and I'm relieved. I've been able to release it from my body and watch it all take its place.

And within myself it's all becoming clear. My intentions were only good, and they got fucked over. I'll probably never hear from Micki again, but it was nice and comforting for a while, and the subplot was something I loved. And the pain was because of my love and caring for Nancy.

It's after eleven, and Nancy hasn't called back. I seem to know that she's gotten the message and has chosen not to return the call. I've got to do what must be done, even if it means exposing my three-day-old wounds and getting more.

"Nancy."

"Yes."

"This is Fran."

"Hello, Fran."

Something's terribly wrong. This is going to hurt. It's going to be a beginning or an end. I must follow through.

"Do you have a minute?"

"Yes, I have a minute."

"I'm not sure what to say. I'm feeling anger and hostility."

"Why the fuck are *you* hostile?" says Nancy.

"I don't know."

Nancy says it all—that she was surprised at us; there were sides to be taken Monday night, and we took Micki's.

I take a breath. "When I walked into the bathroom?"

"Yes?"

"I—I—I—" Say it, dammit! "I wanted to tell you I loved you."

"I didn't give you a chance," she says.

She goes on again about how wrong we were. I try to explain that we didn't know what we were doing there, we didn't want to be there, and then—what she'd written about me.

"Didn't you know it wasn't for your eyes?"

"Of course I knew that, and I feel terrible and guilty, and that's why I wanted to hide."

"What did it say?"

"How we met, that I thought you were a witch, and now I know that you're not, and feel awful about that, and that—you felt protective toward me and liked me a lot. I never knew that."

"You mean you never felt any warmth from me?"

It sounds so terrible. That isn't it.

"It's just that I've spent all this time realizing I shouldn't look for people to be protective, and you're one of the people who helped me see that."

A pause.

"I'm sorry," I finally say.

"Well, fuck it," Nancy says. "There's something you can do to make up for it. Will you do it?"

"Sure, what is it?"

Nancy's voice has changed and become gentle again—the only way I've ever heard her before.

"Write it for my book. Write everything that's happened up until now."

I'm feeling all sorts of things.

"Okay," I say.

"You're a writer, dammit, and you can do it."

And there's the Nancy I'm accustomed to—pushing, hitting me with a strength that no one else gives, or maybe can give.

"Just watch your semicolons," she says.

"I'm a comma freak."

"I know."

"And that'll make up for it?"

"You don't have to make up for it," she says. "Are you all right?"

"Yeah. I'm all right."

"Are you sure?"

"Yeah."

"Okay," Nancy says.

That means it's time to go.

"Okay," I say.

Nancy kisses me over the phone. I have a thing about getting kissed on the forehead and kissed over the phone. It makes me feel awkward. I'm busy for about three seconds contemplating it, smiling.

"I love you," Nancy says.

"I love you," I say.

I hang up the phone and cry hysterically for a few seconds, letting loose, feeling the relief that was so long and roundabout in coming.

Cassie Davidson: Life Shop

The announcement arrived in the morning mail like an invitation
to a birthday party. *Nancy and Micki request the pleasure of your
company in their life swap.* Hope, my ten-year-old daughter, who
enjoys dressing up as much as any kid and relishes the fantasy of
having a twin, was enthralled. "A life swap," she squealed. "It's
like a costume party" (her favorite kind). Hope gave no immediate
thought to existential questions of identity.

I examined the invitation. *I want to know if people can get out
of their skins,* Nancy's ad had said *(references, lawyers, all safeguards),* and Micki had answered, *I am already out of my skin, and
am willing to try yours.*

Micki, one of the more daring and experimental among my
friends, a sociologist of obvious integrity, was right in there con-
ducting her investigations first hand. When I had last spoken to her
she had been looking for a new job and a new setup for the
following year. Now, I imagined her pleasure on reading Nancy's
ad in *The Voice,* thinking it a godsend. What a good way to satisfy
wanderlust: switch job, residence, friends, identity in a single
move and get a unique angle on the Important Questions at the
same time. She was the perfect person to answer such an ad.
Bravo Micki! Lucky Nancy!

Then I read the announcement again: *life swap, June 11 to 24.*
The proposed switch was not for a year but for two weeks! I had
misunderstood. This life swap was evidently a vacation, not an
investigation. Two weeks would hardly be time enough to become
oriented to a new job, residence, circle of people, skin, let alone
time to feel at home in them. Perhaps time enough for a few good
fucks, maybe even a fast romance; time to sample the local wines
and observe the quaint customs of the natives; but no more.

Well, Micki was a hard-working woman who deserved an interesting vacation. She was not one of those people to take a Carib-
bean cruise or share in a Fire Island beach house. She had no
children to think about, no nuclear family to convince. Why not?
Two weeks in someone else's life, while involving no more risk or
commitment than two weeks in Paris, might be a nice diversion.

Hope took the announcement from my hand and began reading
it aloud. *"You are invited to come along. The rules are simple. Call
us by each other's name, treat us as if we were the person you've
always called by that name, and believe that we're going to do
everything we can to be what the old Nancy, the old Micki are to
you."* She gave me a prodding shove. "Go on, Mom. Call them
up."

I hate to refuse Hope anything, but what could I do? The "simple rules" of the invitation would be impossible for me to follow.
It might be easy enough to pretend a stranger was a friend if the
relationship were governed by conventions. If you were a date or
a lover, say, a boss or an office mate. (I remembered regretfully
the impersonal interchangeability of certain lovers and certain
jobs at one time in my own life.) But if you were intimate friends?
If your intimacy depended on candor and trust? If your friendship
encompassed an exchange of treasured ideas and confidences
which arose out of the unique experiences of a lifetime? That
was precisely the kind of friendship I had with Micki. It was serious; I could not take it lightly. The night we first met, she, another friend Leona, and I had talked about our lives and feelings
till three in the morning. It had been such a rewarding high that
we had agreed to continue meeting as a threesome every month
or so to grapple openly with the Important Questions. We never
wasted time on pleasantries. No, it would take almost as long for
Nancy to be (as the announcement promised) "what the old
Micki is" to me as for the proverbial typewriting monkey to com-
pose *King Lear.*

"Well?" said Hope, with visions of a summer Halloween. "Aren't you going to call?"

Micki, whom I know to be open and introspective—the best kind of traveler—would be sure to get the most out of her vacation. I could hardly wait to hear all about it. But if I called her up, I would reach the false Micki.

"No, honey," I said, "I'm afraid not."

She scowled in disgust. "Just like a grown-up. Spoiling all the fun."

Suddenly I found myself on the defensive. It wasn't fair. I had done nothing. I genuinely wished the swappers a bon voyage. Yet there was my daughter unwrapping two pieces of bubble gum with an accusing look on her face. "Come on now, Hope," I said, and took her on my knee. I tried to explain that though I had enjoyed charades at her age, I no longer had time for them. (Hope made a terrible moue at this and began chewing.) I offered to live as someone else for a while myself—to be Karen's mother for a week and let Karen's mother be me if she agreed—that sounded like fun. (Hope shook her head in a violent *no!*) But as for being supporting cast in someone *else's* switch, pretending some total stranger was an intimate friend or some intimate friend was a total stranger—that was bound to be a bore. If we were allowed to talk about the switch, that might be interesting, but the rules forbade it. If we couldn't be ourselves either, what could we possibly discuss but the weather?

By now Hope was looking painfully bored herself, popping bubbles to distraction. That child simply hates serious discussions. She'd had enough.

"Anyway," I concluded, "I'd call if I could talk to the real Micki" (I'm *not* a bad sport! and I was dying to hear her thoughts on the swap), "but I don't know how to get in touch with her."

"Just call the other one and ask for her phone number," suggested Hope sensibly.

I doubted it would work, but I did want to restore myself in my daughter's eyes. I picked up the phone and dialed Micki's New York number.

"Hi?" I said tentatively when a woman came on. "This is Cassie. Is that Micki?"

"This is Micki."

"Which one?" I felt like a fool.

"Why, is there another?" asked the good woman coyly. It was not *my* Micki.

After an awkward moment, I proceeded. "I called to see—uh, would you mind giving me your friend Nancy's telephone number?"

"Nancy?" said the woman on the phone. "I don't believe I know anyone named Nancy."

It was a toss-up whether I felt more intimidated or stupid. I thought of poor Micki, stranded in someone else's life, perhaps unable to speak the language, with no way for her friends to reach her. "Oh," I said helplessly, "I thought you did."

Hope, who loves nothing more than a good conspiracy, was jumping up and down at my elbow. "Go on," she goaded in a stage whisper, "go on and make a date."

"Shh," I said. The situation was untenable, but what could I do? "I haven't seen you for such a long time, Micki. Maybe we could get together for a fast drink?"

"Yes, I'd love that," said the false Micki.

We arranged to meet at a place within walking distance from my apartment. I dared hope that when the time came perhaps she would be so tired of pretense that she would drop the pose long enough to engage in some genuine exchange with me. She sounded quite nice, actually, and it's not so easy for solitary folks like me to meet congenial new people in New York. Naturally, I could not count on discussing the Important Questions with her right off (if ever: trust is a tricky soul that needs nourishing), but perhaps we could strike some common chord.

"One more thing," I said before hanging up. "I know we're close friends and all, but how will we recognize each other?"

"Oh, don't worry. I'll be wearing my usual Mexican clothes. Old friends like us shouldn't have any trouble."

"Not old," I corrected gently, for Micki and I had actually been friends for less than a year, "but intimate. I'll be wearing my feminist button."

Just in case she intended to carry the pose through to its tedious end, I took the precaution of inviting Leona, who is always good for a little soul-searching, to join us. I love Micki, but this other was an unknown quantity. If everything failed and false Micki insisted on limiting us to those topics available to strangers, at least Leona and I could make contact.

"You were great, Mom," said Hope. Inviting Leona met with Hope's full approval. Since in real life we usually met as a three-some, I was playing according to the rules.

When Arnold came home from work that night, Hope rushed to fill him in on the conspiracy. Micki-Nancy, Nancy-Micki, she kept squealing, and showed him the announcement.

My husband was suspicious. "I bet they're doing it so they can write a book," he said cynically. "You just watch. It's a ripoff."

"A book?" I was shocked. I am a writer myself and know how desperate people can get for book ideas, and the announcement did say Nancy was a writer. But it had never occurred to me that there was some ulterior purpose to the swap. It had seemed its own justification. "Oh no, Arnold. I'm sure they're just interested in exploring the social and psychological possibilities of another life."

"In two weeks?"

"Well, okay. Maybe not. But at least it's a nice vacation. A new place, a bunch of new people. It's not so easy to meet new people in New York, you know. Besides, what would be the appeal of such a book?"

"Come on now, Cassie. Won't they be sleeping with each other's men?"

Hope's eyes widened in renewed interest.

"Yes, but——"

"Mark my words," said Arnold, using the traditional phrase that makes it unnecessary later to say the less acceptable I told you so. "There'll be a book by the time this is over. Wait and see."

Aaron Tyman: Nancy Plays Micki

Micki plays Nancy
and vamps me;
Nancy never does.
Micki answers to "Nancy."
Transmigration
of the soul
is for spirits
not for me.

Letter From Dan(ny)

Dear Nancy,

My "participation" in the life swap has been passive throughout. My attitude is that I had no reason to prevent its taking place but, as I had no respect for the enterprise, I would minimize my involvement. Thus until now I did not accept your offer to write something "to up the truth quotient" in the book. This letter itself is the first and last active participation. I write only to clarify the attitudes underlying my behavior, both in living with you and in negotiating the legalities of this book.

As an author and scholar I strongly feel that people who have ideas, that is, they have something substantive to communicate, should write books. Your enterprise seemed to me from the first to stand this notion on its head. As I saw it then (and still see it now that the swap is over and the manuscript is prepared): You wanted to write a book but had Nothing to say. What to write? What to say? With nothing worthwhile to say, you had to create a gimmick, set up a situation, to give you something to journalize about. Well, you did that grandly. You found something that would possibly be more interesting to you and your readers than your spoiled upper-middle-class life of endless and meaningless consuming: expensive shoe stores, restaurants, bars, and more restaurants seem to fill (?) your life. If you think I'm exaggerating, reread the first part of your story.*

When you got the situation set up, I was inevitably part of it. I tried not to be uncooperative, but was mostly indifferent, not out of any dislike for you but out of a total lack of respect for your endeavor. My lover and I are easygoing people and could easily tolerate you playing games in our house, but you must see why we weren't interested in playing.

Since you have found publishers, and possibly even readers, for this nonsense, I guess I can't accuse you of being silly (it proves you have a good business sense), but it depresses me that the publishing ripoff in America is so blatant and that the public must be so starved for things that they pay any attention to this.

Dan (not Danny!)

*Dan(ny) read the manuscript before he wrote this letter. The other contributors worked in the dark. N.W.

Audrey Evert: Paddy Irish and Gallo Red

My friend Nancy is a masculist—a woman who looks up to men —complete with a letter from Norman Mailer framed and hanging on her bathroom wall. She is a woman who admires prizefighters, horse races, tough-guy newspapermen, Paddy Irish Whisky. Nancy is also a lady. She likes formal evenings, pastel carryalls, flower arrangements. Women's Lib would indict her for schizo-phrenia and then, in its typical fashion, probably send her a lawyer and bail bondsman.

Micki, on the other hand, is a feminist. She has peeked over the edge of her own femininity and vulnerability and found the void, and the void was terrible. She became political, but the void was still there. She has a husband in Buffalo, a lover in her Manhattan apartment, and problems. She has seen hysteria. She is no Ti-Grace.

That these two people could exchange existences, swap their lives, seems like an odds-on favorite for disaster. And it was. They mixed like oil and water or, maybe better, like Paddy Irish and Gallo Red wine (a perennial Lib group favorite), leaving interesting stains on each other's psychic tablecloths. But some good did come out of it. Nancy and I got to be friends, after a fashion. And for a while there, insights of an interpersonal nature fell like rain.

I first met Nancy on a balmy, restless night in early April: the kind of weather that drives you out of doors, pushes crocuses up through the ground, and drives sex molesters to do things they regret. That particular night it had driven me and about fifty other people into the Lion's Head, which had doors propped open and the air circulating.

Sitting at the bar I found Bennett, an old friend of mine. I see Bennett once every three years, and within five minutes we are launched into a discussion of eternal verities. Life, fame, love, art all come tumbling out of Bennett in an optimistic manner. After ten minutes of talking to him, you are joyously, mindlessly exclaiming, "Things are going to be all right."

Into this steamy good will walked Nancy and Trigger Mike Kagan. Nancy appeared to be in a daze, a daze that in all the time I've known her has never really left her. She smiled sweetly and vacantly and cast demure, alluring glances around the room. She was well dressed, well groomed, tidy. She seemed to consider her remarks before making them, and she spoke in paragraphs. Right away I knew I wasn't going to like her.

Since Trigger Mike is a friend of Bennett's and also of mine, the four of us grouped together in a friendly lull. The conversation foundered briefly and settled down on the subject of Nancy's next book. She said she was going to exchange her existence—clothes, apartments, lovers, toothbrushes—with an uptown sociologist. She said she had found her through *The Village Voice*.

After a digestive pause, we all fell down praising the idea. Mike was strangely quiet. "Wow," Bennett said, "that is really a nifty idea, Nance. That is really superb."

"Terrific," I said. "Incredible." Bennett and I were holding each other up, euphorically exclaiming what a fine idea it was, how it offered a rare course in the nature of human potential, had the same fascination as the doppelgänger throughout literature. Right away I got the idea Nancy wasn't going to like me.

"I don't think Nancy likes me," I told Mike a week later.
"Sure she does, kid," said Mike.

"I don't know," I said. "She's sitting over there looking pretty hostile."

"Naw," said Mike. "Really, she likes you."

"I think she thinks I think you're cute," I said. That was a cop-out; I admit it. Still it was easier than explaining alluring glances, the doppelgänger throughout literature. "And I do," I added. "You are cute."

"Aw, shucks," he said. Mike is very loose.

"Look," I said, "I don't care if she likes me or not. But it's kind of awkward, don't you think, since I talk to you, to have her ignoring us?"

The next time I ran into Mike, he was sitting in the Lion's Head with a strange girl, both of them dressed to the nines, looking peculiar. The girl was tall, skinny, with short, curly hair, looking very much like I look as a tall girl when I have short curly hair: like what someone once described as a telephone pole with a bird's nest on top. She was wearing a mostly white thirties dress and would have looked better in a peasant blouse. She looked very uncomfortable. Right away I concluded her to be Micki. Mike was looking very mournful and motioned frantically for me to come over.

"How are you liking the swap?" I asked Micki.

"Well, you know," she said, "I'm trying to deal with it rationally. I'm not doing so well, am I, Trig?"

"You're doing okay, kid." Mike glanced off in the other direction. He offered, "Micki is a sociologist."

"Well, I'm *trying*," she said. "I really *am*. Maybe I'll get the hang of it. Who knows? Who knows?"

Right away also I concluded Micki's mental state was not all it might be. Under a semisane exterior, she had the look of a person who was hanging on to a cliff with bitten fingernails.

"Are you a friend of Nancy's?" she inquired.

"Actually," I said, "you should be chilly to me. Nancy doesn't like me."

"She does *toooo*," protested Trigger Mike.

"Oh, dear," said Micki. "Why is that?"

"I don't know. I think she thinks I think Trig is cute."

"Well, he *is* kind of cute," said Micki, sitting back in appraisal.

"Well," Micki went on, "I'm a feminist, and I think women should talk to each other, so I'm going to talk to you." Mike winced.

"I am too and I do too," I said. "Terrific."

Mike pulled me aside. "Why don't you have dinner with me Wednesday? I can't see Nancy. It'll be the nicest thing that happens to me all week," he said mournfully.

"How's the old hanky-panky aspect going?" I said, referring to Micki.

"We're consummating tonight. Already I'm not looking forward to it."

"Mike," I said, "you have a crummy attitude."

"Well, I can't help it. She's not trying at all. She's not trying to be like Nancy. She's just being herself. She just talks about herself all the time."

"That should be interesting, something new."

"Yeah, well——"

Next Monday, Nancy and Mike were in the Head. Nancy was wearing a peasant blouse. "You're not supposed to be here, are you?" I asked her.

"No," she said. She looked about as mournful as Micki and Mike had the week before. "But, it sure as hell beats some of the places I've been of late."

It was the most real statement I had ever heard out of Nancy.

"Trig says you think I don't like you," she said. There was an uncomfortable pause. "I really do," she said. "I don't know; I have a lot of trouble talking to women. I don't make friends with women easily."

To say that Nancy and I were bosom chums since that moment would be nice for dramatic purposes, but it would be a lie. Her "man's woman" philosophical position I find indefensible. Still, it isn't ideology so much as personality that determines what we are. Nancy and I, on two different sides of the philosophical fence, have a lot in common, even an ex-lover or two. Micki and I, sharing philosophy and sympathy, will probably never see each other again, since our personalities cause us to lead different lives. And Nancy, if not the most let-it-all-hang-out-honest feminist, is at least an interesting case.

"How are things going with the swap?" I said to Nancy a little while later. She and Mike had gone off near the jukebox to confer.

"Not good at all," she said.

"Micki is calling up all of Nancy's friends and telling them she's schizo," offered Mike.

"She's sitting in my house right now, wearing my clothes, having a party for my friends, telling them all I'm a schizo," Nancy marveled. "*I'm* a schizo! And she wants to save my soul."

"Wow," I said.

"I'm dying to go over there and find out what's happening, but I don't know. What do you think?"

"It's a good idea," I said.

So, after some short preparations, off we went: Nancy, me, Trigger Mike, a girl named Roz, and my friends Jay and Bernie.

"The kid may look okay," Trig said to me, "but she's really very hurt and disappointed."

When we got there, it was clear that Micki was worse. In fact it was clear that Micki was coming apart at the seams, cheerfully strewing bits of her stuffing at bystanders. She didn't look at all happy to see us. She and Nancy embraced awkwardly, and the room immediately set itself up like a theater. Five people extended themselves across the couch, and Mike sat in a nearby chair. Nancy sat in a shelf seat (offstage) in the opposite corner. One shaggy-haired person, whom logistics had left behind, sat in the middle of the floor with a bottle of apple juice.

"How have you been, Micki?" I said. Somebody had to do it.

"Not so good," Micki said.

"Yeah," Mike said.

"I've been trying, actually, but it's been very hard. Like the first day I came in here. I tried to figure out what Nancy would do. I figured if you have an answering service, that the first thing you would do when you come in the door is call it, right? So I did, and there's a message from Magda, so I call Magda and say, 'Thank you for leaving the message.' And Magda says, 'Nancy would never say that—thank you for leaving a message.' I mean, I can't win."

"That's pretty terrible," said Mike.

"Don't keep riding me, Mike; you just cut it out. Then," she continued, "Mike *locked* me in the house all Tuesday morning. I was a *prisoner* here."

"Come on, you weren't going anywhere," Mike said.

"Well, I might have, and I couldn't have if I wanted to," she said.

"Oh, Micki, you are so fulla shit," Mike said. "Fuck you."

"And I'll never do *that* again, either."

"That's fine with me. It's nothing I have any desire to repeat."

"Mike, you are one of the worst people I've ever met. If you want to trade insults, just get me started, just get me started. You're a male chauvinist pig, and all you do is talk about yourself all the time."

"Tough talk, tough talk," Trig said.

She haranged off for a minute, to the whole room, in a high close-to-breaking voice. "I am desperately trying to be objective and analytical, and I am getting completely incoherent." She tried to go on, but nothing came to her, and she sank cross-legged to the floor next to the shaggy-haired person with the apple juice. I became quite fond of her in that minute, nutsy, boggled, and incoherent on the floor, a shining symbol of all our inabilities to cope.

Minutes later, she got up, and she was gone.

Nick's Journals 6/12 and 6/15

6/12

Utter panic at Tard's on Sunday. She looked particularly cute and irresistible, a little more blonde and stupid than usual, gorgeous in a *Finzi-Contini* blouse and white pants. This creature had to be returned fully intact. I could have burst from high blood pressure and stomach jumpies as I looked around the Tard pad, where my sensibilities had been restored earlier in the day after I had been let down by an old New York girl friend and others. Nancy, like my parents, is great not just because she is great, but because she is fun to discuss ideas with, share things with—art, politics, literature. It's not just personality (though it helps).

Yesterday tried to call New Tard. I realized that I did not in fact feel that Nancy was away. Complete ease in dialing YU 2–XXXX. The phone number has taken on a personality of its own. I call it, and I know what *my* voice will be like when she answers. I know the exact position of the phone, the way N will pick it up (usually tripping gracelessly into position); I can sense every corner of the apartment, the Münter, the kitchen, the grass seat on the bench, the new sofa, the bar with the wire kangaroo, the record jackets lying on top of the records, the leather-bound books I gave Nancy as a Sarah Lawrence graduation present, each object on the too dark gray tea table. And familiar little YU 2–XXXX, one of my favorite tunes. Nancy may get out of her skin, but some of us can continue to be in it and enjoy it.

Good talk with New Tard today. I tried to sound as if I were speaking with the same Nancy as on Sunday, asking her how Micki was and what she had for lunch at the Exchange, talking about Trigger Mike. Micki was Micki when she asked me certain questions—how did the TV work?—and told me that she had been afraid about Mike but had found him great. This is of course not what N would have said but what M living in N's life would say, and we did have to be Nick and Micki when I told her the best way to get to Hartford. But I felt relieved because Micki had a warm glow and a sweetness to her voice, and I knew that Nancy was not doing this with a neurotic *schmegeggy* and that Micki would take care of things and herself. When I said that she should let me know if something turned up for Thursday and she couldn't come to Hartford, it was perfect that she giggled and said, "But, darling, how could anything be more important than you?"

It's all fun, a brilliant experiment, less scary now that we are in it and the end is in sight, a great idea of a way to travel, truly to expand, to overcome all of our existential loneliness or to discover that it cannot be overcome. We long to read every book, meet every person, travel to every place, know everything, and this seems like a new and maybe better way to do the same thing. I can feel warmth over the phone, security because I can dial that number and say "Tarducci"—much better than having real Tard someplace not great or in a bad mood, and I don't think I'll worry as much about New Tard's ups and downs, be quite as upset if she sees Jack Barleycorn again (but who knows, I may yet find that I react the same). It is all a little spacing out, and the phone call was strange because Micki was Nancy but was also Micki needing to have me straighten out certain details, perhaps needing me to be kind in some special way.

Mummy and Daddy will be taking us for dinner on Thursday. One thing the swap does for all of us in supporting roles is give us an extra chance to appreciate every detail and aspect of our own dailiness. Having dinner with my family becomes a real adventure because I'll see it all through someone else's eyes. I'll look at my own personality, humor, manners, role in Tard's life through new eyes; we all will. I hope I can resist the temptation to be too good, too well behaved, too on-vacation. I've told New Tard to tell Mummy she is almost out of Shalimar.

6/15

(Journal for this day originally written in a blind exhaustion and panic and marked NOT TO BE PRINTED AS WRITTEN. But now, with the coolness of retrospect—)

I had told her that she would recognize me at the Hartford train station because I looked like 1955 and would be in front in an orange MG. I, of course, would know her by her clothes. I first saw her coming down the steps from platform 4. (I realize now that she could not have realized that for me an arrival at the Hartford train station means thoughts of Russian novels—especially in the winter, when the Tardess wears her Mongolian lamb coat—or perhaps of the imitation Richardson aspects of the building itself; for her, it was only psychology and the swap itself on the brain.) As I went to meet her, she was really Tard and me Nick, except that she did not have Tard's pretty face or movement. When I put my arm around her, she was my Tard, in khaki pants with a scarf through the belt loops, wearing a silky white shirt, the pearls she had received as a Confirmation present, the art deco pendant, the smell of Shalimar. And since I really wanted to feel that it was Nancy, I did not look at the slightly squashed fish face.

She was warm and sweet and seemed *très* Nancy until she said, "I didn't bring the Scrabble set because we have so many important things to talk about," at which point I knew this was not Nancy but Micki Wrangler.

We went for a swim at our country club near Hartford. I had decided not to sign her in as a guest; she was Nancy (a member) after all, and the Nancy in the eyes of the club members could not possibly be there that week, and if the rest of the world could go along with it, so could the Board of Rumblestream. I would do anything to sit in on a Pool Committee meeting where it was discussed.

Micki looked cute in the water (although I panicked to see her keep on the pearls and pendant); but it was there that I began to hear an intense stream of conversation in a loud voice which did not cease for her entire visit and eventually made the inside of my ear ache ferociously. She babbled about how Mike was an MCP, how he had made a fool of himself at Frankie and Johnnie's, how he was self-conscious about his body, and I realized from these and other observations and attitudes that Micki was nothing but an invader in my sister's life. (The real N would have swum around while I grabbed her ankles or watched me imitate the Jewish lady's crawl, a technique perfected at our club whereby ladies can keep their hair completely out of the water, paddle their arms without splashing, and keep their kicks nicely submerged.) I knew from the moment her diatribe began that Micki was not becoming Nancy, but play-acting as Nancy, dressing as Nancy, and in that guise remaining Micki to the core. She mainly told me who she did *not* like (people whom Nancy might perhaps have complained about now and then, but ones whom she mainly enjoyed and loved). She was bursting to rip into their weaknesses, to tell me how George Warneke was abusing her, to explain why Mike was a nothing, all in an outbreak from which I could barely make out the details. She did tell me that she liked Abbe.

She spent ages changing at the club; she probably thought that Nancy would take a long time getting ready to go home, but her image of Nancy's vanity was way off base, as N never would have dared to keep me waiting that long, only to come out overdressed and over made up. The minute we got in the house, she asked Mum for Shalimar (as I'd cued her), then started to talk nonstop again (as Nancy never has). She observed the warmth of our family, or so she told me when I took her upstairs to see the bedroom she had had for twenty-four years, the bathroom in which she'd been reading a soggy copy of *Waiting for Winter* for nearly that long. I attributed the nonstop blabber to her nervousness, and I would say that as we started out for dinner, we were all prepared to give her the benefit of the doubt.

There was, of course, for all of us, an interest in hearing about Nancy's life from another point of view, and I think it took us all a while (really until the next day) to realize what we were up against. At dinner she repeated to my parents all of her complaints about Mike and George, calling them demanding, unrewarding, and insufficiently bright. We are not inclined to be cruel, but I think we would have preferred any of them to her at the table with us at that point. She ordered crab fingers as an appetizer—my little Princess never would have done *that* at an inland Swiss restaurant

—and managed to stretch out dinner interminably with her jabbering and ordering of all sorts of things. Dad kept telling her to eat, and Mummy explained that Daddy gets restless at long dinners.

Micki darted across the table, "Why is it up to Daddy? Why doesn't Mummy decide these things as well?" Then she asked Mummy what sort of painter she would have been as a man (could Bryn Mawr '63 really produce these clichés?), and I said that if Mummy had been a man she would have had to work for a living, instead of being able to hire help at home and paint as she loved. Mum agreed. Intense Women's Lib conversation sans humor, no Nancy shyness or sweetness, and lots of talk about her—Micki's —childhood. (Mum had said—anything to calm her down—"Now, Nancy, tell us about Micki's background.") Micki told us—and at this time the life swap became nothing but a game in changing the subject of each sentence to make it "she" instead of "I," with tears accompanying it all. After a while Dad turned to her and said, "You know, darling, in all of the years I've known you, I've never seen you talk more and eat less."

At one point during dinner, my father's tennis partner and his son came over to say hello. We all grinned. Mother cocked her head back, took in a deep breath, and said, "Steve—I'd like you to meet—Well, Steve, you remember our daughter, Nancy, don't you?" (The real one and he had been debating constitutional law only a few weeks earlier.) He looked as puzzled as could be. Dad said, "You remember—we told you, didn't we?"

"You I know for sure." Steve smiled at me, then left the sentence hanging. We all smiled. We felt we had given him something to brew over during dinner. Then Micki went right back to her political-professional analysis of the life of someone with whom we had all shared so many dinners and trips and years of love, cutting into her with the genius and sensibilities of a robot.

When we were walking out of the restaurant, Micki half crying on Mum's shoulder as she described her own mother's suffering, Dad—who is the sweetest of men (not saccharine, but kind) and usually very soft-spoken—turned to me with the greatest line of the swap, his face drawn with restless anger: "Your goddamn sister made me miss 'Kung-Fu.'"

On the way out to my cabin in the country, I had the great pleasure of having Miss Liberated Honest Open and Free tell me that she was in love with my mother, and she made it very clear that this meant physically. (Her attitude now was a no-nonsense one; she seemed to want to separate herself from the swap and the frivolous, dishonest, self-deceiving girl whose weaknesses she had so brilliantly been pointing out during dinner. She, Micki, would only be honest henceforth. I was to use her real name, meet her real self.) She told me that Mum was in love with her, too, to which I replied, "In that case, she certainly doesn't know it, and probably never will."

Micki also gave me the benefit of her professional analysis of the family, on what problems Nancy must have because mother is more attractive and poised than she, too much to live up to. I attempted to explain to Micki that in fact Mother's mother had been extraordinary in ways totally different from Mum herself, that Nancy had qualities my mother did not approach, but it wasn't worth the effort; I was tired, drawn; there was no one who listened, no one worth talking to, no purpose to indulging in family intimacy with this presumptuous bitch.

By the time we got to my little house, three small rooms filled with American primitive antiques and some great modern art on the edge of a wildlife reserve, I was still tempted to treat her as Nancy, but she wouldn't play cribbage or let me read or talk with her as I do with N. I showed her around, and she helped me place a fantastic sculpture by Richard Stankiewicz for which I had just finished repainting the stand the night before. We placed it perpendicular to the entrance, so that its explosive forms cascade down as one walks into the room. It may have been the most productive thing to come out of the swap. Her sense of form was a plus I never expected.

We went outside, and when I put my arm around her and started to get aroused, I knew once again that this was not Nancy. She then changed her blouse in front of me in my bedroom, and with her large dark thick tits in my face, she asked if Nancy would change in that way. (Nancy might change in the same room, but in another part and with her back turned. I told Micki this.) Suddenly it seemed that there might be a way to salvage the wretched evening (it would be worth a lot in anecdotes anyway), and I began to put on the charm—I showed off different things around the house, opened a cold bottle of Verdicchio. I said that we should get into bed, read or watch Watergate on TV. I explained that Nancy and I sometimes shared the big double bed.

But the Nancy act was completely over. Micki lay there talking on, and half in hopes of silence, I pounced on top of her, instantly aroused again, trying not to think that this girl was in any way supposed to be my sister, or even that she was fish-faced Micki Wrangler. I really don't go for instant sex, but once every few months it's nymph-and-satyr time again, and I'll go after anyone, so I whipped off my underwear like a prep-school boy let loose with his first girl on a prom weekend. She called time; when she had turned off the lights and the TV and finished undressing, I'd started to think about the whole situation, and I rolled over on my back uninterested. I never turn off the lights, anyway.

Micki then decided it was time to teach me about sex. She lay there on her back, described her lovers, and assured me that I had a far better body than any of the men in Nancy's life. I may have made fun of the athletic abilities (if you can call it that) of some I've met, but I've never been too eager for the rundown on them as lovers. Micki assured me with great pride that, unlike my sister, she had men who were veritable Charles Atlases and that the lover whom she lived with had a prick 6½ inches in diameter. I had to hear about all the problems this posed for him and for her, although of course I was mainly thinking that my dear little sister might need surgery. Bryn Mawr then realized that she meant circumference rather than diameter—she hadn't known the difference between the two words, realized which she had been able to measure with a tape. I heard that Mike was out of shape and didn't have a real ass, about how she gently seduced Abbe, whom Nancy had always intimidated by seeming too experienced, about how she made Aaron Tyman very happy, whereas Nancy wore too much Shalimar. And now she would do for Nancy's kid brother lots that Big Sis had never provided. But whether it was ice cubes or a mini hair dryer or her teeth that she was humoring me with, my ears were ringing as much as my cock with the lecture—always in clinical terms—on why I was enjoying myself and how Peter loved to be scratched firmly way at the back of his balls and how Nancy would benefit from knowing the bodies of Micki's men and discovering what kindness really was. She told me that she really loved me and being in bed with me, and that she'd learned to "relate to her own cunt" by getting to know other women's, but she was desperate when I told her that I kept no special lubricating creams around; she always finds it tough to keep going without them.

I had tossed all night, and I could have done without our morning shower together. She spent most of breakfast trying to find something with which to remove her eye makeup; Her Femininity settled on Mazola oil. I put on my most baggy, cuffed pants, thin-lapeled, slightly grease-stained old green dacron suit, and worn-out Weejuns to restore myself to puritan perfection for the work day and drove Micki off to the bus. She was obviously wrought by the whole experience; she dreaded going back to Nancy's New York life, wanted to stay or return to my parents and me, kept talking about how much she loved Mum. She cried most of the way in. Despite all her revelations, there had been no real intimacy for me. I was nothing but dragged out as I left her at the bus station.

A few hours later I called Dr. Wrangler at Hawthorne College and told her secretary that it was Mr. Finsterwald on the line. I heard the code name announced, and then Nancy was on, and I was doing my best to explain that I hoped she wasn't torturing herself following the swap rules because Micki was breaking them right and left. I also had to tell dear little Sis that there was someone who seemed dead bent on destroying her life piece by piece and who was in a pretty damn good position to try it. I avoided calling Micki for the next few days and was happy to be out of her reach at a wedding in Vermont and my old tennis camp in New Hampshire that weekend. I decided that I would have to get out of taking her to see friends of Nancy's and mine the following weekend, but I hoped that the sociology expert who sounded like a garbage disposal would be returned to the life she missed so badly before then and that Nancy's great life would be restored intact to its proper owner.

PARTING

Summer broke today. I went to Chinatown for lunch with Susie, brown and buoyant after two months in Italy, then I walked home slowly to celebrate the almost-fall air. Susie and I had talked at lunch about why neither of us wants to live in New York anymore, but everything tugged at me as I came uptown, made me think I might never be able to leave. The light in lower Manhattan. Nancy Whiskey Pub, which I've always meant to visit, on Lispenard and West Broadway. The name Lispenard. The way the city seemed to break open, yield itself, as I angled up Sixth Avenue. The hopscotch squares painted on the pavement of Sullivan Street. A cabby on MacDougal warning a kid on a bike about cabbies. The smell of frying sausages. A fortune-teller calling out from her storefront: "Come on in, dear. I see something good for you today."

My mind made one of those leaps minds make, and I started thinking about Ben Rothenberg, about how I had been able to leave him and not turn back, even though I loved him. I realized that I would, after all, be able to leave New York, and the life I've loved here, and the man at the heart of that life but not of my future. "Let it happen and let it go," my friend Ruthie from Cambridge once wrote in a poem. I had always liked that line, but it took the life swap to teach me that those words are sanity itself. One may grieve for what is over. One may not cling to it.

All summer long I've been making notes about what the life swap was and what it taught me and what new questions came flying off it. I planned to sit down on the first almost fall day and work the notes into an essay that would change everyone for evermore, but now it's that day, and I'm of another mind. Either it's plain what this book is about, or it will never be plain. Enough to share one last piece of blue paper:

Quotations to consider for up front

"A sentimental person thinks things will last—a romantic hopes against hope that they won't."—F. Scott Fitzgerald, *This Side of Paradise*

"Immortality is but ubiquity in time."—Herman Melville, *Moby Dick*

"What man has made, man can change."—U.S. Chief Justice Fred M. Vinson, speech at Arlington Cemetery

"A stomach-ache is your fault. If a manhole cover blows off, sails up ten stories, and decapitates you in an elevator, it's your fault."—Alan Harrington, *The Revelations of Dr. Modesto*

"We can exist in harmony with reality—which is to say we can be happy—only if we admit the tenuous quality of reality; if we perceive the close affinity between actuality and dream."—Edgar Mittelholzer, *Shadows Move Among Them*

"The most important laws and facts of physical science have all been discovered."—Albert A. Michelson, *Light Waves and Their Uses*

I like all those quotations very much, but the last is my favorite and the one I would probably have used if I'd used any. What I like about it is that it was published in 1903.

Scientists, sociologists, theologians, psychologists, moralists, and revolutionaries, too—everyone is always trying to tell us that all the evidence has been weighed and the world is square. It's octagonal, isn't it, dearheart?

978-0-595-37821-0
0-595-37821-8

Printed in the United States
92253LV00004B/1-39/A